Making the Impossible Possible

Leading Extraordinary Performance—the Rocky Flats Story

Kim Cameron and Marc Lavine

16
EasyRead Large

RHYW

Copyright Page from the Original Book

Making the Impossible Possible

Berrett-Koehler Publishers, Inc.
235 Montgomery Street, Suite 650
San Francisco, California 94104-2916
Tel: (415) 288-0260, Fax: (415) 362-2512
www.bkconnection.com

Ordering information for print editions
Quantity sales. Special discounts are available on quantity purchases by corporations, associations, and others. For details, contact the "Special Sales Department" at the Berrett-Koehler address above.
Individual sales. Berrett-Koehler publications are available through most bookstores. They can also be ordered directly from Berrett-Koehler: Tel: (800) 929-2929; Fax: (802) 864-7626; www.bkconnection.com
Orders for college textbook/course adoption use. Please contact Berrett-Koehler: Tel: (800) 929-2929; Fax: (802) 864-7626.
Orders by U.S. trade bookstores and wholesalers. Please contact Ingram Publisher Services, Tel: (800) 509-4887; Fax: (800) 838-1149; E-mail: customer.service@ingrampublisherservices.com; or visit www.ingrampublisherservices.com/Ordering for details about electronic ordering.

First Edition
Paperback print edition ISBN 978-1-57675-390-3
PDF e-book ISBN 978-1-60509-707-7

2010-1

Production management by Westchester Book Group. Cover design by Richard Adelson.

This optimized ReadHowYouWant edition contains the complete, unabridged text of the original publisher's edition. Other aspects of the book may vary from the original edition.

Set in 16 pt. Verdana

RHYW

TABLE OF CONTENTS

We wish to dedicate this book to the remarkable men and women who truly made the impossible become possible. This includes a wide variety of individuals and groups—each of whom played a key role in achieving what no one believed could occur—employees working at the Rocky Flats facility itself; the activist community; local, state, and federal governmental agencies; members of the U.S. Congress and the state of Colorado governor's office; members of community groups in towns and cities surrounding Rocky Flats; state and federal regulators; and leaders in Kaiser-Hill and CH2MHill. Without significant contributions by each of these constituencies, this success story would never have been possible.

Acknowledgments

We want to thank CH2MHill for supporting the Center for Positive Organization Scholarship at the University of Michigan's Stephen M. Ross School of Business. The support of CH2MHill, the parent company of Kaiser-Hill, which was the primary contractor responsible for closing Rocky Flats, helped us conduct this research. We are grateful to the management of both CH2MHill and Kaiser-Hill for participating in this research effort as well as for making available to us an extensive collection of stakeholder interviews. Our focus in this book is on the day-to-day organizational dynamics at Rocky Flats, so we concentrated our interviewing efforts on site-based groups. Access to more than 24 hours of videotaped interviews with a broad range of stakeholder groups allowed us to greatly enrich our perspective by gaining the insights of members of local government, former gubernatorial staff and leaders, congressional officials, EPA staff, environmental and community activists, and key site staff members no longer working at Rocky Flats. This data broadened the scope of the research and strengthened our understanding of the processes and activities that occurred in communities, government agencies, regulatory agencies, and the facility itself. We also wish to thank staff members from both the federal and site offices of the U.S. Department of Energy for their participation in this endeavor, and, in particular, the rank and file and leadership of

United Steelworkers Local 8031 for their participation. We wish to thank Nancy Tuor and Allen Schubert for their efforts in reading the manuscript to identify factual errors. Despite their best efforts, and ours, mistakes may remain, and we take full responsibility for them.

We wish to express our profound gratitude to our spouses and families who have offered inspiration, tolerance, and understanding during the time-intensive process of conducting this study and writing the book. For Kim this includes Melinda, the mother of seven beautiful children—Katrina, Tiara, Asher, Cheyenne, Brittany, Austin, and Cam. For Marc this includes his wife, Jennifer, as well as his parents and many friends and mentors. These people contribute to the quality of our work and the quality of our lives.

An Introduction to the Impossible

Once in a great while we find an organization whose performance is so much better than expectations that it is difficult to believe that this level of success is possible—for example, the Revolutionary Army in 1776, the John Wooden–era UCLA basketball teams, or the success of the Grameen Bank movement. Most people hold in their minds standards of what excellence represents, and when we encounter performance that markedly exceeds those standards, we are left to wonder how such an aberration is possible.

This book tells the story of positively deviant performance—the achievement of extraordinary success well beyond the expectations of almost any outside observer. We present the story of an organization that reached a level of performance that was considered impossible, so that adjectives such as "spectacular," "extraordinary," "remarkable," and "astonishing" are apt descriptors. Our account describes how a single organization experienced a devastating loss—the loss of mission and subsequent languishing performance—and then, despite its problematic circumstances, achieved a level of success well beyond expectations.

Simply put, this organization accomplished what most knowledgeable people thought was impossible. The story examines the key enablers that account for this extraordinary level of performance. We explain the leadership principles that can be helpful to individuals in other organizations who are interested in fostering their own spectacular success.

Rocky Flats

This book examines the cleanup and closure of America's most dangerous nuclear weapons production facility. This facility, located near the eastern slope of the Rocky Mountains in Colorado, produced plutonium and enriched uranium triggers for nuclear weapons from 1952 to 1989. Every nuclear weapon in the current U.S. arsenal contains triggers produced at Rocky Flats. Employees worked with the most dangerous materials known to mankind, and an ABC *Nightline* program in 1994 identified several buildings on the site as the "most dangerous buildings in America" because of the radioactive materials being handled, the threat of a disastrous nuclear accident, and the possibility of radioactive pollution escaping and contaminating the surrounding area.

The Rocky Flats site consisted of approximately 800 buildings, with about 3 million square feet under roof. Located on the 6,000-acre site was an enormous amount of hazardous material—tons of weapons-grade nuclear material including plutonium and enriched uranium, tens of thousands of cubic meters of transuranic acid waste and low-level radioactive liquids, and rooms in some buildings that had radioactive pollution levels reaching beyond infinity on the measuring devices. Contamination existed in walls, floors, ceilings, ductwork, surrounding soil, and, potentially, groundwater. Environmentalists, citizen action groups, state regulatory agencies, federal oversight agencies, and Congress all were understandably distrustful, skeptical, and largely antagonistic toward Rocky Flats. The largest industrial fire in the nation's history had occurred at the site in 1969, and other accidents in the 1950s and 1960s were viewed as evidence that this site was intolerably dangerous. Protests, lawsuits, and an adversarial climate were continuously associated with Rocky Flats. Antagonistic and hostile relationships existed with regulators. A combative stance had been adopted toward the activist community. Noncooperative relationships existed with surrounding states and with other Department of Energy (DOE) sites, resulting in a siege mentality—razor wire fences and guards toting M-16 rifles—that kept outsiders at a distance.

The three unions representing workers—steelworkers, construction workers, and security guards—also had antagonistic relationships with contract company managers, so that formally filed grievances were common among the workforce. Safety was significantly worse than the average at other government facilities and in the construction industry in general. A climate of secrecy, insularity, self-protection, and resistance to change inhibited any hope of a major transformation.

In 1989, because of suspicion that unreported pollution might be occurring, the FBI raided the facility and suddenly shut the place down. Workers immediately lost a mission to perform and were accused of being criminal polluters. In 1992, the Rocky Flats nuclear weapons program was permanently discontinued by order of President George H.W. Bush, so the possibility of continuing to do the jobs for which they were well trained was completely eliminated for Rocky Flats employees.

More radioactive waste existed at Rocky Flats than at any other facility in the country. Consequently, DOE conducted a careful study of the residual pollution at the site in 1995 and concluded that the cleanup and closure of the facility would require more than 70 years and cost at least $36 billion. Similar estimates were developed for thirteen additional DOE sites throughout the United States. An RFP (request for proposal) containing these estimates was circulated to potential contracting companies. The company that won the contract in 1995 was Kaiser-Hill.

What makes the story of Rocky Flats worth telling is the extraordinary level of success achieved—success in terms of speed, quality, efficiency, productivity, innovation, and profitability. As the largest and most complex environmental cleanup project in U.S. history, Rocky Flats was the first nuclear weapons facility to be decommissioned and closed anywhere in the world. But the complexity and uniqueness of the task is not the key message. Rather, the story is worth telling because the entire project was completed *60 years early* and at a *cost savings of approximately $30 bil-*

lion in taxpayer funds. In contrast, the other DOE clean-up sites are approximately on-time (or late) and on-budget (or over) in accomplishing the same kinds of tasks.

By October 2005, all 800 buildings had been demolished, all radioactive waste had been removed, and all soil and water had been remediated to a level that exceeded original federal standards for cleanliness by a factor of 13. Simply stated, the impossible was achieved at Rocky Flats. Not only did Kaiser-Hill accomplish what had never been done before, but it was done in a time frame and at a cost that defied any reasonable expectation. To repeat, the other DOE clean-up sites are approximately on-time (or late) and on-budget (or over) in accomplishing the same kinds of tasks. The story of Rocky Flats represents one of the most dramatic examples of organizational success in history. In a *New York Times* report (2005:A21) on the day of project completion, Senator Wayne Allard of Colorado called the project "the best example of a nuclear cleanup success story ever."

Explaining Extraordinary Success

The book explains how this success occurred. It highlights the key *enablers*—the levers, techniques, and practices—that explain how this extraordinary performance was realized. Our aim is to help leaders identify which enablers are most effective in producing transformational change and how they can create outstanding success. It is important to point out that these leadership principles are not intended to be restricted to a single organizational type or to a single circumstance. Using Rocky Flats as the backdrop for these leadership principles does not constrain them to a nuclear facility. Rather, the principles that emerged from this investigation may apply in many circumstances and to a wide variety of leaders. We hope that leaders will find them helpful in situations where transformational change is required, major challenge is encountered, or the opportunity to do something great is present.

Success this dramatic and extraordinary cannot be explained by a few simple rules of thumb or a "top 10" list. Rather, the enablers that account for this kind of success are numerous and sometimes complex. We organize them into four basic themes by utilizing a well-developed theoretical framework. Our intent in using this framework is to highlight the general leadership principles that underlie the key enablers. That is, we want to help leaders understand how the enablers work and how they can produce extraordinary performance. This theoretical framework—*the Competing Values Framework*—is explained in chapter 4.

The story of how the impossible became possible at Rocky Flats is told from the standpoint of the individuals who were involved in the change. Adopting this approach provides a glimpse of how people experienced this dramatic change, what strategies were being contemplated, and what factors the participants themselves believed were the keys to success. It also highlights the fact that no successful change in organizations—at least no significant transformational change—is due to a lone heroic leader or to a single vision developed by an individual at the top. It is commonplace to identify single leaders as the chief architects of spectacular successes, and we often attribute remarkable organizational achievements to a sole person's talents or genius. Icons such as Jack Welch at General Electric, Steven Jobs at Apple, Bill Gates at Microsoft, Fred Smith at Federal Express, Sam Walton at Wal-Mart, Warren Buffet at Berkshire Hathaway, and a host of others are credited with being the chief explanations for the remarkable achievements of their respective companies.

On the other hand, the story of Rocky Flats is a story of many leaders, many interwoven activities, many constituencies, and many heroic endeavors that all combined to produce a remarkable story of success. In our account of the Rocky Flats transformation, we rely largely on the words of the participants in the project—the leaders who accounted for its success. We do not tell the story in a linear fashion or as a novel might unfold. Rather, we reproduce quotations and observations from a variety of individuals. These people represent a broad spectrum of participants, including federal government oversight personnel from DOE and the EPA, local elected officials, state officeholders, members of the U.S. Congress and their staffs, representatives of environmental and citizen watchdog groups, managers and supervisors working in the Rocky Flats facilities, union leaders, and union members doing the daily work of cleanup and closure. We use direct quotations and some paraphrased observations from these individuals, all of whom provide unique perspectives, insightful descriptions, and helpful explanations for the success of this remarkable endeavor.

Positive Deviance

From our analysis of these interviews as well as from a variety of additional sources of data, we were able to draw some conclusions about how Kaiser-Hill was able to achieve such spectacular success at Rocky Flats (see appendix 2 for a description of the data sources and data analysis procedures). Of course, we risk grossly oversimplifying the key reasons for success by attempting to identify one summary statement that characterizes what was learned from our in-depth investigation. Nevertheless, it is clear to us that the overarching leadership lesson learned from Rocky Flats can be summarized in a single statement, although it belies the complexity that undergirds this straightforward observation:

> *The impossible was made possible by adopting an abundance approach to change rather than a deficit approach.*

An abundance approach to change is deceptively simple. It refers to the striving for positive deviance, pursuing the best of the human condition, and working to fulfill the highest potential of organizations and in-

	Negative Deviance	Normal	Positive Deviance
Individual:			
Physiological	Illness	Health	Vitality
Psychological	Illness	Health	Flow
Organizational:			
Revenues	Losses	Profits	Generosity
Effectiveness	Ineffective	Effective	Excellence
Efficiency	Inefficient	Efficient	Extraordinary
Quality	Error-prone	Reliable	Flawless
Ethics	Unethical	Ethical	Benevolence
Relationships	Harmful	Helpful	Honoring
Adaptation	Threat rigidity ⇧	Coping ⇧	Flourishing
Approach:	*Problem solving gaps*	*Abundance gaps*	

(SOURCE: Cameron, 2003)

dividuals. An abundance approach focuses on resilience, flourishing, and vitality, rather than mere goal achievement. It pursues extraordinarily positive individual and organizational outcomes. An abundance approach stands in contrast to a problem-solving or a deficit-based approach to change. Rather than being consumed by difficulties and obstacles, an abundance approach is consumed by strengths and human flourishing. Rather than an exclusive focus on problem-solving, an abundance approach pursues possibility-finding. Rather than addressing change that is motivated by challenges, crises, or threats—in which the role of the leader is to effectively address problems or deficiencies—the abundance approach addresses affirmative possibilities, potentialities, and elevating processes and outcomes.

One way to illustrate the abundance approach is to consider figure I.1, which represents a continuum of deviance (see Cameron, 2003). Usually the word "deviance" connotes a negative condition, so labeling someone a deviant usually represents a negative evaluation. However, the basic definition of deviance is merely an aberration from the norm or a violation of expectations. Therefore, deviance can occur as a positive aberration from normal conditions as well as a negative aberration, as represented in Figure I.1.

Look first at the top line in the figure. This continuum contains three points—one anchoring the left end (negative deviance), one the middle point (an absence of deviance or a normal or expected condition), and one anchoring the right end (positive deviance). Consider the top line of the figure body first. It refers to *physiological functioning.* When it comes to physical health, the large majority of medical research, and almost all of a physician's time, is spent helping people move from the left point on the continuum (illness) to the middle point (health). The middle point represents an absence of illness or injury, or the normal condition. Pharmaceutical companies allocate billions of dollars a year to develop compounds that assist individuals in moving from the left point to the middle point—to an absence of illness or a reduction in symptoms of illness. Almost all physiological research, in other words, focuses on the gap between the left point and the middle point. Unfortunately, much less is known about how to get people from the middle point on the continuum to a state of wellness, vitality, or Olympic fitness on the right end. Once people feel well, they usually don't see a doctor, and almost no medical scientists study them. Moreover, almost no (legal) pharmaceutical compounds exist to foster a physiological condition that might be described as positively deviant vitality. We know more about solving physiological problems than about creating vitality and flourishing health.

Psychologically the same thing is typical. More than 95 percent of psychological research published in the last 50 years has focused on closing the gap between the left point on the continuum and the middle point—that is, focusing on how to overcome depression, anxiety, stress, or emotional difficulties (Seligman, 2002b). Once psychological and emotional health is at the middle point—no illness or psychological difficulties—it is very seldom the subject of serious scientific investigation. Little is known about how to get people from a condition of mental and emotional health to a state of flourishing, positive energy, or what is sometimes referred to in psychology as "flow" (Csikszentmihalyi, 1990). Most of what we know about human physiology and psychology is how to overcome weakness or illness so that we can reach a state of normality, or an *absence* of deviance.

Now consider *organizations* and the common motivations and approaches used to change them. Organizations, by definition, exist in order to *organize.* They are fundamentally mechanisms to control human activity, or to reduce deviance from expectations. By definition, they reinforce the middle point on the continuum—organizing reduces variation. Usually organizational change is motivated by ineffective, inefficient, or unprofitable performance, mistakes or unethical decisions, conflict-ridden or rigid relationships, or problems being encountered. Leaders in organizations are usually astute in diagnosing key challenges, major obstacles, and important difficulties. The leader's job is often defined as defining, diagnosing, and overcoming major obstacles and closing deficit gaps. Effective leaders are typically defined as effective problem-solvers.

The gap between the middle of figure I.1 and the right-hand side, however, is an *abundance gap*—the difference between successful performance and spectacular performance. The organization is motivated to change from being profitable, effective, efficient, or reliable in performance, for example, to being extraordinary, flawless, generous, or benevolent. Outcomes produce positive benefit for more than the organization itself, and a condition of abundance makes possible the flourishing and success of others outside the organization as well.

The abundance approach motivates change in organizations based on the pursuit of a greater good and an opportunity to achieve positively deviant results. Benefits extend beyond the immediate time frame and beyond the advantage of those directly involved. The results possess profound purpose because they are connected to important personal values and to the core meaning of the organization. The abundance approach assumes that human flourishing, virtuousness, and the best of the human condition are the outcomes being pursued (see Cameron, Dutton, & Quinn, 2003; Cameron, Bright, & Caza, 2004).

The Rocky Flats story is a story of abundance and positive deviance. The extraordinary success achieved extends well beyond even the most optimistic estimates of what would constitute a successful outcome. At the heart of the Rocky Flats success story lies an approach to change that led to positive deviance—extraordinary success well beyond expectations for effective change. Rocky Flats succeeded because it was, fundamentally, a transformation driven by the closing of abundance gaps rather than the closing of deficit gaps. Simply put, an abundance approach made the impossible possible.

Leadership Enablers and Principles

Although there are a large number of interesting aspects of this story of success, we concentrated our study on the enablers that leaders used to spark positively deviant performance. Our research uncovered 16 such enablers, and they are discussed in detail in chapters 5 through 8. These enablers are the levers that leaders used to accomplish their objectives. Most important, these enablers can be summarized as four general themes that appear to contradict each other.

One theme focuses on innovation, risk-taking, visionary thinking, and symbolic leadership, whereas another theme focuses on the opposite—maintaining stability, carefully controlling processes, precise objectives, and financial discipline. Pursuing these two themes simultaneously—that is, fostering chaos and control at the same time—helped foster positive deviance. A third theme focuses on supportive interpersonal relationships, developing human capital, openness, and nurturing a collaborative culture, whereas a fourth theme focuses on the opposite—power and politics, pressure to perform, striving for wealth, and external stakeholders. Pursuing these two themes simultaneously—that is, fostering collaboration and competition—helped explain positive deviance at Rocky Flats.

These *enablers* are translated into a set of key leadership *principles* that emerged from the analysis of Rocky Flats. Twenty-one such principles are identified and are summarized in the last chapter. Leadership principles are basically prescriptions for achieving extraordinary performance. They offer a perspective on how leaders can behave if they are to implement an abundance approach to change. These principles are contrasted with conventional leadership principles in order to highlight the uniqueness of the abundance approach. Our intent is to provide general guidelines that leaders who desire to create extraordinary success can adopt in almost any setting.

It should be pointed out that whereas abundance-oriented leadership principles are contrasted with more conventional principles, this is not to say that abundance should be pursued exclusively or as a substitute for conventional leadership. Rather, abundance practices focus on creating a condition of virtuousness and achieving positively deviant performance, but the extraordinary success at Rocky Flats often required both conventional and abundance practices. At Rocky Flats, these contrasting leadership practices were frequently pursued concurrently. We summarize the general leadership principles associated with the abundance approach in figure I.2, and contrast them with conventional leadership principles.

To repeat, making the impossible possible often required both types of practices, but it is the abundance practices that are the most unusual and that distinguish Rocky Flats from most organizational change efforts. Leaders who produce positive deviance and achieve extraordinary performance will be required to adopt an abundance approach to change, and this book highlights the leadership principles that form the foundation of that approach. In the chapters that follow, we explain why the abundance approach leads to extraordinary performance, and we highlight the key enablers that leaders can use to realize this level of success.

Structure of the Book

Figure I.3 identifies the structure of the book. We begin by addressing the question *How did extraordinary performance occur at Rocky Flats?* The answer, as mentioned above, is the implementation of the abundance approach. The next question is *Why does the abundance approach work? What explains its remarkable success?* After answering this query, a third question is addressed: *What levers can leaders use to achieve similar results?* This leads us to an explanation of enablers of success. Finally, we address a fourth question: *What are the prescriptions for extraordinary performance? What is different from conventional leadership?*

Figure I.2 CONVENTIONAL LEADERSHIP PRINCIPLES COMPARED WITH ABUNDANCE LEADERSHIP PRINCIPLES

Conventional Principles	Abundance Principles
General Leadership Principles	
Problem-solving and deficit gaps	Virtuousness and abundance gaps
A single heroic leader	Multiple leaders playing multiple roles
One leader from beginning to end	A continuity of leaders
Congruence and consistency	Paradox and contradiction
Principles Related to Visionary and Symbolic Leadership	
Left-brain visions—logical, rational, and sensible—with SMART goals	Right-brain visions—symbolic, emotional, and meaningful—with profound purpose

Conventional Principles	Abundance Principles
Consistency, stability, and predictability	Revolution and positive deviance
Personal benefits and advantages	Meaningfulness beyond personal benefits
Organizations absorb the risks of failure and benefits of success	Employees share the risks of failure and rewards from success
Principles Related to Careful, Clear, and Controlled Leadership	
Downsizing at the expense of people	Downsizing for the benefit of people
Commitments and priorities based on environmental demands	Unalterable commitments and integrity at all costs
Managing the contractor, attaching resources to performance	Managing the contract and ensuring stable funding
Ultimate responsibility and accountability for measurable success at the top	Responsibility and accountability for measurable success for everyone, including workers, managers, regulators, community organizations, and funders
Adaptability and addressing work challenges as they arise	Engaging only in value-added activities
Principles Related to Collaborative, Engaging, and Participative Leadership	
Building on and reinforcing the current culture	Introducing challenges that the culture cannot address
Decision-making and leadership at the top	Employee and union partnerships in planning, decision-making, training, evaluation, and discipline
Need-to-know information sharing and physical separation	Early, frequent, and abundant information-sharing with colocation
Long-term employment, personal relations, and the use of specialists	Long-term employability, professional relations, and retraining

Conventional Principles	Abundance Principles
Principles Related to Rigorous, Uncompromising, and Results-Oriented Leadership	
Managing the media	Openness with the media early and often
Keeping adversaries at a distance and using protective political strategies	Making adversaries stakeholders, building relationships, and using positive political strategies
Clear, stable performance targets that meet standards coming from the top	Escalating performance, virtuousness, and positive deviance targets from multiple sources
Organizational financial benefit from outstanding success	Financial generosity and benevolence with employees

Chapter Overviews

In chapter 1, we describe in more detail the conditions that were encountered by Kaiser-Hill managers when they arrived at Rocky Flats in July of 1995. Had Rocky Flats been operating normally—for example, normal levels of productivity, normal employee morale, normal safety records, normal relationships with external constituencies—the closure and cleanup of the facility still would have been given a low probability of success. No similar job had ever been achieved before, and no one knew for sure how to accomplish this task. But the facility was not operating normally. It was in a disastrous condition, so just getting performance to an acceptable level would have represented a remarkable accomplishment. Chapter 1 outlines why this case represents an instance of making the impossible possible—achieving levels of performance well beyond normal. In addition, this chapter explains in some detail what an abundance approach to change is and why it leads to remarkable performance.

QUESTION:
How did extraordinary performance occur at Rocky Flats?

↓

ANSWER:
The abdundance approach

↓

QUESTION:
Why does the abundance approach work?
What explains its remarkable success?

↓

ANSWER:
Heliotropic effects
Amplifying benefits
Buffering benefits

↓

QUESTION:
What levers can leaders use to achieve similar results?

↓

ANSWER:
Key leadership roles and 16 enablers

↓

QUESTION:
What are the prescriptions for extraordinary performance?
What is different from conventional leadership?

↓

ANSWER:
21 abundance leadership principles

Figure I.3 THE STRUCTURE OF THE BOOK

The contract signing between Kaiser-Hill and the Department of Energy marked the beginning of the saga at Rocky Flats. In 1995, few, if any, predicted a successful outcome, given the multiplicity of obstacles and difficulties facing the organization. Chapter 2 provides a more detailed description of the conditions under which the facility was operating prior to the intervention of Kaiser-Hill. A brief history of the Rocky Flats facility is provided, beginning with its creation in 1951, and we discuss in some detail the difficulties presented to the new Kaiser-Hill management team when they arrived on the scene. In this chapter we also discuss some possible rival hypotheses that some individuals might claim negate or dismiss the remarkable success achieved at Rocky Flats.

In conducting our investigation of Rocky Flats, it was difficult to ignore the impact of certain leaders and leadership practices on the success of the change effort. Quite frequently in our interviews, employees cited the *roles* played by certain leaders as being particularly important. Chapter 3 explains and elaborates some of these leadership roles that differentiate abundance-oriented leaders from more traditional leaders. These leaders had special impact on the success of the project, and although only a sample of the leaders are identified by name, they represent successive CEOs at Rocky Flats, congressional and Senate leaders, DOE and EPA leaders, and leaders within Kaiser-Hill's parent company, CH2MHill. Key leadership principles are illustrated in the comments made by and about these leaders.

It is easy to become overwhelmed with the litany of leadership enablers and principles recounted in this book. Hence, we have organized them into clusters with similar themes. For example, in figure I.2, the first four leadership principles refer to a general leadership orientation. The next four principles cluster into one group relating to *visionary and symbolic leadership.* The next five principles relate to *careful, clear, and controlled leadership.* The next four principles relate to *collaborative, engaging, and participative leadership.* The final four principles relate to *rigorous, uncompromising, and results-oriented leadership.* The enablers of extraordinary success are embedded within these themes.

Identifying these clusters is based on the *Competing Values Framework*—a powerful tool to help interpret complex arrays of information. This framework has been the subject of research for a quarter-century and has proven to be of great value in understanding leadership and organizational performance (see Cameron & Quinn, 2006; Cameron, Quinn, DeGraff, & Thakor, 2006; Quinn, 1988). In chapter 4 we provide a more detailed explanation of the Competing Values Framework.

Chapters 5 through 8 identify and illustrate the four general categories of enablers of positive deviance. Chapter 5 illustrates the four enablers associated with visionary and symbolic leadership: *facilitating innovation, risk-taking, visionary thinking,* and *symbolic leadership*—a clear, shared vision; symbolic leadership activities; innovation and creativity; and meaningful work. Chapter 6 illustrates the four enablers associated with careful, clear, and controlled leadership: *maintaining stability, carefully controlling processes, precise objectives,* and *financial discipline*—goal clarity; new contracts and an interagency agreement; detailed planning, "projectizing," measurement, milestones, and accountability; and stable funding. Chapter 7 illustrates four enablers associated with collaborative, engaging, and participative leadership: *supportive interpersonal relationships, developing human capital, openness,* and *nurturing a collaborative culture*—organizational culture change; collaboration; trust and credibility; and human capital and social relationships. Chapter 8 illustrates the four enablers associated with rigorous, uncompromising, and results-oriented leadership: *power and politics, pressure to perform, striving for wealth,* and *external stakeholders*—external stakeholder engagement, external political strategies, bold action and pressure to succeed, and incentives to perform.

Chapter 9 summarizes and elaborates the key leadership principles learned. Principles that may be generalizable to other settings and implemented by leaders in other kinds of organizations are underscored, based on the enablers that were illustrated in the previous chapters.

Appendix 1 presents some of the contrary perspectives regarding Rocky Flats' performance. Some constituencies remain skeptical that enough has been done, that anything of value can be learned from a nuclear arsenal, or that the truth has been told. We try to represent their perspectives in this appendix.

Appendix 2 provides more detail about the data sources used in this investigation as well as the data analysis procedures used to generate our conclusions.

1

Explaining the Impossible—Positive Deviance and the Abundance Approach

In March of 1951, the U.S. government's Atomic Energy Commission publicly reported that it would build a highly secure nuclear weapons plant in Colorado. The facility would be located on former ranching land just 16 miles northwest of downtown Denver, at the base of the beautiful Flatirons, on the eastern slope of the Rocky Mountains. The site was known for it's rocky but flat terrain. The Cold War was escalating, and stockpiling a nuclear arsenal was considered the primary means for keeping the world safe for democracy. The threat of a retaliatory attack with nuclear weapons was seen as the major defense against Soviet aggression. The site—labeled Rocky Flats—is owned by the U.S. Department of Energy (DOE) and was managed by a series of weapons contractors during its years of active operation: Dow Chemical (1952–1975), Rockwell International (1975–1990), EG&G (1990–1995).

The facility began active operation in 1953, producing triggers for nuclear weapons. The site functioned at peak capacity and was known as, arguably, the most productive and efficient facility in the world until 1989, when it was abruptly closed. Seeking evidence of environmental violations, the FBI raided the facility on June 6 and shut down production on the spot. A subsequent grand jury investigation found no evidence of the feared widespread environmental contamination, but the contractor at the time (Rockwell International) agreed to an $18.5 million fine nevertheless, principally for failure to maintain adequate records. In the wake of the FBI raid and shutdown, a new contractor was brought in to manage Rocky Flats. Between January 1990 and June 1995, that firm (EG&G) focused primarily on keeping the site secure and maintaining the facility in a safe configuration. A search for a new contractor was initiated in 1995, and in July of that year Kaiser-Hill was awarded a five-year contract to clean up Rocky Flats.

Kaiser-Hill was initially a joint venture between ICF Kaiser Engineers and an environmental engineering firm, CH2MHill. After ICF Kaiser declared bankruptcy in 1999, Kaiser-Hill became a wholly owned subsidiary of CH2MHill. We recount the story of how Kaiser-Hill, facing enormous challenges and obstacles, made the impossible possible.

Challenges

Kaiser-Hill was awarded the contract to clean up and decommission the Rocky Flats nuclear production facility, an ominous task. First, this project represented the first cleanup and closure of a nuclear weapons production facility anywhere in the world. No one in the industry knew how to accomplish this task. No one had ever taken down a plutonium production facility before. Moreover, the parent company of Kaiser-Hill—CH2MHill—was an engineering and environmental firm, had little experience in nuclear cleanup, and it possessed no experience on a project of this scale. Taking on this task represented an enormous risk for the company as well as for the federal government. According to the former CEO of Kaiser-Hill and a DOE executive:

> If you would have asked me two months after I signed the contract, would I realistically have imagined the outcome that's occurred, I would have said "no." I hoped it would happen, and I wanted the contract to support it, but I wouldn't have bet you a nickel that it could have been done.
>
> Contributor 23—Senior Executive, DOE

Second, the majority of the workforce on site was represented by three unions—steelworkers, building trades, and security guards—which had a history of antagonistic relationships with the management of the previous contracting firms. Grievances were common—in fact, 900 unresolved grievances had been filed by the time Kaiser-Hill took over the project in 1995—expectations of lifelong employment were the norm, and a high degree of pride existed among the workforce regarding the skilled work they performed. Multiple generations of employees worked at Rocky Flats—grandparents, parents, and children—and it was expected that the project would continue for several more generations. The facility represented as close to a guarantee of lifelong employment as it was possible to find. Changing procedures was likely to foster serious dissent among a proud, closely knit workforce, not to mention strong resistance to any major alteration of the organization's mission. The arrival of a completely new management team onsite was not likely to produce immediate cooperation and collaboration; rather, obstinacy and recalcitrance were the most likely reactions.

Third, the site included a 385-acre production area surrounded by more than 6,000 acres of open space called the buffer zone. During its operation, the production areas were surrounded by three razor wire fences, prisonlike watch towers, and security guards toting M-16 rifles to prevent entry by those on a suicide mission or other subversives. Several buildings had installed inhibitors to prevent air attack via helicopter landings and theft of dangerous materials. Visitors entering the facility passed through four security stations and received a "Q" clearance (requiring a full investigation of at least the past 10 years of their personal lives). A culture of secrecy, protection, and concealment was dominant at the facility. Employees were prohibited from describing of their work to outsiders, so they became socially isolated and largely dependent on coworkers for social support.

Fourth, the site was one of the most polluted nuclear facilities in America. More than 21 tons of weapons-grade nuclear material was present. At least 100 tons of high content plutonium residues existed on the site without a treatment or disposal path. At least 30,000 liters of plutonium and enriched uranium solutions were stored in tanks and pipes, some of them leaking and some buried in unmarked locations. More than 500,000 cubic meters of low-level radioactive waste and nearly 15,000 cubic meters of transuranic waste were stored in 39,500 containers. The national press had labeled the site the most dangerous place in America because of its radioactive pollution and the possibility of a major nuclear accident. Several rooms in production facilities had been permanently sealed because of the high levels of radioactivity, which exceeded "infinity" on the metering devices. With a plutonium half-life of more than 24,000 years, the rooms were likely to be polluted forever. Unknown levels of contamination were present not only in the buildings—walls, floors, ceilings, and ductwork—but also in surrounding soil and, potentially, groundwater. Cleaning up such a site in any reasonable amount of time was highly improbable.

Fifth, long-running battles had been fought between Rocky Flats contractors and government regulatory agencies, environmental groups, community representatives, and concerned citizens. Broad public sentiment was that the facility was a danger to surrounding communities, and countless demonstrations by numerous groups had been staged from the 1960s through the 1980s to protest nuclear proliferation, pollution, secrecy, and environmental endangerment. A demonstration involving more than 10,000 people occurred in 1969, for example, after the worst industrial fire in history exposed the possibility of plutonium residues escaping into a wide area of surrounding terrain. The facility was almost in a state of siege by outside agencies and a concerned citizenry in 1995 when Kaiser-Hill was given control.

Sixth, for years, Rocky Flats had argued that it was regulated by the Atomic Energy Commission, and therefore the project was not subject to the inspection and oversight of the Environmental Protection Agency (EPA). In fact, because of national security provisions, EPA inspectors had to be blindfolded when visiting specific parts of the facility because they were not allowed to see certain top-secret weapons materials. As might be expected, this treatment led to suspicion of rules violations and secret pollution. Litigation and congressional pressure led to the EPA's obtaining partial jurisdiction over Rocky Flats, and a surprise raid by the FBI in 1989 led to an immediate suspension of work. In the public's eye, employees were transformed overnight from patriotic heroes engaged in winning the Cold War to polluting criminals threatening the safety and health of the surrounding communities. They were completely barred from continuing production work and from accomplishing the organization's mission. From 1989 to 1995, no production work was accomplished at the facility as employees waited for permission to resume operation but had no authorization to do so. The workforce actually doubled in size during that period because of the requirement to produce an overwhelming number of documents verifying pollution levels, procedures, and new nuclear compliance guidelines.

Figure 1: Protesters at Rocky Flats

In 1992 President George H.W. Bush announced the permanent closure of the facility as a result of the abandonment of the W-88 nuclear warhead program, but no action was taken to change the work scope from what had been outlined since 1989. Hence, the workforce was without a mission, thwarted in its desire to restart the production facility, uncertain if an alternative use for the facility would be specified, and closely scrutinized by regulatory agencies that required large numbers of environmental reports and safety studies. Employees produced documents, monitored conformity, and created reports, but they had no meaningful work objectives.

Seventh, the federal government was skeptical of the ability of any firm to successfully complete the cleanup, and the ability to receive the necessary funding to accomplish closure was dependent on the confidence of Congress and other federal agencies. In 1995, it was not at all certain that the necessary support would be provided. According to one of the DOE regulators on the site:

> There was nervousness in Congress about giving this project a big pot of money. They were asked: What kind of controls are we going to have?
>
> Contributor 19—Senior Executive, DOE

The Government Accountability Office (GAO) also was skeptical that the cleanup and closure could be completed, and as recently as 2001, a GAO report estimated the probability of completing the project by the end of 2006 at less than 15 percent. Cost overruns and missed deadlines were highlighted as problematic. In the state of Colorado, similar doubts were expressed. After the agreement with Kaiser-Hill was signed, a senior official in the Colorado Department of Public Health and Environment (CDPHE) reported:

I had staff in the division who really felt we had sold out the project.

Contributor 27—Senior Manager, CDPHE

The Contract

The Department of Energy awarded a contract to clean up the site to Kaiser-Hill in 1995, after a competitive bidding process. This was the first performance-based contract issued by the Department of Energy to encourage work toward closure rather than merely to manage ongoing operations. This contract ran for five years, allowing the Department of Energy an opportunity to evaluate Kaiser-Hill's performance. In 2000, Kaiser-Hill was awarded a no-bid closure contract—in which the goal of closing the facility was added to the goal of cleaning it up—as a result of its performance in the previous five years. The rationale was that the bidding process was too costly and too time-consuming, so the contract was awarded based on the merits of the first five years' performance. That contract was to extend through the end of 2006.

In 1995, the U.S. Department of Energy's Office of Environmental Management issued a Baseline Environmental Management Report, titled *Estimating the Cold War Mortgage,* which provided a detailed estimate of the cost of closing facilities involved in Cold War weapons research, production, and storage. This report covered 13 facilities located throughout the United States. With reference to Rocky Flats, this analysis produced an estimate of a minimum of 70 years and a cost of more than $36 billion to close and clean up the Rocky Flats facility. Completion was estimated, optimistically, to occur in the year 2065. One high-ranking DOE official commented that 70 years was a gross underestimate and predicted that the more realistic number was 200 years to completion.

Extraordinary Results

In light of these ominous challenges, the prospects of a successful closure and cleanup of Rocky Flats within 70 years were by no means guaranteed. What makes this story worth telling is that the entire project was completed 60 years early and at almost $30 billion savings in taxpayer funds. Other DOE clean-up projects in the United States—with similar estimates of time frame and budget—have not come close to the success achieved at Rocky Flats either in terms of time frame or budget.

As the world's first nuclear production facility to be cleaned up, Rocky Flats represents a one-of-a-kind example of extraordinary success. The facility was closed and cleaned up, and will become a wildlife refuge, in a fraction of the estimated time. All structures were demolished, all surface waste was removed, and the soil and water were remediated to better than initial federally mandated standards by October 10, 2005. The estimated cost for the project is $3.9 billion (approximately $7 billion in total, including the expenditures in the years before Kaiser-Hill took over the project), a small fraction of initial federal estimates. The entire site will be transformed into a wildlife refuge a year sooner than even the most optimistic estimates as recently as 2003.

Many critics from citizen action groups, the environmental community, local and state governments, city administrations, and regulating agencies went from being protesters and adversaries to being advocates, lobbyists, and partners. (Appendix 1 highlights some exceptions, identifying contrary points of view regarding Rocky Flats success.) Relations with the three unions (steelworkers, security guards, building trades) improved from 900 grievances to a mere handful per year, and the leadership of the steelworkers union described union-management relations as the best they had seen in their careers. A culture of lifelong employment and employee entitlement was replaced by a workforce that enthusiastically worked themselves out of their jobs as quickly as possible. Remediated pollution levels surpassed initial federal standards by a multiple of 13, and safety performance exceeded federal standards twofold and the construction industry average fourfold. A $300,000 rebate in workers' compensation insurance premiums was received because of the excellent safety record. More than 200 technological innovations were produced in the service of faster and safer performance. The theme of the facility, "making the impossible possible," represents performance that exceeded even the most optimistic estimates by a wide margin.

After the first five years of Kaiser-Hill's management, one former DOE regulator, on a return visit to the Rocky Flats facility, commented:

> The radiation was so high in [Building] 771 that we couldn't even measure how high the radiation was in there. Yet, I was in that building this morning! It was so exciting to me; because that was the vision we had when I was here. Now to drive around the rest of the site and see all these other buildings that are pads now—there is nothing but grass where there were buildings and laboratories of plutonium—to see the progress that we made the last five years is just absolutely astounding. No one said we could do it. But they're doing it. They're doing it. The workers are doing it!
>
> Contributor 21—Manager, DOE

Figure 1.1 summarizes key performance changes that occurred from the time Kaiser-Hill initiated the project in 1995 until 2005. It highlights the dramatic success achieved on a variety of criteria—timeliness, budget, productivity, labor relations, safety, and outcomes—over the 10-year period after Kaiser-Hill began managing the facility.

Summary of Outcomes

Despite the unusually difficult environment that characterized Rocky Flats at the outset of 1995, the extraordinary results achieved by a remarkable organization are summarized in figure 1.1. The project was completed in one-sixth the time and at less than one-sixth the cost compared with the original estimates. Pollution was mitigated from the most dangerous levels in America to a condition safe enough for a wildlife refuge and nature center. Despite a work scope in which the slightest error could have been disastrous, as well as a set of tasks that had never been completed before, safety performance improved from levels worse than industry and federal averages to more than twice as good as those benchmarks. Safety improved fivefold, in fact, compared with the safety records previous to 1995, when absolutely no cleanup or closure work was being done.

Employee layoffs and downsizing are likely to create bitterness, resistance, and deteriorating performance in organizations (see Cameron, 1994, 1998). Yet, at Rocky Flats the workforce was incrementally reduced over the 10-year period from over 7,000 employees to zero with no strikes, a dramatic reduction in grievances, and labor relations rated by both union and management as the best in their careers. External constituencies—including citizen groups in the surrounding communities, Colorado state officials, regulators such as the EPA, and the supervisory DOE—became partners, collaborators, and contributors to the success of the project. This situation represents a dramatic transformation from a history of 10,000-person protests, lawsuits, an FBI raid, court battles, and the legislative pressures that characterized these relationships in 1995.

Figure 1.1 ROCKY FLATS BEFORE AND AFTER THE CH2MHILL CONTRACT

Performance Criteria	Beginning (pre-1995)	Conclusion (2005)
Estimated time for completion of closure	70 years	10 years
Estimated closure budget	$36 billion	Just over $6 billion
Pollution levels	"Most dangerous rooms in America" DOE standard=651 pCi/gm	Safe enough for a wildlife refuge. Residual Soil Action Levels=50 pCi/gr
Safety TRC=Total Recordable Case rate (# of occupationally related incidents requiring more than basic first aid)	TRC Jan. 1996=5.0 (construction industry avg. 4.5)	TRC July 2004=1.0 (construction industry avg. 4.0, DOE avg. 2.0)
LWC=Lost Workday Case rate (restricted days away from work)	LWC July 2004=0.2 (construction industry avg. 4.0, DOE avg. 0.8)	LWC July 2004=0.2 (construction industry avg. 4.0, DOE avg. 0.8)

Performance Criteria	Beginning (pre-1995)	Conclusion (2005)
Statistic is calculated by rate for 100 FTE=# injuries/illness-esx200,000 man hours		$300,000 workers comp insurance rebate
Number of employees	3,500 during production, approximately 8,000 after shutdown and before cleanup	Steadily declining, with consistent layoffs through completion in 2005
Labor relations	900 employee grievances in 1998	"A handful a year." A union steward reported: "The best labor-management relations I've seen."
Relations with communities	10,000 protests; mistrust and little information flow to communities	Model stakeholder dialogue structure Frequent collaboration
Relations with the state of Colorado	Adversarial. Asserted that the Atomic Energy Act shielded Rocky Flats from state oversight	Cooperative and positive. State government officials were instrumental in securing federal support and helping regulators and contractor work collaboratively
Relations with federal regulators: DOE and EPA	EPA requested FBI raids that shut down the facility in 1989.	Site is a pioneer and a benchmark within DOE and EPA for cleanup and closure
Productivity	Between shutdown and closure announcement, almost no work was carried out	Exceeded the accelerated closure schedule in terms of both time and cost

Performance Criteria	Beginning (pre-1995)	Conclusion (2005)
Organizational culture	Secrecy, highly compartmentalized, assumptions of lifelong employment, low morale after shutdown	Collaborative, pride in closure, increased transparency, optimistic vision with a meaningful purpose

Rocky Flats represents a story of almost unbelievable performance in the face of serious adversity, and it would represent extraordinary performance even if the circumstances had been benevolent. This book recounts how these remarkable outcomes occurred, that is, the leadership principles and the key enablers that accounted for them. Exceeding almost every expected level of performance makes Rocky Flats an *extreme case*—an example so different from the norm that examining its features brings into stark relief particular features that may be hidden in normal organizations and under usual circumstances. The remainder of this chapter explains how this positively deviant performance occurred and the abundance approach that accounted for it.

The Abundance Approach

As mentioned in the Introduction, the fundamental explanation for extraordinary performance at Rocky Flats was the adoption of an *abundance approach to change.* An abundance approach refers to an emphasis on achieving the best of the human condition, striving for positive deviance, and working to fulfill the highest potential of organizations and individuals. It focuses on thriving outcomes and on virtuousness, and it stands in contrast to a problem-solving or deficit approach to change. The latter approach focuses on identifying and solving problems, addressing deficits and weaknesses, and overcoming challenges and obstacles.

For example, most leaders of change have been trained to recognize and define problems. They usually assume that leading change means overcoming obstacles that stand in the way of achieving a new vision (Kotter, 1996). A well-known national problem-solving approach to change is widely applied (Burke, 2002; March, 1994; Mitroff, 1998). This classic problem-solving model—taught almost universally in management development programs, change programs, and decision-making training—relies on four fundamental steps.

First is identifying and defining a problem accurately. When attempting to understand an organization, for example, typical questions might include What are the major challenges being faced? What are the competitive threats? Where are the problems? What key obstacles must be addressed? The second step relies on generating alternative solutions to the problem—based on root causes, if possible—so that convergence on a solution is not premature. Brainstorming techniques and group participation methods are often used to ensure that more than one alternative solution to a problem is considered. The third step focuses on evaluating and selecting the best alternative. Such evaluation addresses whether or not the chosen alternative really does solve the problem, achieves stated goals, does not create unwanted latent effects, and will be accepted by the individuals involved. The fourth step involves implementing the chosen alternative solution and following up to ensure that the problem or obstacle is really resolved.

This problem-solving approach relies on the assumption that an important job of the change leader is to identify and resolve problems and challenges that stand in the way of progress. The goal is to achieve a successful change, usually defined as effective, efficient, or advantageous performance. A large majority of leaders' time and attention is usually focused on this approach when they are attempting to lead change.

In contrast, the abundance approach—which does not *substitute* for the problem-solving approach but *supplements* it—focuses on closing the gaps between acceptable performance or even successful performance, and spectacular performance or even virtuous performance. It emphasizes positively deviant accomplishment rather than normal or expected accomplishment. It focuses on positive possibilities rather than deficits. In the Introduction, we showed a deviance continuum, with illness, problems, and difficulties on the left-hand side and normal, expected, and successful performance in the middle. We labeled the gap between the left side—problems or challenges—and the middle point—successful performance—as a *deficit gap.* Closing deficit gaps refers to solving problems and overcoming obstacles. Most academic research and most leadership focus are aimed at these kinds of gaps.

Figure 1.2 A PROBLEM-SOLVING APPROACH TO CHANGE COMPARED WITH AN ABUNDANCE APPROACH

Problem-solving Approach	Abundance Approach
Identify Problems and Challenges	Identify Extraordinary Success
• Identify key problems and challenges	• Describe peak experiences
Identify Alternatives and Cause Analysis	Conduct an Analysis of Enablers
• Generate alternative solutions based on root causes	• Identify enabler of the highest past performance
Select Optimal Solution	Identify How to Create Sustainability
• Evaluate and select the most optimal alternative	• Identify what could be continued and replicated in the future
Implementing and Following Up	Designing a Positive Future
• Implement the solution and follow up to ensure problem solution	• Design interventions that create an ideal future with extraordinary performance
Basic Assumption	Basic Assumption
• Our job is to overcome major problems and challenges	• Our job is to embrace and enable our highest potential

On that same deviance continuum, the right-hand side represents a virtuous condition—that which is positively deviant, flourishing, and life-giving. Working to achieve this kind of extraordinary performance was referred to as closing *abundance gaps.* An abundance approach to change focuses on achieving positive deviance, or the best of the human condition. It means not only doing well, it means creating goodness that extends beyond the immediate and beyond tangible achievement (Cameron, 2003). Figure 1.2 provides another way to summarize the differences between these two approaches to change (Cooperrider & Whitney, 1999). The basic assumption of the problem-solving approach to change is *Our job is to overcome major problems and challenges.* The basic assumption of the abundance approach is *Our job is to embrace and enable our highest potential.*

An abundance approach to change is similar to, and relies on, some of the same assumptions as Appreciative Inquiry (AI), a change tool introduced and made popular by David Cooperrider (for example Cooperrider & Whitney, 1999). It also draws on the strengths-based work being produced by the Gallup Organization (e.g., Buckingham & Clifton, 2001), the virtue ethics literature (Caza, Barker, & Cameron, 2004), the positive emotions work of Fredrickson (2003), and the broad field of positive psychology (e.g., Seligman, 2002b). It is a central part of the research agenda in the *Positive Organizational Scholarship* movement (Cameron, Dutton, & Quinn,

2003). The abundance approach offers its own unique perspective in these research streams, as will be illustrated in the chapters that follow.

One main message of this book is that focusing on abundance gaps produces a *heliotropic effect* (Cooperrider, 1990; Darwin, 1989) which, in turn, produces *amplifying* and *buffering* benefits. Emphasizing abundance gaps, in other words, unleashes positive potential that leads to extraordinary performance. It explains how the impossible was made possible at Rocky Flats. We explain why this occurs in the following section.

The Heliotropic Effect of Abundance

To explain the heliotropic effect, let us pose a question: What happens over time when you put a plant in a window? The answer, of course, is that the plant begins to lean toward the light. That is, a natural tendency exists in every living system to be inclined toward positive energy—toward light—and away from negative energy or from the dark. The reason is that light is life-giving and energy-creating. All living systems are inclined toward that which gives life.

The heliotropic effect is evident in many ways within individuals and organizations—physiologically, psychologically, emotionally, visually, socially, and so forth (see Cooperrider, 1990; Cameron, 2003; Bright, Cameron, & Caza, 2006). In the section that follows, we illustrate the heliotropic effect as it affects individuals, and in the one after that, we review evidence of the heliotropic effect in organizations. Several scientific studies are summarized with the intent of explaining how an abundance approach helps produce positively deviant outcomes. These examples serve as the explanation for how an abundance approach created extraordinary performance at Rocky Flats. The chapter concludes with a brief discussion of the amplifying and buffering benefits of an abundance approach to change.

Individuals. At the individual level, the heliotropic effect may be manifested physiologically as the *placebo effect.* That is, if a person believes a medication will be effective, it will, in fact, produce the desired effect about 60 percent of the time. One classic example involved a woman who entered the hospital suffering from uncontrolled vomiting. Her muscle contractions couldn't be halted, and she continued to regurgitate over and over. The medical professionals gave her medication designed to stop the vomiting, but nothing was effective. Finally, she was offered a new "miracle drug," just developed, which the doctor claimed to be 100 percent effective for her specific symptoms. Within 20 minutes of taking the drug, her vomiting stopped completely. The surprising part of this incident, however, is that the drug given to her was ipecac syrup, a medication designed to *induce* vomiting. The power of the placebo effect overcame not only her physiological symptoms—which she couldn't control—but also the effects of the medication itself (Ornstein & Sobel, 1987).

Psychologically, the heliotropic effect is manifested as the *Pygmalion effect.* That is, our systems respond not only to our own positive expectations, but also to the expectations of others. Literally hundreds of studies have confirmed the Pygmalion effect in individuals ranging from airline pilots and welders to preschoolers and high school athletes. The best-known studies have been conducted with elementary school children. To illustrate, assume that we have a normal group of students and three teachers who are naïve to the experiment. The first teacher is told that he or she will be assigned to a classroom filled with extraordinary performers who have very high IQs and a history of success in the classroom. The second teacher is told that he or she will be assigned to a classroom of students with enormous diversity in ability and experience—some extremely bright, some who have struggled a great deal in the classroom, and some who are normal. The third teacher is told that he or she will be assigned to a classroom of challenged students who come from underprivileged backgrounds, and have a history of failure and difficulties in the classroom. We allow the three teachers to teach for a year, and then we give all of the students a standardized exam. Statistically significant differences appear in the results. The students taught by the first teacher score above average;

the students taught by the second teacher have average scores; the students taught by the third teacher score below average. The expectations of the teacher account for the differences in performance, and those expectations are more powerful than any other single factor, including actual IQ scores (Rosenthal & Jacobsen, 1968). If the teacher thinks that the children are bright, then they are.

The heliotropic effect is also manifested *emotionally.* That is, many studies have documented the fact that people with positive emotional states and optimistic outlooks experience fewer illnesses and accidents and, in fact, enjoy a longer and higher quality of life. Depressed, anxious, or angry people get sick more often than happy, joyful, upbeat people, even when exposed to the same cold virus, and they tend more often to be in the wrong place at the wrong time and to experience accidents. One of the most intriguing studies illustrating the emotional manifestations of the heliotropic effect was a study of Alzheimer's disease among 678 elderly nuns who were members of the School Sisters of Notre Dame and ranged in age from 75 to 104. What was especially intriguing about the study was a finding based on the journals and diaries kept by 180 of these women when they entered the convent 60 years earlier. Some of the women recorded thoughts like this: "I am so grateful to enter the convent. This is a dream come true for me. What a wonderful blessing." Other women recorded thoughts like this: "This will be a sacrifice.

It's going to be difficult, but I have committed myself, and I'll follow through." The first group displayed "positive emotional content," whereas the second group did not. Six decades later there was a significant difference in the numbers of nuns alive in each group. Two and a half times more nuns had died in the second group than in the first, and in every decade there was a significant and increasing difference in mortality rates. Positive emotions simply predicted longer life spans (Snowden, 2002; Danner, Snowden, & Friesen, 2001).

The heliotropic effect can manifest itself in *visualization.* When people visualize themselves as succeeding—they see themselves hitting the ball, clearing the bar, making the shot, getting the right answer, or recovering from illness—they tend to succeed significantly more than otherwise. For example, assume that we wanted to help a group of people improve their bowling scores. We could promise everyone a reward—say $100—if they could improve their scores by an average of, say, 10 pins over several weeks. To conduct the experiment, we would have each person bowl three games while we videotaped the games. Then, for half the group we would show them videotape of the frames when they made strikes or spares—that is, when they knocked down all the pins. For the other half of the group we would show them videotape of when they did not make strikes or spares. Each person would watch the videotape, practice for several weeks, and then come back and bowl three more games. The results of the experiment would reveal significant differences between the two groups. Those who watched themselves succeed would improve significantly more than the other group; in fact, improvement among the weakest bowlers would exceed 100 percent (Kirschenbaum, 1984). Visualizing success leads to success.

Still another set of studies shows the heliotropic effect that occurs when individuals are exposed—even briefly—to *virtuous, optimistic, positive behaviors* (see Ryff & Singer, 1998; Emmons, 2003; Seligman, 2002a). For example, let us assume that we wanted to divide a group of people in half. We would ask each person to keep a daily journal. One group would be asked to write down each day three things for which they were grateful. The other group would be asked to write down three things for which they were not grateful, or three things they wished had not happened that day. Alternatively, we could ask one group to record the three best things that happened to them that day and the other group to record the three worst things that happened to them that day. We would then expose them to several experimental conditions. For example, we would give everyone a flu shot, and a week later we test for the number of antibodies in their systems. The first group—exposed to gratitude and optimistic conditions—would be healthier than the second group. When confronted with a difficult mental problem, the first group would remember longer, use more information, display more mental acuity, and express more creativity than the second group. A significant difference would also exist in the amount of illness experienced by the members of each group as well as in their productivity at work. That is, exposure to a virtuous condition such as gratitude—even briefly—tends to unlock the heliotropic effect (Emmons, 2003).

The heliotropic effect also occurs through *positive energy.* Most people have been exposed to someone who is energizing, uplifting, and life-giving. We tend to flourish in their presence. We also have encountered people who are the opposite—they drain our energy and are life-depleting. Baker, Cross, & Wooten (2003) found that network maps could be produced for groups and organizations that diagram the energy networks among individuals. The results look like an airline system map, with some people being like hubs, having a large number of positive energy connections, and others being more peripheral. The results of this research show that people who are positive energizers—they uplift, strengthen, and encourage others—are much higher performers at work than normal people. Moreover, a person's position in an energy network is four times more important in accounting for performance than position in the information network or the influence network. It is more important to be a positive energizer than to have a title or a senior position in the hierarchy. Moreover, organizations that are high performing have three times more positive energizers than normal organizations. Positive energy, simply stated, unlocks the heliotropic effect.

Additional evidence could be cited to confirm the association between a positive or abundance approach and the heliotropic effect within individuals—including the strengths-based findings of the Gallup Organization (Buckingham & Clifton, 2001), the high-quality connections research of Dutton and Heaphy (2003), and the positive emotions work of Fredrickson (2003). Each of these streams of research confirms the conclusion that emerged from the studies cited above: namely, that a focus on the positive and on abundance unlocks the heliotropic effect. People do better physically, mentally, socially, and emotionally when exposed to abundance.

Organizations. The trouble is, organizations are not the same as individuals. Many findings that apply to individuals do not apply to organizations, and one cannot automatically draw the conclusion that just because something applies to a person, it will also apply to an organization. If fact, skeptics might appropriately raise questions such as: Aren't most organizations fraught with problems? Can any leader afford to ignore difficulties? Is an abundance approach to change just a whitewash of serious challenges? Won't any organization fail if it fails to focus on its weaknesses and liabilities? In light of major challenges faced by most organizations and most leaders, what is the relevance of an abundance approach?

Several studies have been conducted by Cameron and colleagues (for example, Cameron, 2003; Cameron, Bright, & Caza, 2004; Bright, Cameron, & Caza, 2006; Gittell, Cameron, & Lim, 2006) which do, in fact, support the impact of a positive, abundance orientation on organizational performance. That is, an abundance approach does appear to be associated with high levels of performance in organizations. A few of these studies are summarized in order to provide additional evidence for the association between abundance and the heliotropic effect.

One investigation was conducted by Marcial Losada (Losada & Heaphy, 2004) in which 60 top management teams came together for their annual planning-budgeting-evaluation meeting. Their work was performed in a setting where investigators could observe and code their communication events. Unknown to the team members, each organization's performance was categorized on the basis of productivity, profitability, and other outcome data. On these various outcome measures, if the organization scored above average, it was classified as high performing. If the organization scored below average, it was classified as low performing. There were 19 high performing, 26 medium performing, and 15 low performing organizations observed.

One category used to code teams' communication was the number of positive statements made, versus the number of negative statements, as they were engaged in their work. A positive statement expressed approval, support, appreciation, agreement, and so on. A negative statement expressed disapproval, contradiction, disagreement, anger, and so on. Executives in high-performing firms made five times as many positive statements as negative statements. Executives in low-performing firms made three times as many negative statements as positive statements. As a nonlinear dynamics study, the pattern of positive communication unfolding over time in the high-performing firms was significantly different from what emerged in low-performing firms, so the results did not occur merely because people tend to talk more positively when things go well. The study's conclusion was that this positive-to-negative communication ratio is by far the strongest predictor of organizational performance.

Coincidentally, a study conducted by John Gottman (1994) of recently married couples produced similar results. Couples who had been married between one and five years held a conversation in which they discussed a controversial topic in their relationship—child rearing, finances, time at work, or whatever. The conversation was recorded for 15 minutes. Gottman then followed the couples over a period of ten years and could predict with 95 percent accuracy who was still married and who was happily married, based on that 15minute conversation a decade earlier. The predictive ratio in the interaction was five positive statements for every negative statement. The key message in these two studies is that positive communication tends to produce positive outcomes, and in the Losada study, the outcomes generalize to the entire organization. An abundance approach to change puts its greatest emphasis on the positive, and positivity produces the heliotropic effect.

Another set of studies investigating the impact of the abundance approach was conducted among organizations that had recently downsized (see Cameron, 2003). The problem with organizational downsizing is that it almost always produces negative effects—most notably, the destruction of interpersonal relationships, shared values, trust, loyalty, and commonality of culture and values; reduced information-sharing and increased secrecy, deception, and duplicity; increased formalization, rigidity, resistance to change, and conservatism; increased conflict, anger, vindictiveness, and feelings of victimization; and increased selfishness and voluntary turnover, as well as deterioration in teamwork and cooperation (Cole, 1993; Cameron, Kim, & Whetten, 1987). As a result, most downsizing firms experience a deterioration in performance. (It was expected, based on these findings, that Rocky Flats would deteriorate in performance as the layoff activities associated with closure began.)

The studies summarized below do not examine causal relationships between abundance and high performance, but they do produce evidence that is suggestive of such a relationship (see Cameron, 2003). For example, in one study, two organizations (one in health care and the other in engineering) that

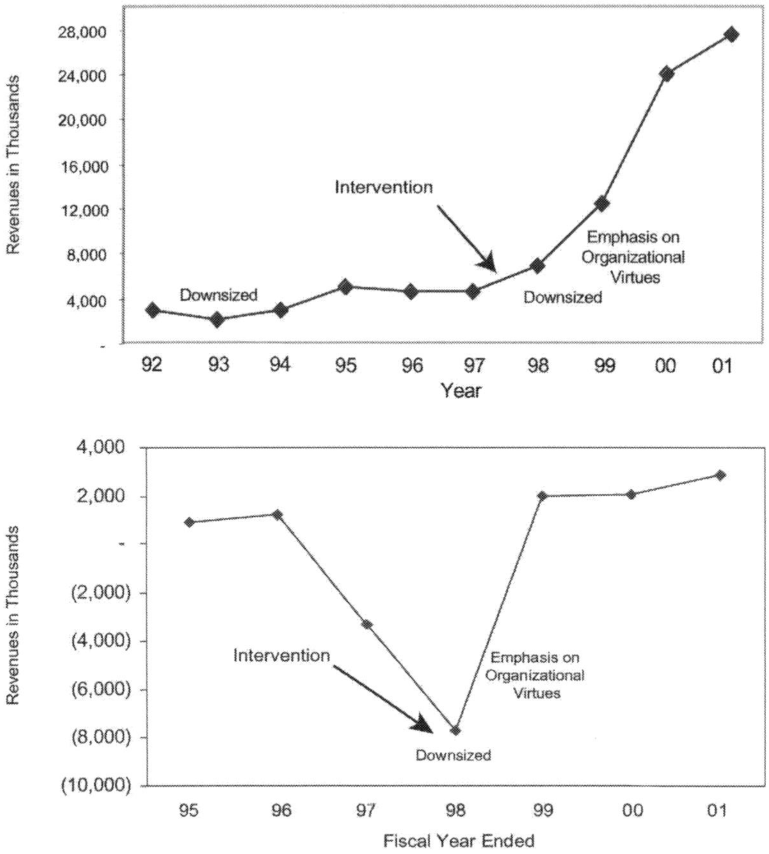

Figure 1.3 INTERVENTIONS TO FOSTER AN ABUNDANCE CULTURE

had recently engaged in downsizing experienced a major intervention focused on enhancing an abundance orientation. Fostering organizational virtuousness—as indicated by an emphasis on compassion, integrity, optimism, trust, forgiveness, and kindness—was implemented by the senior leadership team, and measures were taken of various indicators of an abundance approach. Figure 1.3 summarizes the results of the leadership interventions. Both organizations dramatically improved their financial performance. These results do not prove that abundance caused a heliotropic effect in organizational outcomes, but the results are suggestive.

Another study was conducted among seven organizations competing in the same industry. In each of these firms, performance measures were gathered—productivity, profitability, quality, customer satisfaction, and employee loyalty—as were scores of the extent to which an abundance approach typified the firms. Abundance was indicated primarily by high scores on certain organizational virtuousness factors—for example, fostering compassion, integrity, optimism, trust, forgiveness, and kindness. Figure 1.4 illustrates that the relationships between abundance and performance are quite strong. The higher the abundance scores—as indicated by organizational virtuousness—the higher the performance.

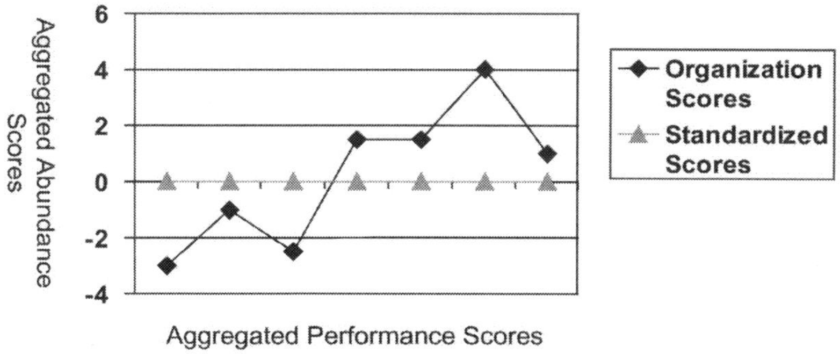

Figure 1.4 RELATIONSHIPS BETWEEN ABUNDANCE AND PERFORMANCE

A third study used the same outcome measures and the same indicators of abundance, but this study was conducted with a large sample of organizations across 16 industries (for example, retail, automotive, consulting, financial services). Large multinational

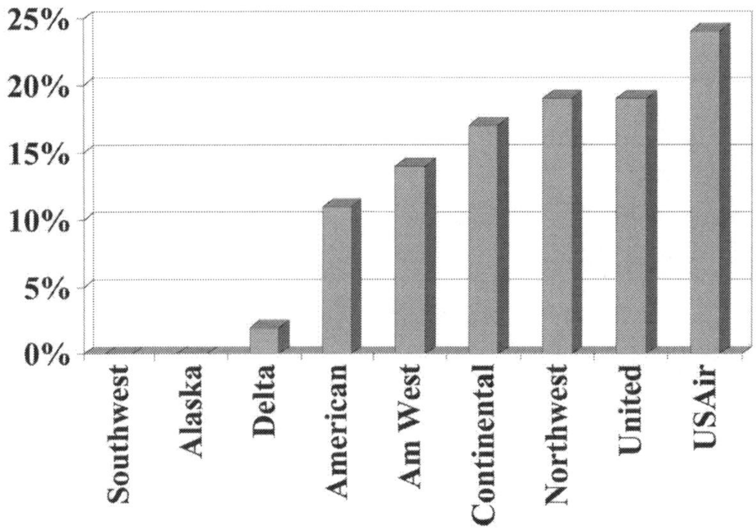

Figure 1.5 DOWNSIZING AMONG U.S. AIRLINES AFTER SEPTEMBER 11, 2001

firms were represented as well as medium, small, and even not-for-profit organizations. All of these organizations had been engaged in recent downsizing, so all were predicted to show a deterioration in performance. Statistical results revealed, in fact, that when controlling for all other factors, downsizing did lead to deteriorating organizational performance. However, statistically significant relationships were found between organizational virtuousness and profitability. Organizations scoring higher in virtuousness were more profitable, and, when compared with competitors, industry averages, goals, and past performance on perceptual measures, virtuousness mitigated the negative effects of downsizing. Higher abundance (virtuousness) scores were associated with higher performance.

Again, no one of these studies can claim to prove that virtuousness produces higher organizational performance, or that abundance causes a heliotropic effect in organizations. However, taken as a group, they are suggestive that such a relationship may be present.

A study of the U.S. airline industry after the September 11 tragedy adds to the evidence that positivity, virtuousness, and abundance produce higher levels of performance for organizations. Gittell, Cameron, and Lim (2006) studied the reactions of the nine major U.S. carriers after the terrorist attacks in 2001. Ridership fell to zero for the first week or so after the event, of course, but when people were permitted to fly again, only about 80 percent of previous passenger levels were attained in the subsequent year. The major airlines found themselves with 20 percent too many gate agents, flight attendants, mechanics, pilots, and planes. The logical strategy was to downsize. This was the strategy implemented by almost all of these airlines, as illustrated in figure 1.5.

In particular, short-haul routes were the hardest hit during the first year after the tragedy, since many people preferred to drive or take a bus or train rather than to board an airplane. The hassle factor associated with stepped-up security was a key reason why more short flights were canceled than long-haul flights. The two airlines that were most affected—since they relied

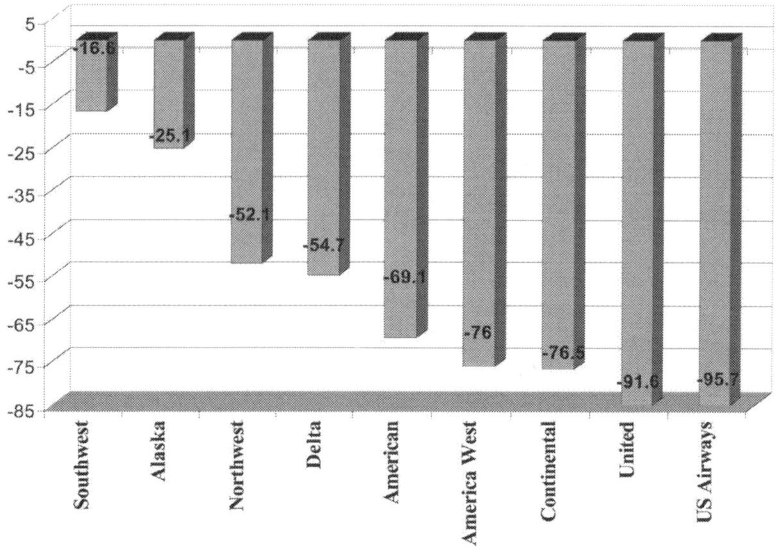

Figure 1.6 SHAREHOLDER VALUES, SEPTEMBER 2001–SEPTEMBER 2002

most heavily on short flights—were Southwest Airlines and US Airways.

The difference between these two firms was marked, however, in the extent to which they relied on an abundance approach. US Airways laid off more than 20 percent of its workforce and imposed force majure, which allowed it to avoid paying severance benefits to laid-off employees. Southwest Airlines, on the other hand, decided to not lay off a single employee. Despite losing several million dollars a day, CEO Jim Parker said:

> Clearly we can't continue to do this indefinitely, but we are willing to suffer some damage, even to our stock price, to protect the jobs of our people.

The reason given for this approach represents an abundance-oriented approach—virtuousness, focusing on the good, and aiming at producing human flourishing.

> We could have furloughed at various times and been more profitable, but I always thought that was shortsighted. You want to show your people that you value them, and you're not going to hurt them just to get a little more money in the short term. Not furloughing people breeds loyalty. It breeds a sense of security. It breeds a sense of trust.
>
> CEO, Southwest Airlines

The problem with an abundance approach to change in the airline industry (or any industry), of course, is that Wall Street doesn't care. Shareholder value and a return to stockholders are the key benchmarks of success. Whether an abundance approach is used or not is largely irrelevant to investors. In fact, an abundance approach to change, or fostering virtuousness in organizations, seems a bit too syrupy and saccharine for most senior leaders who are pressured to produce short-term financial results. As illustrated in figure 1.6, however, it was the abundance approach that produced the highest financial payoff in the airline industry. In fact, this study found that the correlation between increases in shareholder value and the use of an abundance approach was 0.86 in the first year after the tragedy, and it remained that way through 2005. Wall Street rewarded abundance and virtuousness the most.

Amplifying and Buffering Benefits

One reason that organizations do better when exposed to abundance and virtuousness—that is, a reason that the heliotropic effect works in organizations as well as with individuals—is its *amplifying* and *buffering benefits.* Simply stated, when an abundance approach is implemented in organizations, positive consequences are amplified, and they become self-reinforcing. Similarly, the organization becomes buffered from negative consequences and develops hardiness (see Cameron, 2003; Bright, Cameron, & Caza, 2006). There are at least four explanations for why these benefits occur: *the generation of positive emotions, the formation of social capital, the demonstration of prosocial behavior,* and *the creation of resiliency.*

Positive emotions. An abundance approach to change and the facilitation of virtuousness in organizations produce positive emotions in individuals which, in turn, lead to an amplifying effect. When organization members observe compassion, experience love, or witness spectacular performance, for example, they are inspired, increase their pride in the organization, enhance their enjoyment of the work, and elevate their satisfaction with the job, and thereby they experience "love, empathy, verve, zest, and enthusiasm ... the sine qua non of managerial success and organizational excellence" (Fineman, 1996:545). Several studies (George, 1995; Fineman, 1996; Seligman, 2002a) have demonstrated that this amplifying effect is emotionally disseminated throughout an organization by way of a contagion effect. That is, the entire organization is influenced positively when an abundance approach is pursued, especially by individuals in leadership positions.

Social capital. A second reason for the amplifying benefits of an abundance approach is its association with the formation of social capital. Social capital refers to the development of positive relationships among employees. Building social capital reduces transaction costs, facilitates communication and cooperation, enhances employee commitment, fosters individual learning, strengthens relationships and involvement, and, ultimately, enhances organizational performance (Adler & Kwon, 2002). Experiencing an abundance approach, with its emphasis on virtuousness, creates a sense of attachment and attraction toward virtuous actors (Bolino, Turnley, & Bloodgood, 2002), which in turn helps members of an organization experience an urge to join with and build upon the contributions of these others (Sethi & Nicholson, 2001). Organizations function better when members know, trust, and feel positively toward each other, and an abundance approach creates the conditions for that to occur.

Prosocial behavior. An abundance approach tends to foster prosocial behavior or behaviors that benefit other people. Several authors have pointed out that individuals engage in prosocial behavior because of an intrinsic motivation toward helping others, among other factors (e.g., Batson, 1994). "Evidence on impulse helping suggests that ... individuals may be genetically disposed to engage in impulsive acts of helping" (Krebs, 1987:113). Observing and experiencing virtuousness helps unlock the human predisposition toward behaving in ways that benefit others. Studies reported by Cialdini (2000) and Asch (1952) support the idea that when people observe exemplary or moral behavior, their inclination is to follow suit. Positive spirals of prosocial behavior tend to flow from abundance-oriented behavior.

Resilience. An abundance approach also buffers organizations from harmful events by fostering resiliency. Seligman and Csikszentmihalyi (2000) pointed out, for example, that the development of abundance and virtuousness serves as a buffer against dysfunction and illness at the individual and group levels of analysis. They reported that the positive dynamics associated with abundance were found to be prevention agents against psychological distress, addiction, and dysfunctional behavior. Learned optimism, for example, prevents depression and anxiety in children and adults, roughly halving their incidence over the subsequent two years (Seligman, 1991).

Similarly, at the group and organization levels, an abundance approach enhances the ability to absorb threat and trauma and to bounce back from adversity (Dutton, Frost, Worline, Lilius, & Kanov, 2002). It serves as a source of resilience and "toughness" (Dienstbier & Zillig, 2002) that fosters a sense of collective efficacy, thus helping the organization absorb misfortune, recover from trauma, and maintain momentum in difficult circumstances. Abundance helps replenish or renew organizations. That is, observing or experiencing the abundance approach fosters positive energy and, hence, replenishes the human capital needed to capably absorb or recover from damage (Dutton & Heaphy, 2003).

Summary

In this chapter we addressed the question *How did extraordinary performance occur at Rocky Flats?* We provided more detail regarding why this case represents an instance of making the impossible possible—achieving levels of performance well beyond normal. Never had such a task been undertaken. The obstacles and difficulties at the facility were enormous, so just meeting expectations for a 70-year, $36 billion cleanup would have represented a remarkable success. However, the fact that success was achieved 60 years early, $30 billion under budget, and with significantly better quality standards than originally required would be unbelievable if it hadn't actually happened. The primary reason for this success was the implementation of an abundance approach to change—a positive emphasis, or an emphasis on achieving the best of the human condition, striving for positive deviance, and working to fulfill the highest potential of organizations and individuals. Adopting an abundance approach to change unlocks the heliotropic effect in individuals and organizations. The heliotropic effect not only produces elevated performance but also provides amplifying benefits—escalating, self-reinforcing performance—and buffering benefits—the development of resiliency and the ability to absorb negative influences. Subsequent chapters illustrate these effects at Rocky Flats.

Among the conclusions to be drawn from this explanation are the following:

- ***The impossible is made possible by the abundance approach to change.***
- ***An abundance approach to change helps produce the heliotropic effect.***
- ***Unlocking the heliotropic effect in organizations, and among employees, leads to extraordinary performance.***
- ***Adopting an abundance approach produces amplifying and buffering benefits, so an upward spiral of improvement can be created as a result of abundance leadership.***

2

Impending Disaster—A Brief History of Rocky Flats

Rocky Flats had a history of excellent production-performance during its years of operation. The workers involved in production were considered the best in the world, and the site never missed a production goal. However, because of the extraordinary security and secrecy required at the site, the public tended to hear about Rocky Flats only when problems occurred. Unfortunately, some of the largest and most serious environmental and industrial accidents in U.S. history occurred at Rocky Flats, so it became a focal point of activism against the dangers of radioactive emissions as well as nuclear proliferation in general.

The public's image of Rocky Flats was based largely on trepidation and controversy. These perceptions came to a head when the site was raided in 1989, and the active mission of the facility was abruptly halted due to alleged environmental law violations. Internally, the climate at Rocky Flats deteriorated substantially because employees were no longer permitted to do the work they were trained to do, even though the site continued to operate over the next six years until a closure agreement was reached. During this time, the site functioned without a clear mission, and no progress was made toward cleanup or finding a transitional use for the facilities. Neither the public nor employees were satisfied with what had become of Rocky Flats.

This period had enormously detrimental effects on employee morale and self-confidence, and on the organization's culture. Moreover, external constituencies—multiple federal, state, and local groups—were embroiled in criticism and condemnation. The transformation at Rocky Flats is especially remarkable, therefore, because positively deviant performance emerged from a history of entrenched difficulty. What follows is a brief history of the site's operation prior to 1995 and the circumstances from which extraordinary success was achieved.

Operating Overview

On March 23, 1951 a front page article in the *Denver Post* announced that the Atomic Energy Commission would build a top-secret nuclear weapons plant in a rocky but flat ranching area in Jefferson County, Colorado (Obmascik, 2000). The skyline of Denver is visible from the production area although most Denver residents were unaware of its existence. Rocky Flats began operation in 1953 and was in production until the 1989 raid. From the 1950s until 1995, the facility was managed by a principal contracting company with experience in defense contracting and weapons manufacturing.

From 1951 to 1977 Dow Chemical managed the facility; from 1977 until 1989 Rockwell International was the managing firm; and from 1989 until 1995 EG&G was the primary contractor.

The 350-acre production section contained hundreds of different kinds of structures (3 million square feet under roof) in its industrial area, which was surrounded by the open space buffer zone. The property has small streams and a reservoir and had wastewater treatment and power substations, a fire department, and a medical office. Rocky Flats was, during its first 30 years, a small full-service city.

At the height of production, the site operated with almost 8,000 employees, and the plant was in 24/7 operation, steadily producing "the most deadly devices ever invented" (Obmascik, 2000). Rocky Flats employees converted plutonium into among the "most highly engineered devices ever manufactured"—plutonium pits, or triggers, for nuclear bombs (Obmascik, 2000). A hollow sphere that varies in size "from a grapefruit to a soccer ball," a plutonium pit explodes with the power of a Hiroshima bomb (Obmascik, 2000). Rocky Flats workers processed, purified, and machined the plutonium pits which served as the triggers to unleash the firepower of thermonuclear weapons. These bombs were 600 times stronger than the atomic bombs used during World War II. Each pit possessed the explosive equivalent of 15,000 tons of TNT (Obmascik, 2000).

Figure 2: Rocky Flats site with the Denver skyline

By 1957 Rocky Flats "had become the linchpin in the nation's nuclear bomb system" (Obmascik, 2000). According to declassified reports from DOE, approximately 70,000 pits were manufactured from 1953 to 1989. The plant also manufactured other weapons parts using uranium, beryllium, stainless steel, and other materials. According to the Colorado Department of Public Health and Environment (CDPHE, 2004), more than 8,000 materials were used or stored at Rocky Flats, including plutonium, uranium, beryllium, tritium, carbon tetrachloride, and dioxin. Prior to its closure, many tons of weapons-grade nuclear material and hundreds of tons of contaminated nuclear waste were present on the site, more plutonium residues than at any other DOE nuclear manufacturing facility.

Security at the site was exceptionally high. A *Denver Post* reporter, Mark Obmascik, who visited the site described approaching the site as follows:

> Visitors must pass through as many as four security stops before entering any classified section of the complex. Rocky Flats spends $55 million a year on security. At the first Rocky Flats checkpoint, to protect against terrorist suicide missions, guards with submachine guns swab dust from the steering wheels and doors of visiting cars to check for explosives residue.

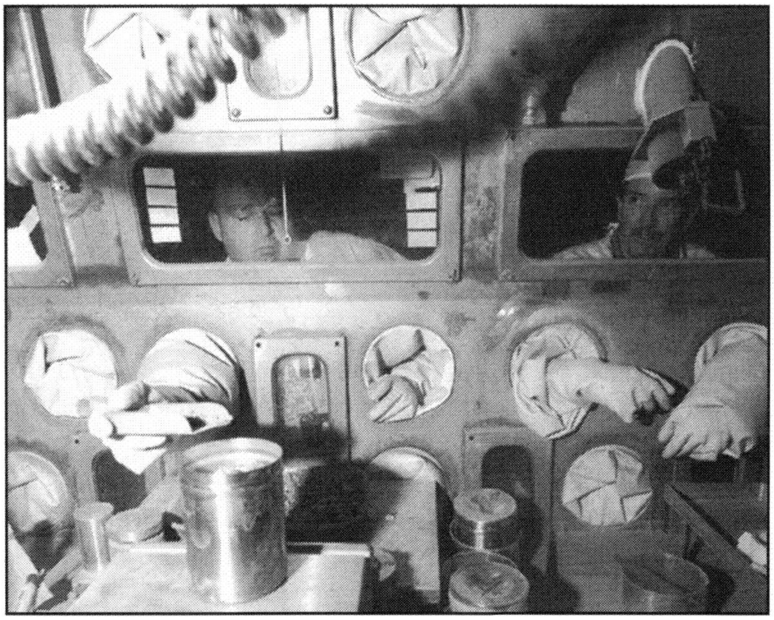

Figure 3: Handling radioactive material inside a glove box

> The second checkpoint is staffed by more armed guards, who screen visitors with metal detectors and scan fingers and palms with a computer that matches handprints with government records. Most people who proceed through

Figure 4: A security guard with loaded M-16 rifle

this guard station already have received a top secret "Q" clearance, which requires a full investigation of at least the past 10 years of their personal lives.

A third checkpoint just outside a plutonium building screens the visitor's necklace of five or so security badges to make sure the person is allowed inside. Some buildings also post a fourth security station, where more guards with submachine guns check visitor badges behind a portal of bulletproof glass and 4-inch-thick metal doors.

> The perimeter of the 385-acre pit production area is surrounded by two razor-wire fences, security cameras and prisonlike watch towers with more armed guards. To foil helicopter landings, deterrents are stationed on the roofs of several buildings. (Obmascik, 2000)

The Most Dangerous Rooms in America

Figure 5: Storage facility before cleanup

Not only could the weapons components produced at Rocky Flats cause enormous destruction, but the materials at the site posed a substantial risk to workers and surrounding communities. While some level of radioactivity occurs naturally in the background environment, a number of studies posit that inhaling even one plutonium particle increases cancer risk. The half-life of plutonium is 24,360 years. In addition to plutonium, many of the thousands of chemicals and radioactive materials used at the site carried significant health risks. While the site was often the first in the world to adopt health protocols—such as the use of advanced radiation monitors—many substances were used prior to a time when risk was adequately known or protocols were put in place (CDPHE, 2004).

Figure 6: Storage facility after cleanup

The probability of making the site safe again was, in practical terms, virtually impossible. Rocky Flats had been labeled as the most dangerous place on the continent in the 1994 exposé, and it was not likely that such a condition could be altered easily or quickly. The sealed "infinity rooms" were likely to be polluted forever because of the lengthy half-life of the radioactive contaminants contained in them, but more importantly, the exact level of pollution could not even be assessed on metering devices.

Patriotism and Pride

Despite the dangers involved in production, the highly skilled employees were extremely proud of their role in "keeping the country safe during the Cold War." The weapons production of Rocky Flats was critical to the U.S. Cold War strategy from the 1950s through the 1980s, which was based on the notion of national defense through nuclear deterrence. In addition to its patriotic mission, the workforce took great pride in the quality and productivity of their manufacturing operation. While the site didn't command the same status within the DOE complex as Los Alamos or other better-known facilities devoted to research, the workforce never missed a production quota during its years of operation and had the highest production quality of any DOE facility. Four officials in the steelworkers union said, for example:

> We have a history of doing good work here. We have done work that no one else on the planet could perform. We had the most up-to-date machine shop in the world before the raid and closure announcement.
>
> Contributor 12—Union Officers, Kaiser-Hill

And the site CEO stated:

> We machined tolerances that no one else in the world was capable of.

Environmental Hazards and Growing Public Awareness

The site saw itself as operating under the protection of the Atomic Energy Act. That is, because of the importance of its mission for national security, the site was not required to comply with environmental laws administered by the Environmental Protection Agency (EPA) or submit to regulation and oversight by other federal or state agencies.

The site operated in such secrecy until 1969 that the full nature of its mission was not well known by the public. On Mother's Day, 11 May 1969, a plutonium briquette spontaneously ignited, causing what at the time was the largest industrial fire in U.S. history (Obmascik, 2000). The fire caused "more than $200 million worth of damage in today's dollars" (Obmascik, 2000). This accident focused significant public attention, for the first time, on the potential for hazardous emission releases from Rocky Flats. Independent analyses of soil samples collected near the plant after the fire confirmed that radioactive materials had escaped. As a result, public mistrust and protests over how the plant was managed and operated gained momentum. Demonstrations of more than 10,000 people occurred at the site, which became a focal point for individuals and groups concerned about nuclear proliferation, environmental degradation, and social justice (Cooney, 1987).

The investigation of the fire also revealed that previously undisclosed accidents had occurred at the site. As a result of independent measurements of soil contamination after the 1969 fire, the public learned about earlier plutonium releases and a previous plutonium fire. On 11 and 12 September 1957, a plutonium fire, started in a glove box (a metal enclosure in which plutonium was handled and machined), burned for 14 hours. Sometime prior to 1968, a storage area was found which contained approximately 5,000 30- and 50-gallon leaking steel barrels filled with waste oil and solvents that were contaminated with plutonium and uranium. Acids created in these waste barrels caused extensive corrosion. An estimated 5,000 gallons of plutonium-contaminated waste oil leaked from the corroded drums into the soil. When Rocky Flats staff monitored and mapped the area in July 1968, they found soil contamination covering 261,000 square feet (6 acres), with the highest plutonium concentrations in the top inch of soil. Windstorms in late 1968 and early 1969 blew plutonium-contaminated soil particles onsite and offsite, affecting a much larger area (CDPHE, 2004).

Additionally, government-sponsored investigations by independent third parties after the end of the site's active operation in 1989 determined that the filtration system used to collect airborne plutonium from the production process did not collect all such matter, and small amounts were released into the environment through rooftop vents. Moreover, large quantities of the carcinogenic solvent carbon tetrachloride had been released over many years (CDPHE, 2004).

An Unprecedented Response to Secrecy

Despite these major environmental incidents, Rocky Flats had adamantly maintained that it was not subject to oversight by the EPA or Colorado Department of Public Health and Environment because of provisions of the Atomic Energy Act. A former Congressional staff member, and later a Kaiser-Hill manager, noted:

> Through my years on the Hill I would say that the relationship deteriorated and deteriorated and deteriorated. At the beginning DOE and the contractor just sort of stiff-armed the public and the regulators. They had been operating in secrecy since the mid-50's and they basically saw no reason to do anything else. They thought they were covered by the Atomic Energy Act, that they did not have to comply with environmental laws, that this whole environmental angle was a nuisance and something that they could just hold up the shield of the Atomic Energy Act and protect themselves. It went from bad to worse, and there was so much secrecy.

Contributor 5—Manager, Kaiser-Hill

Because such stiff-arm tactics often did not work, the reaction at Rocky Flats was to invest in public relations activities aimed at putting a positive spin on these events.

> We were involved with the site at a period when the site was very combative. They saw the regulators and the activist community as enemies. They had 43 people doing community relations to try to spin things that were failing at an alarming rate.

Contributor 5—Manager, Kaiser-Hill

The adversarial nature of the relationship between Rocky Flats and these external constituencies led to even more misunderstanding and miscommunication. Rather than improving public relations and building positive images, secrecy, defensiveness, and concealment produced the reverse. One incident highlights the problem of the emphasis on secrecy and suppression of information.

> I'll give you an example. There was so much secrecy that frequently they didn't even know what the public knew or didn't know. EG&G [the contractor prior to CH2MHill] came in as contractor, and I was on the environmental monitoring council. I had asked a question about plutonium that was unaccounted for. This was the plutoni-

> um-in-the-ducts issue, and we had been told, "Oh, maybe two grams, 2.8 grams. That's what we think we've seen in the ductwork." So, the deputy on the contractor's side came to talk to the council, and I asked the same question. He said, "Well, I don't know whether I can tell you. It may be classified, but I'll call you back." He called me back the next day and said, "It's about 28 kilos." That was a thousand times what we'd been told previously. He didn't understand that this was the story that was going to be on the front page. He had looked at a previous report that said as many as 100 kilos, but he didn't know that that number had never been out in the public. He felt that the number he was giving me was a small number. Meanwhile, I fell off my chair and was on the phone with the *New York Times* reporter two seconds later. It was on TV and radio pretty much the entire next day.... The headline in the *New York Times* the next day is, 60 pounds of plutonium in the ducts.... They didn't even know what was out and what wasn't.
>
> Contributor 5—Manager, Kaiser-Hill

The results of local, state, and federal litigation produced rulings in the late 1980s that allowed both the EPA and the state of Colorado to obtain regulatory jurisdiction at Rocky Flats, in addition to the authority of the Department of Energy. Based on the strenuous efforts of Rocky Flats management to maintain a veil of secrecy, and reports of flagrant environmental violations, the EPA launched a criminal investigation into the operations at Rocky Flats. An EPA official assigned to Rocky Flats in 1988 described the threatening environment that characterized these investigations:

> In 1988, when I arrived in Denver, there was a considerable controversy going on at the Flats. As you know, one of the first briefings I got was from the criminal office. They told me they were going to do the flyover. They told me that they were going to be flying over restricted zones, and it was possible that the plane would be shot down. This was all in my early briefing. So, anyway, there were very tense moments in the early days because of the criminal investigations.

Contributor 34—Regulator, EPA

Operation Desert Glow

On 6 June 1989, in an unprecedented move by law enforcement against a federal facility, agents from the Federal Bureau of Investigation, the Justice Department, and the Environmental Protection Agency launched a raid on Rocky Flats—dubbed Operation Desert Glow—to investigate allegations of environmental crimes. The site's nuclear mission was immediately halted.

In March 1992, following a grand jury investigation, a plea agreement between the U.S. Department of Justice and the site contractor, Rockwell International, was announced. Rockwell International paid a fine of $18.5 million. The site was designated a Superfund hazardous waste site and was slated for cleanup. Rockwell International was replaced as the site manager by EG&G.

Employees continued to report to work, but no production mission existed for them to achieve. Because no advance warning of the raid had occurred, systems were shut down midprocess, so some radioactive materials were left unstabilized and safety hazards increased rather than decreased. The facility became a liability to DOE, the state of Colorado, and the employees. The work stoppage also brought significant changes to the workforce and took an enormous emotional toll. As one executive at Rocky Flats put it:

> This was a very talented and proud workforce during the Cold War. They took a lot of pride in the work they were doing and the contributions they made. They went literally overnight with the FBI raid from being heroes to being goats. They didn't have a lot of meaningful work to do for quite a period of time.

Contributor 9—Senior Executive, Kaiser-Hill

An Organization Adrift

Despite the fact that production had been halted at Rocky Flats, the contract structure of the facility was designed to reward speed of production, not cost savings. Thus employees still reported to work each day. Federal contracts were structured on a "cost-plus" basis, so that reimbursement to the managing firm was based on the expenses incurred. High-quality work and timeliness of output were more important than cost efficiency, so the primary issue of negotiation in DOE contracts was the percent of overhead to be awarded to the managing firm. One former DOE manager of Rocky Flats explained the process:

> There was a process we called the award fee contract. They got cost plus award fees, so they got reimbursed for all their costs, whatever they were. If they went from 3,000 to 7,000 employees, they got paid for that, even if they weren't accomplishing anything more than they did with 3,000 employees.
>
> Contributor 21—Manager, DOE

The workforce actually increased during this period even though no production work was accomplished. Approximately 3,500 employees worked at Rocky Flats during the prime years of production. However, after the FBI raid in 1989 and the subsequent escalation in regulation and jurisdictional entities involved at Rocky Flats, employment rose to almost 8,000 employees. Between 1989 and 1995, the managing firm, EG&G, added employees in anticipation of the resumption of production activities. DOE was headed at the time by Admiral Watkins from the U.S. Navy nuclear program, and far more stringent compliance standards were imposed on the Rocky Flats site. The site was redefined as a nuclear facility instead of a production facility, so a new set of standards and activities was required. Even items such as pens and gloves had to be compatibility tested and standardized. This resulted in a marked increase in the demand for reports, assurances, and accountability from CDPHE, DOE, and the EPA. The costs associated with federal reimbursement therefore continued to escalate. A senior DOE manager at Rocky Flats reported:

> They had spent billions of dollars, and the ... staff had grown from 3,000 to well over 7,000 people. In five years they hadn't done anything except paper studies. That was, in part, in response to working with the state and the EPA. These agencies had set up something like 200 milestones that were all paper milestones. It was: "Do this study; do that study." The truth was, we couldn't keep pace with those studies. The site was basically shut down, in the sense that it was just going no place. No work was getting done.

> No waste was being cleaned up. Nothing was being produced.
>
> Contributor 21—Manager, DOE

Between 1990 and 1992, it was assumed that Rocky Flats would resume production activities, even though no clearance had been received to do so. After the unexpected shutdown in 1989, much work had to be accomplished to get the facility ready to resume production, and close scrutiny by regulators added massive requirements for measurement and accountability. As a result, the workforce was, by and large, prohibited from accomplishing anything meaningful. An assistant to a congressman explained:

> After the raid in 1989, nothing was going on at Rocky Flats. It was just sitting out there, and nobody knew what to do with it. Most of what was happening after the raid was dealing with grand jury investigations.... It was just a time of confusion, lack of direction, aimlessness.
>
> Contributor 33—Assistant to a U.S. Congressman

The EPA team leader at Rocky Flats since 1995, commenting on the workplace culture at that time, observed:

> When I first started there, I was impressed, or rather I was astonished, by how little work was going on. My first tour at the site, I looked around

> and the lunchrooms were full of people playing cribbage and the like, and it just didn't look like any work was going on.

Contributor 35—Regulator, EPA

To be fair, this condition mainly described the nonproduction side of the facility. In the plutonium buildings, employees were working 90-hour weeks under enormous pressures to prepare for resumption of production under a new set of standards. They were required to engage in tens of thousands of surveillance activities relating to ventilation systems, air pressure, fire systems, and so on. Approximately $700 million was spent annually to keep the facility heated, ventilated, and secure, even though no substantive work was being accomplished. That is, Rocky Flats continued to be a major expense in the budget of DOE even though no progress could be detected.

A senior DOE manager provided a description of the organization's loss of direction once its mission became defunct:

> Rocky Flats basically drifted. There was no place that it was going, and there were no shores that it was heading to.

Contributor 14—Manager, DOE

No one was satisfied, of course, with a site that had no mission, continued to be a potentially dangerous environmental threat, and spent hundreds of millions of federal dollars on nothing more than documents and reports. On the other hand, crafting a new mission was a major challenge. It was not clear that pouring more resources into Rocky Flats would create a return on the investment or that progress was possible. Workers assumed that despite rhetoric to the contrary, the site would eventually resume its production role. The idea of permanent shutdown was vehemently resisted. The multiplicity of problems associated with Rocky Flats made closure and cleanup seem intractable. A senior official at DOE described the attitude of state and federal officials regarding the facility:

> There had been some improvements in public perception ... to move the site more toward cleanup, but there was still a heavy influence of this idea that Rocky Flats represented bad people who used to make nuclear bombs who had poisoned the environment....
>
> It was a site that had tremendous problems. There was little hope for success, where the only news that was generated was bad news.... It was an intractable problem. It was going to be with us forever. It was never going to get solved. And all the time it would be with us, it would be a source of bad news. So that led Colorado elected officials to take the position that we want as little to do with this as possible. And it led national decision makers to take the view that on the one

hand we don't want to invest anything in Rocky Flats because it will be a bad investment, but on the other hand if we neglect it entirely, something really bad could happen and we'll be responsible for it. So there was this tug-of-war as to what to do that led to an extraordinary amount of micro-management out of Washington. But in any case, nobody in 1995 looked at Rocky Flats as an opportunity for success.

Contributor 16—Manager, DOE

Certain Closure

The anticipation that Rocky Flats could be prepared to restart production was dashed in 1992 when President George H.W. Bush announced the cancellation of the W-88 warhead program. This resulted in the end of an active nuclear mission for Rocky Flats, and the certainty that the facility would permanently close. With the end of the Cold War, the country's program of nuclear weapons production would not begin again.

We got to a position where we realized that Rocky Flats was never going to restart, so it was a decision of where do we go from here? It got very frustrating for us in the governor's office because a number of people had different ideas about what to do. We knew the mission was over and we were going to transition to something else; the problem was, nobody knew what that something else was.

Contributor 33—Assistant to a U.S. Congressman

In 1995, DOE's Office of Environmental Management issued a Baseline Environmental Management Report titled *Estimating the Cold War Mortgage.* This report provided a detailed estimate for the cost of closing facilities involved in Cold War weapons research, production, and storage. The report provided a much more precise and detailed estimate for the costs of closure for more than "120 million square feet of building and 2.3 million acres of land—an area larger than Delaware, Rhode Island, and the District of Columbia combined." The report posited that closing facilities and safely addressing nuclear waste would require "substantial resources comparable to the level of effort expended for the nuclear weapons production and research activities" (DOE, 1995).

This report put the price tag for cleanup and closure at Rocky Flats at $36 billion. The estimated time frame, as stated before, was 70 years. The report acknowledged that even though these estimates were more precise and data-driven than any previous estimates, there were still several unknowns. Technical remedies did not exist to address some problems, and a variety of issues associated with cleanup could not be fully defined at the time of the estimate. A 70year time horizon also introduced uncertainties into the cost and schedule estimates. More than $55 million had already been spent on security alone at Rocky Flats, however, so DOE had an incentive to do something with the site for cost-saving reasons alone.

The State of Rocky Flats in 1995

EG&G (the contractor managing the site after the raid and stoppage in 1989) was replaced in 1995 by Kaiser-Hill. Prior to awarding the contract, full awareness of the conditions at the facility was lacking. Several specific aspects of the situation that Kaiser-Hill encountered upon arrival at Rocky Flats are described below.

Management Systems. By 1995, when Kaiser-Hill took over the project, the inefficiencies in procedures and processes were out of hand. Without spending constraints, little incentive existed to capitalize on cost savings, coordinated systems, or synchronization. These inefficiencies were major stumbling blocks to accomplishing work in an economical and timely manner. One senior manager stated:

> If I look back on 1995, when I got here, what frustrated me the most was that in my area of responsibility, every system and process was broken. I dealt with things like four different e-mail systems, two platforms, average age of a PC was seven years old, I had mainframes in three different states, I had a procurement system that had never passed a certification under the procurement rules. Our HR program was designed for

> one company, but we had multiple contractors here. It just went on and on and on. It didn't matter where I was. Wherever I turned, it didn't work. We basically had to completely rebuild everything. But we had to do it while we were still running. I had to change payroll. I had to do invoices while I still ran cost. From the beginning it was probably the greatest and the most frustrating challenge I've ever had in my career. But it was the most rewarding because nobody had ever done this before. We knew we were on the cutting edge all the time.
>
> Contributor 6—Senior Executive, Kaiser-Hill

Nuclear Waste. Over the years, many buildings had been converted into waste storage facilities. Barrels containing chemicals and radioactive solutions were stacked floor to ceiling in these structures, and contamination had occurred in walls, floors, ceilings, ductwork, and surrounding soil. No blueprint drawings of the miles of duct work and piping, structural upgrades, ventilation systems, or building refittings had been preserved, primarily so that security would not be compromised if such plans fell into the wrong hands. Exactly what was contaminated, where, and to what extent was not known and was difficult to determine. More than 3 tons of plutonium had purposefully been stored in preparation for what was thought to be an eventual return to production in addition to the tons of other kinds of nuclear materials. Because oxidized plutonium catches fire, such storage presented an ongoing and precarious security concern.

Figure 7: Storage of radioactive waste prior to 1995

No one had ever demolished and cleaned up a building contaminated with plutonium before, so no precedent existed for processes or procedures. Moreover, many buildings were constructed to withstand a Russian bombing attack, so walls were several feet thick and reinforced to withstand explosions or implosions. Buildings had been modified repeatedly over the years with little or no documentation. Finding a way to safely dismantle these structures—many of which were highly contaminated—was a task that no one had ever attempted and no one was trained to do.

Figure 8: Uncovering buried radioactive waste

Bureaucracy. In light of prior accidents, EPA violations, and unknown levels of contamination, the EPA and CDPHE had put enormous pressure on the facility to produce documentation of environmental compliance. The facility had become immersed in responding to demands for production reports, measurements, and compliance with regulatory guidelines. An EPA oversight officer described the environment this way:

> DOE, in fifty years of working in secrecy, developed an incredible bureaucracy and an incredible set of rules for doing work that no longer applied to cleaning up and closing down a site. They were all written around the manufacture of nuclear weapons. Once you shifted your priorities, shifted your focus from manufacturing weapons to actually decontaminating and closing down a site, a

> lot of those guidelines and rules no longer applied.... It would take 35 or 40 men to move one drum from building 776 to 371 because they had to have, you know, 20 guards standing around and 15 guys with clipboards watching. While maybe that's the proper precaution for moving a plutonium pit from one building to another, it's incredible overkill for moving a drum of low level waste.
>
> Contributor 35—Regulator, EPA

One DOE official stated:

> When they had 3,000 employees, at least they were producing the components of the nuclear weapons. When they had 7,000 employees, they were doing studies. And these studies weren't getting anywhere. In fact, they were missing their deadlines with the regulators and were getting fined.
>
> Contributor 21—Manager, DOE

To be fair, a DOE official reported that no objective criteria existed to determine acceptable or unacceptable performance. The site was immersed in drafting reports and producing paperwork, but few objective standards existed against which performance could be benchmarked. People didn't know how they were doing or whether or not they were making progress.

Depending how they woke up that morning, DOE would make a judgment as to whether that was good, bad, or how much they deserved—70 percent or 90 percent, or this amount of dollars.... DOE would look at the report and say, "No, it needs more work, go back to the contractor." Then they had to go to EPA. EPA would look at it and say, "No, I think you need to do a little more work." When I got here, we were late on more than half of the 200 milestones, and we looked ahead and we said, we're going to be late on the remaining milestones, because of paper studies. The paper studies were subjective.

Contributor 21—Manager, DOE

Safety. At the time Kaiser-Hill began gathering data in 1995, the recordable incident rate (safety record) at Rocky Flats was worse than that of the commercial construction industry. Specifically, the total recordable case rate (safety incidents) was 5.0, compared with a 4.5 average in the construction industry and a 3.0 incident rate across other DOE sites. This poor safety record was especially notable since no production was taking place in the facility at that time. OSHA officials had been barred from entering the site by Rocky Flats employees arguing that OSHA had no jurisdiction, and only 60 individuals were monitoring safety concerns in a facility with almost 1,000 buildings and that was handling radioactive materials, highly toxic chemicals, asbestos, beryllium, hydrochloric acid, and other dangerous materials. A union official reported that Rocky Flats workers had handled almost every dangerous chemical produced in the United States. One elected official, a member of the state's Health Advisory Panel, stated:

> Some of the safety-related matters were not enforced to the extent that they should have been. The culture was one of getting it done at any cost.
>
> Contributor 26—Community Representative

Moreover, safety was not carefully monitored because of the confusion surrounding regulatory responsibility. Dispersed and confusing accountability among the various regulatory agencies led to poor reliability onsite. One state official said:

> The regulatory climate was chaotic. We could never figure out who was responsible for what, what the cleanup levels were, who had the oversight, and so forth. So, from a community perspective—it might have been otherwise from a regulator standpoint—it appeared to some of us that we didn't know who to talk to if we had a problem.
>
> Contributor 26—Community Representative

The Public. The relationship between Rocky Flats and the public at large had deteriorated into an antagonistic and hostile one. One DOE official stated:

> There was never a period of time when I worked at Rocky Flats when we didn't have one or another serious controversy with the community.
>
> Contributor 21—Manager, DOE

An EPA official described the sources of that antagonism:

> In the early days, our whole relationship was just pure hell. There were major problems with contractors. There were major personality problems with senior management. There was a tremendous amount of defensiveness over the fact that Rocky Flats insisted that we had no jurisdiction at all in dealing with them.... they basically took the position that EPA rules did not apply to them because they were national security. Everything was national security. We could do nothing. In fact, most of our inspectors didn't even have access to the site.
>
> Contributor 34—Regulator, EPA

From the early years of production until Kaiser-Hill was awarded the contract, environmental groups, antiwar groups, antinuclear groups, chambers of commerce in surrounding communities, city councils, county commissions, the public media, the state health department, the EPA, and DOE all played adversarial roles. Protests, lawsuits, and even harassment were not uncommon. As many as a dozen citizen action groups were organized in opposition to Rocky Flats, and, as mentioned before, relationships between Rocky Flats and almost all outside constituencies were poor. One DOE manager described the situation in 1995 this way:

> When we came in 1995, the relationships with the regulators and with the community were really fairly rocky.... The community was not satisfied with the progress and information they were receiving, and the relationship with regulators was one of enforcement as opposed to working together to solve a problem.... The relationships during that time were very confrontational. When I was from the state, we believed that the site was doing everything in its power not to comply and to ignore us.... There was the feeling that in order to get the site to do the right thing, you had to hammer them, and so that meant enforcement actions and penalties.... So the environment was really pretty bad going all the way up to 1995.

Contributor 8—Manager, Kaiser-Hill

Relationships of distrust and skepticism had long been the norm with federal agencies, the local community, and interested citizen groups. Hence, the existence of resistance to change was at high levels.

> One of the difficult obstacles was that the original accelerated concept was so radical that, in part, it was hard to get people to take it seriously. When you talk about taking a closure schedule and cutting it from 70 years to 7 years and achieving the same outcome, it really is almost unbelievable. "How in the world could they do that?" So we met a lot of really heavy skepticism. I mean, I know there were a number of people at [DOE] headquarters, in Congress, and in the congressional staffers who originally thought this was just some marketing scheme that we had dreamed up in order to get more money for the site.
>
> Contributor 9—Senior Executive, Kaiser-Hill

External support and the ability to call upon outside agencies for assistance and cooperation, therefore, were highly tenuous as Kaiser-Hill embarked on its task at Rocky Flats.

The Workforce. Between 1989 and 1995, there was little to celebrate among the workforce. Aimlessness, micromanagement, and outside agency encroachment, coupled with a negative public image, made for poor morale among the workforce. Steelworker union officials described their own feelings at the time:

> It was difficult to feel like we were criminals when the FBI raided Rocky Flats. We then felt even worse when the announcement was made to close the place in 1992.

Contributor 12—Union Officers, Kaiser-Hill

Without meaningful work or a clear mission at Rocky Flats, labor/management relations had deteriorated. By the 1995 contract signing with Kaiser-Hill, hundreds of unresolved grievances had been backlogged. A climate of resistance and recalcitrance existed, especially among the unionized workforce. The prior site manager, EG&G, had made little observable progress at the site, and Kaiser-Hill had no prior experience in weapons production and very little in nuclear site cleanup. A predictable consequence was that employee trust and confidence in management would be at an all-time low. One consultant described the labor conditions at the beginning of the 1995 contract period:

> You have to remember that when CH2MHill came in, in 1995, you had a new management team of, you know, 50 people who were imposed on this existing structure. The existing structure had its own culture, and employees had been told that it was going to take 75 years to clean up the site. It was going to cost 40, 50, 60 billion dollars, and they and their children would be able to work at Rocky Flats forever. The employees and the

> union members had been working for companies that build weapons, and here you have an environmental company coming in to head a new contract. There was an enormous amount of distrust ... with the contractor coming in and trying to impose a whole new set of values and a whole new vision for the site. So it was incredibly, I think, exciting for the management team, but it was clear that there was a lot of hostility among the ranks.
>
> Contributor 5—Manager, Kaiser-Hill

Hostility and recalcitrance on the part of employees was understandable, based on the description of a senior DOE manager upon his arrival in 1995.

> I think I had to go through four checkpoints to get to my own office. Visitors to the manager's office had to be escorted from the front gate by a security officer carrying an M-16 rifle. So, for outside visitors, especially for some of these citizen groups, it was very intimidating. It certainly was not an environment that was conducive to talking to the manager about what the issues were. There were stories in the newspaper almost on a daily basis about all the things that were going wrong at Rocky Flats, and how no one trusted anybody, and there was no credibility, and no work was being done, and we were wasting all of this money.

In other words, access to managers was restricted, most executives were housed in a separate headquarters building with little direct contact with the workforce, and a brand-new management team had been assigned to the site. It is understandable that a workforce used to time frames that included lifelong, and even multigenerational, employment would simply adopt the attitude that they would wait out and passively resist the new team from Kaiser-Hill. No incentive existed to do otherwise.

The Culture. During the production years at Rocky Flats, the sensitive nature of the projects on which employees were working led to a culture of secrecy. Very little information was disseminated either among workers or to outside constituencies. National security concerns prohibited individuals from sharing information with spouses and even colleagues working in the same facility. One DOE official noted:

> The culture of Rocky Flats and the culture of the entire weapons complex was built with walls between sites, walls between facilities, and walls even between operations in same facilities. So, the culture was very secretive, and it needed to be that way because we were building nuclear weapons. That permeated through the site where husband and wife working in the same facility might not have not known what the other was doing, and for a very good reason. So the culture

> was a chopped culture. It was a culture, in the early 1990s, of "we're here to build weapons." That was a culture passed down from generation to generation.
>
> Contributor 14—Manager, DOE

The highly skilled nature of the work being performed, coupled with the limited amount of interaction that could occur with individuals outside the Rocky Flats facility, led to a very tight-knit culture. Predictably, social relationships as well as professional relationships were restricted to Rocky Flats employees. One outside consultant described the consequences:

> One of the things that was stunning to me, coming in from the outside, was how many plant members were married to one another. One of the reasons that happens ... was they couldn't really talk about what they were doing outside, and they not only had to run this very tight, closed culture on the site, but there were generations of families who worked there. There was very little play between the Rocky Flats workers and the greater Denver Metropolitan area.
>
> Contributor 5—Manager, Kaiser-Hill

Traditionally, employees had been proud of the mission of the facility and of the competence of the workforce at Rocky Flats, and over time, the assumption that Rocky Flats represented lifelong employment began to grow. No one else knew how to do the job that was being performed so well at Rocky Flats. Multiple generations of workers were employed, so Rocky Flats not only became a full-service society, but it took on the multigenerational characteristics of a self-sustaining community as well. A former member of the governor's staff and a U.S. congressman put it this way:

> So many of the workers at Rocky Flats have been here their whole lives, and for many of them, their parents or grandparents were at Rocky Flats since it started. So you grow up in that culture, and there's a lot of pride in that culture, and the culture was that you could work next to somebody for 20 years and you didn't talk about what you did.
>
> Contributor 24—Community Representative

In this kind of cohesive culture, loss of mission was especially unsettling. One DOE manager said:

> That was a culture where it was passed down from generation to generation. For a lot of the folks who worked at Rocky Flats, their parents and their grandparents worked at Rocky Flats, and they assumed their children and grandchildren would be working there, too, in supporting the mission. That all changed in 1992 when President Bush canceled the project.

> I don't think we recognized at the time how big that change was going to be.
>
> Contributor 14—Manager, DOE

In our interviews conducted onsite, it was common to learn of whole families that worked on the site as well as several generations in the same family. Workers repeatedly told us that they had assumed that the site would continue to provide employment for many generations to come. The loss of an active mission, therefore, destroyed the employment plans not only of onsite employees but also the culture of multigenerational families.

One consequence was that the organization lost energy and drive. Individual initiative and creativity were replaced by a culture of apathy and irresponsibility. Between 1989 and 1995, the formerly vibrant culture became a culture of apathy and recalcitrance.

> DOE would tell employees what to do and how to do it, so all they had to do was whatever DOE said. Then they weren't responsible for anything because it was always, "DOE told me to do this, and DOE told me that." They got paid for showing up, not necessarily accomplishing anything; they got paid for just showing up.
>
> Contributor 21—Manager, DOE

Considering Rival Explanations

In light of the tremendous difficulties faced by the Rocky Flats facility in 1995, legitimate questions can be raised regarding whether the final cleanup and closure accomplishment is really valid. The claim that Rocky Flats achieved spectacular success previously considered to be impossible will justifiably invite skepticism. It is important, therefore, to consider alternative explanations for these results. Plausible alternative explanations might include the following:

1. The initial closure estimate of 70 years and $36 billion was grossly inflated; therefore accelerated cleanup and closure were not so exceptional after all.
2. The closure and cleanup project at Rocky Flats was carried out to very different specifications than the initial estimate, which could explain time and money savings.
3. The Rocky Flats closure plan involved cutting corners—for example, sacrificing safety—to carry out accelerated closure.
4. Other DOE sites have achieved, or are now achieving, similar levels of performance, so this achievement is nothing exceptional.

We briefly consider each of these possible explanations. First, the initial estimate stating that it would take 70 years and $36 billion to close Rocky Flats appeared as part of the Baseline Environmental Assessment conducted by the Department of Energy's

Office of Environmental Management. This estimate went much farther than previous estimates to precisely calculate the cost and schedule of closure. While the cost of closing Rocky Flats, along with other former Cold War facilities within the DOE nuclear complex, provoked a public policy debate about the cost of "the Cold War mortgage," the estimate was not criticized by Congress, DOE, EPA, the state of Colorado, or citizen action groups as an overly cautious or invalid estimate. There is no evidence to suggest that the estimate itself was unrealistic or based on false premises. In fact, some environmental groups advocated a multigenerational approach to cleanup to ensure that pristine levels of decontamination were achieved. The point is, 70 years was not an unrealistic estimate of the time required. The 13 other nuclear facilities were given similar time frames.

Second, an alternative rationale for extraordinary performance could be that the site was cleaned up to different specifications than the original plan. A site could be cleaned up to differing levels of residual contamination. In the case of nuclear sites, the question is, what level of background radiation will remain once cleanup is complete? The accelerated cleanup did, in fact, differ from the initial closure specifications, but the variance was on the more rigorous side of the equation. That is, the overall level of background radiation that remains is substantially less than the original proposal. The original DOE contract and allocated budget specified 651 radioactive picocuries per gram to remain in the soil. This is called the residual soil action level (RSAL). As pointed out earlier, the RSAL actually achieved at Rocky Flats was 50 picocuries per gram. In this sense, the cleanup was even more stringent than the original standard, despite the fact that the budget and initial plan allowed for the much higher level. Whereas disagreement may exist about what RSAL level is most appropriate over the long term, it is clear that Rocky Flats exceeded the standard that was originally dictated in the federal contract.

In addition, the DOE-EPA-CDPHE contract stipulated that RSAL levels would be remediated to safer levels than had been present before 1995, but it did not obligate Kaiser-Hill to remove radiation at soil levels deeper than 10 feet. Because virtually no contamination penetrates beyond the first few feet of soil, and because of the geologic stability of the site, this remedy was considered to be a better environmental outcome than the original plan. Massive excavation and soil disturbance might have done more harm than good by distributing radioactive contamination, so assuring safe RSAL levels down to 10 feet is a standard superior to the original plan developed at DOE. While the issue of cleanup levels is of fundamental importance from a long-term health and safety standpoint, and some stakeholders contend that cleanup levels should still be improved, from the standpoint of alternative explanations, this would not explain such a dramatic achievement of success.

A third alternative explanation—that Rocky Flats cut corners to achieve efficiency gains—could be deemed both true and false. Employees developed numerous technological and process innovations that greatly increased the productivity of the site. This means that in several areas, they cut corners by markedly increasing efficiency. The safety record at the site improved from worse than the construction industry average—during the period when work had stopped and no production was taking place—to twice as good as the industry average two years after Kaiser-Hill began to manage the site. Kaiser-Hill increased expenditures on safety personnel and training and decreased the number of safety incidents. Given the level of protocol in operating a nuclear facility, a serious safety infraction could have shut the site down for months. Compromising on safety—either in personnel or in environmental remediation—was not a logical strategy to achieve accelerated closure.

In addition, a series of innovations in the processes used to dismantle more than 1,000 contaminated glove boxes created efficiencies that led to a 25-fold increase in productivity. In other words, if cutting corners refers to weakening standards of performance, then Rocky Flats was not in the corner-cutting business. If cutting corners means improving efficiency, then Rocky Flats is a prime example of corner-cutting.

Fourth, the performance at Rocky Flats could be alternatively explained by the fact that similar success also occurs normally at other DOE sites. That is, this story is best characterized as standard operating procedure—nothing extraordinary occurred at Rocky Flats. As is illustrated in chapters 7 and 8, however, no other DOE site has functioned at the same level or achieved the same cost and time targets as Rocky Flats. One high ranking official in DOE commented in 2004:

> Current DOE projects are not being pursued in the same way as Rocky Flats. In fact, there may be a regression toward the old way of doing things instead of toward the Rocky Flats approach.
>
> Contributor 23—Senior Executive, DOE

The average number of employees at other sites throughout the DOE complex exceeds that at Rocky Flats, and the safety record at Rocky Flats exceeded the DOE complex rate by 1999 and continued to be better through the end of the project. In other words, none of these explanations, alone or together, can explain 60 years of time savings and more than $30 billion in cost savings.

Summary

In 1995 Kaiser-Hill management encountered an organization that one executive described as "a bankrupt culture." It operated in a physical facility full of storage containers filled with large amounts of radioactive waste and dangerous chemicals, and with contamination in the physical structures and the soil. Employee distrust of the new, inexperienced Kaiser-Hill management team was coupled with hostility toward outsiders who threatened to change the tradition of lifelong employment and the tightly knit culture of secrecy, pride, and insularity. Specific prohibitions had long been in place regarding sharing information with individuals outside the organization, and relationships with almost all external constituencies were adversarial and confrontational. The loss of organizational mission had caused employees to become demoralized, and while costs continued to multiply, no meaningful progress had been made toward production, closure, or cleanup for six years. Employees had transitioned from patriotic heroes to criminals and outcasts. Productivity, efficiency, and safety were all at abysmal levels.

The first DOE manager summarized his assessment of the facility, upon entering Rocky Flats in 1995, in these words:

> In the five years before I arrived, the contractor received over $60 million in incentive fees, and in my mind hadn't done anything. That was my assessment. They had done a lot of paper studies, but they had not shut down. They hadn't drained a tank. They hadn't cleaned up a glove box. Nothing.
>
> Contributor 21—Manager, DOE

The most likely reaction to such circumstances is to be defensive, discouraged, or resigned. On the other hand, one important conclusion to be drawn from Rocky Flats is the following:

> ***Regardless of external circumstances—whether difficult and resistive or comfortable and conducive—adopting an abundance approach to change is always possible.***

In light of the abysmal circumstances present at Rocky Flats, this chapter has considered the possibilities that initial estimates were unrealistic, actual cleanup was inadequate, or the cleanup was largely achieved by dangerous shortcuts. We found no evidence, however, that accounts for Rocky Flats' achievements through such means. Indeed, we found that the scope of actual cleanup exceeded earlier agreements. The most reasonable conclusion is that Rocky Flats represents a remarkable instance of making the impossible possible. This conclusion is partially supported by the inability to explain extraordinary success through rival hypotheses or skeptical assertions, and it is supported by the evidence presented in the following chapters.

3

The Role of Leaders

Rocky Flats is a story of leadership success. There was nothing special about the external environment, the location, the structure, the resources, or other context factors that could have accounted for the results. The individuals involved in the Rocky Flats transformation universally identified the roles played by leaders as a key to success. Positive deviance resulted from leadership actions.

It would be convenient, and much easier to explain, if the success at Rocky Flats could be attributed to the behaviors of one heroic leader, to a single intervention strategy, or to a small collection of powerful initiatives. Complicated transformations are, however, a combination of many factors occurring in collaboration—mutually affecting each other and difficult to distinguish from each other. This was certainly the case at Rocky Flats.

Faced with myriad problems and obstacles—including labor tension, mistrust among external constituencies, lack of know-how, and a nonsupportive public—the leadership challenge at Rocky Flats was daunting. What would lead Rocky Flats from a place of hopelessness, anger, and resistance to a place of positive momentum, optimism, and success? What would be the key levers for change? How could people become committed to closure? Which factors would have to be transformed, and which should be left in place? Who could be relied upon to assist with the change, and who should be removed? Was a successful outcome within the realm of possibility?

This chapter focuses on the question *What levers can leaders use to produce similar results?* Specifically, we focus here on the leadership *roles* that differentiate abundance-oriented leaders from more conventional leaders. Rocky Flats leaders had special impact on the success of the project, and though only a sample of them are identified by name, they represent successive CEOs at Rocky Flats, House and Senate leaders, DOE and EPA leaders, and leaders within Kaiser-Hill's parent company, CH2MHill. Key leadership principles are illustrated in the comments made by and about these leaders and the roles they played.

Enabling Leadership

Successful organizational change is often attributed to a single leader's vision, strategy, charisma, savvy, or sheer force of personality. Heroic figures such as Nelson Mandela in South Africa, Mohandas Gandhi in South Africa and India, Winston Churchill in Great Britain, and Franklin Delano Roosevelt, Martin Luther King, and Abraham Lincoln in the United States are examples of individuals whose single-handed leadership is credited with transforming nations. On the other hand, it is clear that whereas leadership plays a crucial role in any major change, no single individual has sufficient power to bring about large-scale reformation. Successful leadership always emerges in multiple places and among multiple people. Clear targets, consistency of direction, and coordination of efforts are required among the various leaders, of course, but seldom is one individual able to lead a transformation single-handedly.

A clear message from the study of the Rocky Flats transformation is that multiple leaders serving both congruently with each other as well as independent of each other were required to create the successful change. In the quotations that follow, various contributors involved in the transformation—both onsite and in state and federal agencies—credited several individuals or entities with playing critical leadership roles at critical times. No single person was the hero, but many were essential in making the project successful. The quotations highlight the necessary variety of leaders, and subsequent chapters identify the specific actions taken and enablers implemented by these leaders. (Names of specific individuals are maintained in these quotations because none of the people mentioned served as sources for these specific statements.)

First, the leaders assigned by Kaiser-Hill to manage Rocky Flats obviously played crucial leadership roles. The first CEO assigned by CH2MHill to the Rocky Flats facility was Bob Card. (One previous CEO, George O'Brien, had been present for a few months, but he essentially played no role in the cleanup and closure story.) Bob had formerly been one of the top five executives within CH2MHill, and the fact that the company assigned such a senior manager to this project sent an important message to all concerned that the company was taking this project seriously. The Rocky Flats cleanup effort dwarfed previous CH2MHill projects in size and it represented unprecedented risk-taking by CH2MHill. The message was clear that this project was being treated as a high priority, and the firm was making a visible commitment to its success. Concern about the capability of the newly created division—Kaiser-Hill—to tackle this unprecedented task motivated CH2MHill to assign capable leadership to the project as a matter of risk reduction. Bob was replaced by Alan Parker in 1999 when Bob was asked to serve as Undersecretary of Energy in the Department of Energy. Alan was, in turn, replaced by Nancy Tuor in 2003 when Alan was assigned to manage a newly acquired nuclear cleanup project in Idaho. Nancy remained the CEO until closure in October of 2005.

The importance of highly skilled leadership at the top was obvious.

> The leadership from the Kaiser-Hill organization was very important. They were a Denver company who really had an interest in doing things different. They poured their corporate heart into what we were trying to do. They brought some fabulous leadership to the site.

I think if you go back and look at the work that Mark Silverman did in preparing Rocky Flats, and the work that Jessie Roberson did, who is now the Assistant Secretary of Energy, coupled with the vision that Al had, they were extremely important.

Contributor 14—Manager, DOE

Much of the credit, in my opinion, has to go to Bob Card and to Larry Burge for their leadership because, up to that point, there had not been sufficient talent to be able to deliver the kind of project baseline that needed to be delivered to the Department of Energy. Larry was one that just drove this like crazy.

Contributor 7—Manager, Kaiser-Hill

Several people credited Bob Card with helping to create the initial vision that led to spectacular success.

While I'm sure there were enormous numbers of people who participated, it was Bob Card who clearly had the energy and the vision to make a lot of things happen. He wasn't a captive of the DOE system. He was a free-thinker, had the ability to think outside the box, and is certainly one of the brightest people to ever run a DOE site from a management per-

> spective. So, I'd have to say that the people were more important than the instruments.
>
> Contributor 15—Senior Executive, DOE

> The idea to change so fast was Card's. The only people not okay with the pace were Congress, but Congress eventually became an advocate. Al Alm became an advocate. Community and regulators also then became advocates.
>
> Contributor 9—Senior Executive, Kaiser-Hill

A different leadership role was attributed to Alan Parker, and it was just as crucial as that played by Bob Card.

> Alan Parker took over after Bob's vision was stabilized. The processes were in place. The talent was here. Alan institutionalized the culture of improvement and added more incentives. He paid a great deal of attention to the union employees, so union-management relations are now great. That may not have happened under Card.
>
> Contributor 9—Senior Executive, Kaiser-Hill

One key role of top leaders was to ensure that effective leadership was present throughout the organization.

> We changed a lot of people. We had to redeploy people at the top. We didn't necessarily fire them, but the leadership had to be right. We had good solid middle managers. My major contribution was getting the right people at the top.
>
> Contributor 10—Senior Executive, Kaiser-Hill

In addition to leadership from Kaiser-Hill executives, managers assigned to the site from the Department of Energy played crucial leadership roles. Both the site manager and assistant site manager were credited with being highly effective leaders in the early phases of the project. On the DOE side, Mark Silverman, the first site manager, is credited with having had a significant role in the spectacular achievements. He left after four years and was replaced by Jessie Roberson. She served as an assistant site manager from DOE for five years before becoming site manager. She later returned to the Department of Energy in Washington, D.C., as Assistant Secretary for Environmental Management. The combination of strong leadership from CH2MHill, coupled with strong DOE leadership, was seen to be key to a successful transformation.

> In moving forward with the closure of this site, I really give credit to Mark Silverman for organizing the strategy to do that. He was very, very capable at working with the community

leaders. I watched him. He was a mentor for me in this area. I wasn't very experienced. I knew how to work with regulators. I knew what the environmental regulations were. I'm a nuclear engineer. I understand radiological contamination. But I did not have the kind of experience and opportunity to see someone like him do that. He was very good. He actually worked with this management team—the contractor, the citizens, and the local communities—to develop a strategy that everybody owns. It was very, very well done—but painful—but I actually credit him for doing that. That's probably the most important thing.

Contributor 20—Senior Executive, DOE

We had a very strong contractor, and Bob Card came to the Hill often. He briefed the staff. He briefed the members of Congress. He would bring his charts and show us how he was making progress here and how he thought he could move things around. That worked very well. Then when Jessie Roberson went to the field, she was very supportive. She was doing her best to knock barriers out of the way in the DOE bureaucracy. So, Bob would give us ideas. Jessie would try to knock the barriers out in DOE. And I would try to knock them out in Congress. You just felt like

> you were part of the team, and it worked really well.
>
> Contributor 22—Manager, DOE

The roles played by key leaders in the House and the Senate, while seldom publicly recognized, were essential to the success of the project. Senator Wayne Allard and Congressman Joel Knollenberg were particularly important. Being part of the team, "knocking barriers out of Congress," and coordinating visions were all key aspects of successful leadership from Washington. Developing and maintaining support for congressional budget allocations was, of course, a critical feature of their leadership roles. Furthermore, leadership in the Department of Energy was necessary for the successful transformation. Assistant Secretary of Energy Al Alm was a key figure in helping to articulate the goals and aspirations of the project from the outset. Gaining political and economic support from the DOE was a crucial part of the foundation needed for change.

In regard to elected officials:

> One of our early allies was Representative Knollenberg [D-Michigan], who really believed that DOE should do something different in how it dealt with its nuclear legacy. The most stunning thing about his support was that he didn't have a DOE site in his district. But, he was an early

advocate, an early point of light on what were trying to do.

Contributor 14—Manager, DOE

Senator Allard [D-Colorado], of course, made Rocky Flats a priority in his business. Rocky Flats was one of his great focal points.

Contributor 14—Manager, DOE

An advocate in the senior leadership team at DOE was also important.

I mentioned former Assistant Secretary Al Alm, who came back to the Department of Energy in the mid-1990s with his ten-year plan. He was an early visionary, and I like to view what we're doing as merely an extension of what Al's ideas were. Al was a truly remarkable individual who really understood and intuitively had a feeling for where the department needed to go. He provided leadership and vision that we're still following today.

Contributor 14—Manager, DOE

I credit a lot of that success to Al Alm and his leadership. He began to embrace this idea of accelerated cleanup. Because of Al Alm's leadership, the Department of Energy became a key propo-

> nent and ally of our plans, in going out and meeting with the public, and in going out and having conversations with our stakeholders.

Contributor 7—Manager, Kaiser-Hill

The cooperative role of leadership within regulatory agencies was also key.

> That is also true of the regulators. From the time of the FBI raid in 1989 up to 1999, extraordinary support and commitment have been given by the regulators to do the right thing, to regulate the right thing, to focus on the right thing, and to make sure that we kept our word.

Contributor 14—Manager, DOE

One example of how these leadership roles were played is described by Congressman Knollenberg. He took personal responsibility for encouraging and enabling the Rocky Flats project objectives. Regulatory and budgetary hurdles had to be addressed, and a new standard of efficiency in operations of DOE projects had to be established.

> My role was to beat down that regulatory hurdle because they were creating more obstacles than value. That was the big one. It was also to get somebody in the DOE to listen and understand that we wanted to save money. We told them that you've got too many people, period.... No, this

> project doesn't touch Michigan, but it touches the excess, the waste, and maybe even the deceit in government, and there was plenty of that. That's gone from the equation now entirely. Now we can apply these things more effectively in other locations around the country.
>
> Contributor 31—U.S. Congressman

In addition to leadership at the federal level, the governor's office in the state of Colorado became heavily engaged. The state of Colorado matched Kaiser-Hill's commitment to Rocky Flats by assigning a very senior leader—Lieutenant Governor Gail Schoettler—to oversee the project from the standpoint of state government. Schoettler's role was to serve as a liaison and a catalyst to bring the various political entities together.

> I think if you look locally in the state, the support we had from [Lieutenant Governor] Gail Schoettler and the continued support we're having from Governor Owens's office today is extremely important. Without their committed support, Rocky Flats wouldn't be where it is today.
>
> Contributor 14—Manager, DOE

> Lieutenant Governor Schoettler took up the charge again to make sure that what was produced in this vision and the cleanup agreement

actually got implemented.... She took a very active approach to make sure that it would be successful. One of the techniques that she invoked was to gather the communities and local governments around Rocky Flats together to meet on a regular basis. We invited all of the communities—the mayors, the county commissioners, the DOE, the EPA, and the contractor—and we would talk about what was happening, how this was being implemented, where were the roadblocks, what could we do as politicians—the local and the state government elected representatives—to help make this agreement real?

Contributor 33—Assistant to a U.S. Congressman

Continuity in Leadership

Still another of the keys to successful leadership was the continuity of leadership support from the early stages of the project to its later stages. The same individuals were not always in place over that span of time, yet the consistency of vision and support was remarkably stable. Successors took up where predecessors left off, and no subsequent leader created roadblocks or changed directions. In fact, subsequent leaders complemented the attributes of their predecessors by applying new skills that added value to the process. In addition to the presence of individual leaders, the steadiness of leadership over time was a critical factor in maintaining momentum toward success. At any point in time, a successor could have eliminated Rocky Flats from the priority list, diverted personnel or resources, or simply ceased to champion the project. However, leaders from multiple sectors continued to support the Rocky Flats closure initiative, and the momentum was able to continue.

> The first and foremost allies at the Rocky Flats site were always in the governor's office—first Governor Romer and then Governor Owens. They were big supporters. Governor Owens continues to be a big supporter of the cleanup of that site. That made a tremendous difference in terms of our ability to share our views and frustrations, and basically have their commitment to work with us as we tried to find the best way to clean up the site. The regulators—the United States Environmental Protection Agency, the State Department of Health—were incredible partners. The local community turned out to be a much stronger ally than we ever could have imagined. They worked with us to take a look at future uses of the site, letting us know what their greatest concerns were, and then working with us to decide how to fix them. So, within the state I would say it was at three different levels: the governor's office, the regulators, and the local community. Within the Department of Energy we had five Secretaries of Energy who were all committed to pushing the cleanup

> of the Rocky Flats site, starting with Admiral Watkins, followed by Hazel O'Leary, Federico Peña, Bill Richardson, and now Spencer Abraham. Each and every one of them really focused on Rocky Flats and worked very hard to maintain the momentum. They kept pushing constantly for an accelerated cleanup, and that made a huge difference. It was sustained management involvement.
>
> Contributor 18—Manager, DOE

Of course, support from local community groups and backing from the workforce, while not usually associated with leadership in the traditional sense, were important influences on leadership success. Leadership through advocacy, fostering positive energy rather than resistance and negative energy, and executing in the face of adversity were important ingredients in leadership success at Rocky Flats. One of the first moves made by top leaders at Rocky Flats, for example, was to tear down the headquarters building so that all managers had to be relocated to the buildings in which the actual work was taking place. No financial incentive was associated with the elimination of the headquarters building; it was done in order to send a message that the workers in the facilities were the key to success. Managing from afar was no longer acceptable. Locating managers and workers in the same space was an acknowledgment that significant leadership responsibility had to be located in the actual workforce.

Leadership did not occur only at the top. It was demonstrated on multiple levels and included employees who were actually doing the work.

> Then again, it comes down to the people who come in to work every day. Without their advocacy, without their hard work, we just wouldn't be where we are today. I hope we have some footage of these men and women in radiological contamination suits, full-faced respirators, sweating, coming out of these areas soaking wet, working in conditions that few would, few would ever volunteer to do, and working in a such a productive way.
>
> Contributor 14—Manager, DOE

> One of the statements I'll continue to make to people is that we can have a great plan, and we can have money to implement that plan, but if you don't have the human commitment and will to do it, all of that just falls apart. There are key people on this project that made the difference.... I think the personal commitment of key people is what made the difference.... It's the people who are responsible to the general taxpayers for getting it done. If they don't have the will to do it, the plan doesn't matter; it's really the peo-

ple.... I think sometimes we forget the importance of the workers at the site—I mean the federal employees that work for me. I was probably pretty tough on them, but they served both me and the taxpayer extremely well. We asked them to take on a challenge that wasn't what they came here to do, and they did it with tremendous credibility. Also, we asked the labor force to carry out a job, knowing that it wasn't going to go on forever, and they have demonstrated their maturity in doing it with pride. So, leadership is important, but it's the people who actually carry it out and make it happen. We couldn't do it without them. It's always the people that matter.

Contributor 20—Senior Executive, DOE

In addition to leaders onsite, leadership contributing to the success of Rocky Flats was necessary in outside organizations.

I would say the local communities also helped. They had no reason to believe in us, and although we continue to have disagreements, I think they're largely behind us, and they have become one of our best advocates.

Contributor 14—Manager, DOE

Leadership Roles

One way to highlight the importance of leadership at Rocky Flats is to identify the underlying *leadership roles* that each of these various individuals and entities performed. The leadership roles played by these individuals and groups differed in their intent and objectives. At least three different leadership roles were necessary if transformational change was to occur—*idea champion, sponsor,* and *orchestrator* (Cameron, 2005a).

Not surprisingly, the most commonly acknowledged leadership role was the *champion and visionary.* As illustrated by quotations above, this role at Rocky Flats was variously attributed to several individuals, including Bob Card, Al Alm, and Mark Silverman. Each was credited with articulating the vision and championing the idea that the closure and cleanup could be completed substantially faster and at a much lower cost than the federal report had specified.

Idea champions are often the most visible leaders, and they are the ones who receive most of the credit for success, even though each of the three roles is critical. Idea champions are often inspirational leaders who articulate a motivating vision, thus energizing those who listen. For example, "Bob Card clearly had the energy and the vision to make a lot of things happen." Or "Al Alm provided leadership and vision that we're still following today." Idea champions and visionaries also find themselves being warriors in warding off opposition and skepticism. One example of the warrior role associated with idea champions is the following quotation from a manager at DOE.

> Another part of the job was to stand up for this site and fight for this site because we were a threat to the rest of DOE. We said that we didn't need as many federal employees, and we didn't need as many nonfederal or contract employees as they had at the site. I went to DOE headquarters one day for a meeting with all of the field managers and headquarters managers, and said "We don't need so many people. We can do it for less money and with fewer people." Well, that was a threat to everybody else because they had built up these empires of 10,000 employees at Savannah River and 12,000 people at Hanford. Rocky Flats came in and said "We don't need all of these people." But if they don't need them, why do you need them? Well, it was a threat. I think even today some people feel very threatened at DOE because they still have these very large workforces, both federal and nonfederal. So, part of the challenge as a leader, as a manger, is to fight for what needs to be done and what is right. I was very fortunate because I was able to get the support and confidence of the secretary of energy, Secretary O'Leary, very early on, and the assistant secretary for the environment safety and health, Tara O'Toole.

Contributor 21—Manager, DO

Of course, this quotation exemplifying the warrior role also makes it clear that positive deviance—reaching for especially positive and noble goals—often provokes resistance, negative judgment, and opposition on the part of an organization's members.

A second important type of leadership role is the *sponsor role.* Sponsors help acquire resources and support, and they provide encouragement to the visions being advocated by idea champions. Simply put, they sponsor others' ideas, and without this sponsorship, effective change is impossible. Unfortunately, leaders who are sponsors seldom obtain the recognition or accolades that visionaries do, even though their role is indispensable. Several examples of sponsoring leadership were recognized in the quotations above, including Governor Bill Owens—"The continued support we're having from Governor Owens's office today is extremely important"—as well as the regulators (i.e., EPA)—"Extraordinary support and commitment have been given by the regulators to do the right thing."

Another example below illustrates the implementation of the sponsorship role very effectively played by a Colorado state official. Sponsorship in this instance refers not to creating the vision or the objective, but to identifying and solving the problems that stand in the way of progress.

I think what works is getting people to believe that they can solve the problem and that it is their job to solve the problem. It is not their job to hold things up. I think what doesn't work is to let people think that they have an option. You don't have an option when you've got something like Rocky Flats to clean up. You have only one choice, and that is to figure out solutions. So, when we got past the hardened positions into the problem-solving, these were great problem-solvers. They may have really wanted to hold to their positions, but when they had to solve their problems, they did a wonderful job.

Contributor 29—Senior Executive, state of Colorado

The third key leadership role is *orchestrator.* Orchestrators bring together individuals and groups needed for implementation of the vision or idea. Resources are assembled, groups are integrated, political processes are managed, and human effort is coordinated so that progress can be achieved. Orchestrators often cannot articulate the personal vision of idea champions, but they are frequently the ones who make the vision or creative idea become a reality. In the examples above, Lieutenant Governor Gail Schoettler was so identified—"One of the techniques that she invoked was to gather the communities and local governments around Rocky

Flats together to meet on a regular basis"—as was the assistant site manager, Jessie Roberson—"Jessie knocked barriers out of the way in the DOE bureaucracy." An additional example of this orchestrator role is the quotation below, in which the motivation of the orchestrator role is effectively described.

> What were the big roadblocks? Why weren't people getting the problem solved? Because those who were working on solving the problem were extremely capable, very smart, they really understood what they were doing. But it wasn't happening. And so I tried to really get the lay of the land and assess why things weren't moving, and what really became pretty clear is that the sides had hardened their positions and there wasn't anybody who was making the move off of their position. There wasn't anybody who could say "All right, we're going to take this one problem at a time and solve the problem." And that was what my role was. It was to make sure we had people collectively focused on solving the problem, as opposed to defending their positions.
>
> Contributor 29—Senior Executive, state of Colorado

Summary

The analysis of the leadership displayed at Rocky Flats highlights three conclusions that seem clear from participants' observations.

Leadership is embodied in multiple individuals and has multiple sources. No single heroic leader can lead a transformational change, and in effective change, leadership is often exercised simultaneously by multiple disassociated individuals. These leadership efforts must correspond and be coordinated, of course, and a common vision or objective is often an effective way to ensure this alignment. Culture, strategy, and structure can act as alignment mechanisms. At Rocky Flats, multiple leaders were aligned by the common vision of accelerated cleanup and closure, and achieving a standard of performance that far exceeded anything that had been accomplished before.

Continuity and consistency in leadership is required over time. Fast change artists, or leaders who make large changes quickly and then move on, are unlikely to foster permanent transformation. The "program of the month" leader often pursues rapid change, but continuity and consistency are missing. In the case of Rocky Flats, successors in the role of CEO perpetuated the same vision; successors in the Colorado governor's office maintained consistent support; five

Secretaries of Energy maintained a consistent policy toward Rocky Flats; congressional support did not waver over the period of the project; and the initial resistance of the workforce dissipated as new management established credibility and a more collaborative approach.

Three different leadership roles are necessary for spectacular change to occur: idea champion, sponsor, and orchestrator. Idea champions and visionaries are often leaders who inspire others, point toward an energizing future state, and arouse enthusiasm in others. Their vision serves as the glue or the coordinating mechanism that holds together the other leadership roles being exercised at the same time. A second necessary leadership role is a sponsor, or leadership through support, encouragement, and sponsorship of others' ideas. Third is the role of orchestrator, the leader who brings together people and resources in ways that produce results. No significant organizational change will occur without all three roles being performed, and in large-scale transformation, it is difficult for a single person to perform all three leadership roles. At Rocky Flats, these leadership roles were distributed among a variety of individuals who, working congruently with each other, experienced extraordinary success. Some individuals performed more than one of these roles, of course, but usually multiple individuals were required to fulfill the requirements.

4

Competing Values and Paradoxical Leadership

In addition to the existence of certain leadership roles, there is a more extensive answer to the question *What levers can leaders use to produce similar results?* Leaders at Rocky Flats relied on a set of key enablers to create the spectacular results that were achieved. One important purpose of this book is to highlight the enablers that may be generalizable to other settings. Identifying enablers that account for dramatic turnaround and extraordinary performance, however, requires a framework by which they can be organized. Rather than merely listing factors that accounted for the Rocky Flats achievement, we provide a framework that allows us to simplify and categorize the most important factors that explain success. The enablers being identified proved to be vital in turning the impossible into the possible at Rocky Flats—from disastrous performance to spectacular performance.

As mentioned in chapter 1, the framework we chose to organize the enablers is the *Competing Values Framework.* Its purpose is to identify the main themes represented by the enablers. The Competing Values Framework was developed more than two decades ago in an attempt to explain effective organizational performance (Quinn & Rohrbaugh 1983; Cameron, 1986; Quinn, 1988). It was a product of empirical research on the major indicators of effective organizations. It has since been elaborated to include research on a host of other topics, including shareholder value, mergers and acquisitions, approaches to learning, organizational culture, leadership competencies, organizational design, communication styles, organization virtues, creativity, financial investments, and information-processing (see Cameron, Quinn, DeGraff, & Thakor, 2006). In each case, empirical research has confirmed the robustness and applicability of the framework to a broad array of human and organizational phenomena.

The Competing Values Framework

The Competing Values Framework serves primarily as a map, an organizing mechanism, or a sense-making device for complicated situations. It highlights the competing and seemingly paradoxical requirements necessary for achieving high levels of excellence. That is, excellence is always associated with the presence of tension, simultaneous opposites, and paradox (Cameron, 1986), and the Competing Values Framework helps highlight those competing tensions.

From the Competing Values Framework comes a theory about how various aspects of high-performing organizations function in simultaneous harmony and tension. A brief description of the framework is provided as an explanation for how we organized the enablers of successful change at Rocky Flats. Our intent is not to explain the Competing Values Framework in detail—that has been done elsewhere (Cameron and Quinn, 2006; Cameron, Quinn, DeGraff, and Thakor, 2006)—rather, our purpose is to highlight why Rocky Flats achieved such dramatic performance. By applying this framework to the myriad enablers that emerged as important predictors of Rocky Flats' success, it is possible to summarize key themes and simplify leadership principles.

In a nutshell, the Competing Values Framework organizes elements into four categories represented in a 2×2 matrix. It consists of two dimensions—one drawn vertically and the other drawn horizontally—resulting in four quadrants (see figure 4.1).

When studying the effectiveness of organizations more than two decades ago, we discovered that some organizations were effective if they demonstrated *flexibility and adaptability*—the ability to change, adjust, and adapt easily. Other organizations were effective if they demonstrated *stability and control*—the ability to stay the course, resist pressures to drift, and maintain consistency of strategy. Similarly, some organizations were found to be effective if they maintained *efficient internal processes*—the ability to organize, reduce variations and errors, and measure activities; others were effective if they maintained *competitive external positioning* relative to customers and clients—the ability to compete successfully in the

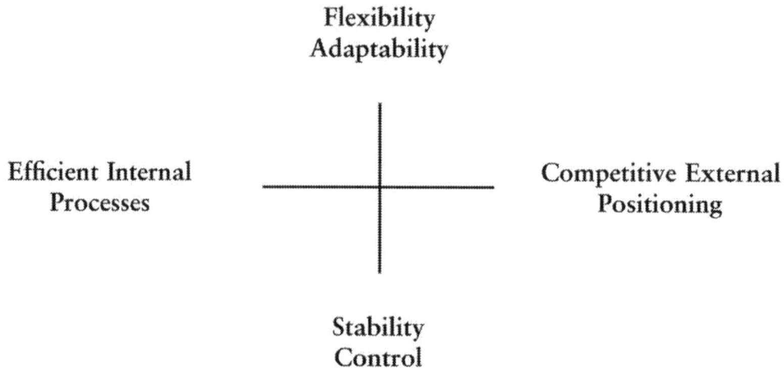

Figure 4.1 CORE DIMENSIONS OF THE COMPETING VALUES FRAMEWORK

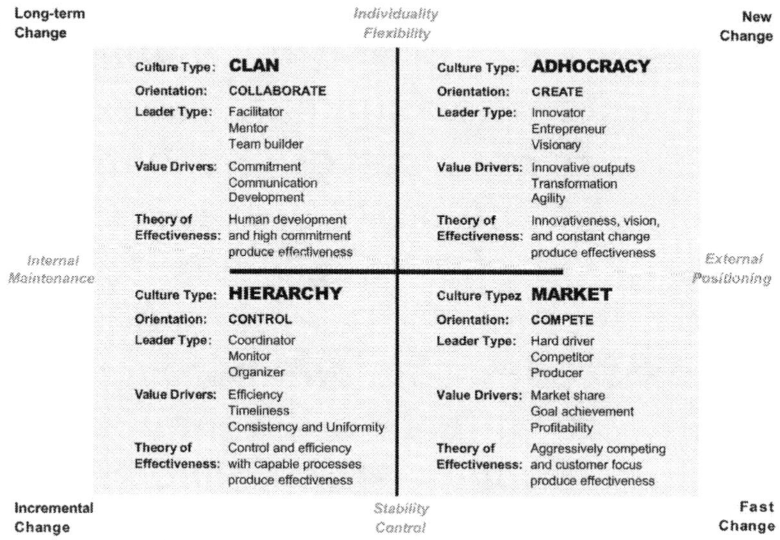

Figure 4.2 COMPARING QUADRANTS IN THE COMPETING VALUES FRAMEWORK

marketplace, create niches, and satisfy external constituencies (Quinn & Rohrbaugh, 1983; Quinn & Cameron, 1983; Cameron, 1986). These differences represent the opposite ends of two dimensions which constitute the rudiments of the Competing Values Framework. The key enablers explaining the success at Rocky Flats can be organized on the basis of these four quadrants.

The Competing Values Framework identifies the basic orientations that emerge in almost all human activity. That is, all organized human activity has an underlying structure. Completely haphazard actions, or randomly dispersed elements, are without organization, so *organization,* by definition, connotes patterns and predictability in relationships. Identifying the underlying dimensions of organization that exist in human and organizational activity is a key function of the Competing Values Framework. It helps uncover the underlying relationships that exist in leadership, learning, culture, motivation, decision-making, cognitive processing, creativity, and so on. Figure 4.2 illustrates major attributes of the four quadrants.

Each of the four quadrants has been given a label in order to characterize its most notable characteristics. When the framework was first developed, labels were borrowed from the organizational studies literature to define each quadrant—*Clan* (upper left), *Adhocracy* (upper right), *Market* (lower right), and *Hierarchy* (lower left). These terms referred to the organizational forms that were described in the scholarly literature and formed the basis for many theories about organizational effectiveness (Quinn & Cameron, 1983). However, the use of descriptive verbs often helps clarify the emphases of each quadrant, so we also use them here—*Collaborate* (upper left), *Create* (upper right), *Compete* (lower right), and *Control* (lower left).

Past research has discovered that most organizations adopt one or more of these quadrants as their dominant culture (Cameron & Quinn, 2006). That is, their values, processes, styles, and assumptions are consistent with one or more of these quadrants, so a culture profile can be developed for almost all organizations. Describing the attributes of each quadrant will highlight its key characteristics and clarify why it is such a useful framework for organizing the leadership enablers that created extraordinary success at Rocky Flats (also see Cameron, Quinn, DeGraff, & Thakor, 2006).

Attributes of Quadrants in the Competing Values Framework

Each of the four quadrants emphasizes a different set of values, strategies, leadership behaviors, and approaches to change.

The Adhocracy or Create Quadrant. This quadrant emphasizes creativity, agility, and constant change. A mantra of this quadrant might be "Innovate, take risks, and envision the future." Organizations that excel in this quadrant effectively handle discontinuity, change, and risk. They allow for freedom of thought and action among employees, so that rule-breaking and stretching beyond barriers are common characteristics of the organization's culture. Organizational effectiveness is associated with entrepreneurship, innovation, vision, and constant change.

Examples of value-creating activities in this quadrant include innovative product line extensions, radical new process breakthroughs (e.g., Polaroid's development of instant photography), innovations in distribution and logistics that redefine entire industries (e.g., Dell, Wal-Mart), and developing new technologies (e.g., gene splicing and quantum computing). Focusing on the strategies in this quadrant enables companies to leapfrog their competitors and achieve breakthrough levels of performance. With regard to the risk and return ratio, the potential payoff is high when creating new value, but so is the probability of failure. Moreover, the pace at which results occur and with which success is achieved is also unpredictable.

Leaders' strategies are aimed at producing new products and services, creating new market niches, and producing value by enhancing the processes by which entrepreneurship can be enhanced in the organization. Elaborating the portfolio of products and services through innovation and helping new ventures to flourish are key challenges of Adhocracy or Create quadrant leaders.

Strategies in this quadrant produce the most value in hyperturbulent, fast-moving environments that demand cutting edge ideas and innovations. Organizations that can predict the future and adapt readily to emerging dynamic conditions will flourish while other organizations are waiting for the uncertainty to diminish. Adhocracy quadrant organizations excel at being pioneers and definers of industry trends. Thoughtful experimentation, learning from mistakes, and failing fast in order to succeed more quickly are typical of successful Adhocracy quadrant organizations.

Individual leaders who excel in this quadrant tend to be gifted visionaries and futurists, inclined toward risk, and unafraid of uncertainty. They are typically adept at creating fantasies, dreams, and visions for the organization. But those dreams and visions are not merely pie-in-the-sky thinking. The ability to stay abreast of changes, remain imaginative, and undertake original actions makes Adhocracy quadrant leaders the darlings of fast-paced industries such as information technology, bioengineering, and communications.

The Hierarchy or Control Quadrant. This quadrant emphasizes efficiency and carefully controlled processes. A mantra for this quadrant might be "Refine, reduce, and perfect." Possessing a substantial degree of predictability and certainty is one of the hallmarks of this quadrant. Organizational effectiveness is associated with capable processes, measurement, and control. Examples of activities relating to value creation in this quadrant include quality enhancements such as statistical process control, cost and productivity improvements, reduction in manufacturing cycle time, and efficiency enhancement measures. These activities help make organizations function more smoothly and efficiently.

Leadership strategies in this quadrant help eliminate errors and increase the regularity and consistency of outcomes. Strategies focus on improving efficiency and cutting costs of operations. The extensive use of processes, systems, and technology is a hallmark of this quadrant. The use of standardized procedures and an emphasis on rule reinforcement and uniformity predominate.

Activities anchored in the Hierarchy or Control quadrant create the most value when failure is not an option—as in industries such as medicine, nuclear power, military services, and air transportation—or in highly regulated or stable environments. Value results primarily from increasing certainty, predictability, and regularity, and from eliminating anything that inhibits a perfect or error-free outcome. Adopting enhanced measurement systems, downsizing, and divesting unproductive units are Control quadrant activities.

Leaders who are most competent in this quadrant tend to be organizers and administrators. They pay attention to details, make careful decisions, are precise in their analyses, and focus on one best way. They tend to be conservative, cautious, and logical as problem-solvers where procedures are followed methodically, and persistence highlights their style. They are often technical experts and well informed. They keep track of details and obtain power based on information control and technical expertise. Documentation and information management are actively pursued.

The Clan or Collaborate Quadrant. This quadrant emphasizes building human capital, developing people, and solidifying an organizational culture. A mantra of this competence might be "Human development, human empowerment, and human commitment." The focus is on building cohesion through consensus, and satisfaction through involvement. Organizations succeed because they hire, develop, and retain their human resource base. Organizational effectiveness is associated with supportive interpersonal relationships, building cohesive teams and teamwork, and fostering high levels of participant engagement.

Examples of activities in this quadrant include clarifying and reinforcing organizational values, norms, and expectations; developing employees and cross-functional work groups; implementing programs to enhance employee retention; and fostering teamwork and decentralized decision-making. Examples include Intel's nonbureaucratic office structure, in which all employees (even former CEO Andrew Grove) work in easily accessible cubicles; the empowering of field managers by CEO Jack Greenberg at McDonald's Corporation; and the large investments in employee training and development by General Electric and Motorola. The activities in this quadrant help to sustain high levels of satisfaction, collaboration, morale, and willingness to commit to the organization and its objectives.

Strategies are aimed at building the human capacity of the organization. Human capital and social capital take priority over financial capital because they are assumed to produce economic returns. Interpersonal skills and competent human interaction are crucial prerequisites to value creation in this quadrant, so leadership strategies emphasize the development of effective relationships. A sense of community, a commitment to culture, and a willingness to cooperate are key outcomes of Clan or Collaborate quadrant strategies.

These strategies produce the most value for organizations when stability must be maintained in the face of uncertainty. Forming effective and long-lasting partnerships across organizational boundaries—inside and outside the organization—is often a requirement for long-term success, and competency in the Clan or Collaborate quadrant is the pathway to achieve that end.

Individual leaders who excel in this quadrant tend to take on roles of parent figure, mentor, facilitator, and team builder. They value shared objectives, mutual contribution, and a sense of collectivity among their employees. They produce working environments that are free of conflict and tension, and organization members tend to be more loyal to the organization and to the team than in organizations emphasizing the other quadrants. Helping individuals develop needed skills, ensuring a fit between job requirements and skills, and fostering life balance all are key objectives of Clan or Collaborate quadrant leaders regarding the individuals for whom they have responsibility.

The Market or Compete Quadrant. This quadrant emphasizes being aggressive and forceful in the pursuit of competitiveness. Organizations that excel in this quadrant emphasize and engender achieving results at all costs. Speed is an essential element in accomplishing goals and maintaining a competitive edge, so "results right now" is a typical demand. A mantra of the Compete quadrant might be "Compete hard, move fast, and play to win." Organizational effectiveness is associated with aggressive action, fast response, and external customer focus.

Examples of value-creating activities belonging to this quadrant include implementing aggressive measures to exceed goal achievement targets, partnering with external agencies, outsourcing selected aspects of production or services, investing in customer-focused acquisition activities, and attacking competitor organizations' market positions. The strategies in this quadrant help position the firm to achieve intended results, exceed expectations, and produce excellent performance in the immediate term. Customers are of highest priority in this quadrant, and they are defined as the ultimate reason for being in business.

Success is traditionally judged on the basis of indicators such as market share, revenues, meeting budget targets, and growth in profitability. Rapid response and speed of action are hallmarks of value-creating activities, and the philosophies of former Chrysler chairman Lee Iacocca—"Lead, follow, or get out of the way"—and former General Electric chairman Jack Welch—"Control your destiny or someone else will"—are typical of the Compete quadrant leadership approach. Taking charge, moving fast, and being aggressive are typical values.

Successful individual leaders tend to be hard driving, directive, and competitive. They welcome challenges and stretch goals, and have high levels of achievement orientation. Type A personalities, assertive behavior, and strong wills characterize Market or Compete quadrant managers. Their power and success are judged on the basis of results, not through their level of effort or the methods used.

Paradox. What is notable about the four quadrants in the Competing Values Framework is that they represent conflicting or contradictory assumptions. Each diagonal quadrant summarizes opposing approaches to leadership, organization, and change. The converse elements in each quadrant highlight one of the most important features of this framework, namely, the presence and necessity of paradox. Past research has confirmed that highly effective organizations are characterized by simultaneous contradictions and competing values (Cameron, 1986, 2005b), and using the Competing Values Framework in this analysis helps uncover the paradoxical nature of excellence achieved at Rocky Flats.

Change Strategies. Figure 4.2 also highlights the different approaches to organizational change that are consistent with each of the competing quadrants. The upper right quadrant, for example, focuses on transformational change—revolutionary, innovative, visionary change—whereas the lower left quadrant focuses on incremental change—small wins, tightening up, and refining. The upper left quadrant focuses on long-term change—creating a foundation, developing resources, deliberate change—whereas the lower right quadrant focuses on fast change—immediate results, rapid implementation, aggressive execution. Although it is not common in organizational change efforts, all four strategies are required if change is to be successful. The story of Rocky Flats is a testimony to that prescription.

Enablers

Our key objective in telling the story of Rocky Flats is to highlight the leadership principles that explain how an extraordinarily successful change process occurred. The leadership principles are based on the use of enablers of successful transformation. Enablers are factors that make change possible. They create the conditions under which the status quo is transformed into a new set of behaviors, cognitions, and outcomes. Enablers produce momentum for change, so that, in combination, they generate inertia that creates a new way of thinking, a new way of doing work, a new way of interpreting success, and a new set of values. Enablers take the form of levers, techniques, and prescriptions that leaders use to produce extraordinary change.

Theme: Supportive interpersonal relationships, developing human capital, openness, and nurturing a collaborative culture *Key Enablers:* Organizational culture change Collaboration Trust and credibility Human capital and social relationships	*Theme:* Innovation, risk-taking, visionary thinking, and symbolic leadership *Key Enablers:* Clear, shared vision Symbolic leadership activities Innovation and creativity Meaningful work
Theme: Maintaining stability, carefully controlling processes, precise objectives, and financial discipline *Key Enablers:* Goal clarity New contracts and an interagency agreement Detailed planning, projectizing, measurement, milestones, and accountability Stable funding	*Theme:* Power and politics, pressure to perform, striving for wealth, and external stakeholders *Key Enablers:* External stakeholder connections Positive external political strategies Bold action and pressure to succeed Incentives to perform

Figure 4.3 THE KEY ENABLERS FOR MAKING THE IMPOSSIBLE POSSIBLE

Using the Competing Values Framework, we organize the key enablers of the success at Rocky Flats into the four quadrants. The four themes that emerge, as mentioned in the Introduction, are *visionary and symbolic leadership* (Adhocracy or Create quadrant); *careful, clear, and controlled leadership* (Hierarchy or Control quadrant); *collaborative, engaging, and participative leadership* (Clan or Collaborate quadrant); and *rigorous, uncompromising, and results-oriented leadership* (Market or Compete quadrant). In the four chapters that follow, we explain the set of enablers that comprises each theme, using the words of the participants in the change effort itself. That is, we rely on the firsthand accounts of participants to describe the means by which Rocky Flats was transformed from a deteriorating and failing organization into an astonishing success. Figure 4.3 lists the key enablers and the overarching themes they illustrate.

Summary

The spectacular performance at Rocky Flats was due to an integrated and mutually reinforcing emphasis in each of the four quadrants. Because diagonal quadrants represent competing or opposite orientations, however, the leadership of the organization had to be paradoxical in order to thrive in such a dramatic way. Factors that compete with one another, or that create tensions in systems, had to be pursued concurrently. Most leaders are inclined to maintain consistency and an unwavering path toward a goal, but positive deviance in organizational performance requires the pursuit of simultaneous opposites (Quinn & Cameron, 1988). A key conclusion to be drawn from this discussion of competing values, therefore, is

> ***The successful leadership of extraordinary change requires the pursuit of simultaneously conflicting strategies.***

5

Key Enablers—Vision, Innovation, and Symbolic Leadership

This is the first of four chapters that address the question *What levers can leaders use to produce similar results?* This chapter addresses the enablers that relate specifically to visionary, innovative, and symbolic leadership.

Among the most significant enablers of success at Rocky Flats was the articulation and reinforcement of a motivating vision of what *could be* in contrast to what had occurred in the past. The articulation of an inspiring vision is an enabler that resides in the Adhocracy or Create quadrant. This quadrant also highlights several additional enablers, including innovation, flexibility, symbolism, and meaning. The forging of vision helped the organization stretch beyond its current performance levels and focus on possibilities more than on probabilities, entrepreneurial activities more than standard operating procedures, and new meanings in place of traditional ways of thinking.

In explaining the spectacular success at Rocky Flats, four categories of enablers in the Adhocracy or

Create quadrant emerged in our analysis—(1) forging a clear and shared vision of the future, (2) symbolic leadership and symbolic activity in support of a changing mission, (3) innovative and creative ideas about work, and (4) creating a new sense of meaning and importance attached to the tasks being pursued. Each enabler is illustrated by quotations from individuals directly engaged in the project.

A Clear, Shared Vision of the Future

The Rocky Flats project began with the reputation of a negative, depressing, doomed-to-failure project. Negative energy, criticism, and cynicism surrounded almost all activities and discussions related to the closure or cleanup. State government as well as DOE officials described Rocky Flats as being anything but a plum assignment.

> It was clear that I was going to be the environmental person for the state of Colorado for Senator Allard when he assumed office. They assigned me Rocky Flats with kind of a chuckle because it was seen as a negative project. I wasn't altogether thrilled with the assignment. I thought it was going to be a lot of drudgery and a failure, and I didn't see the benefit for Senator Allard at the time. Shortly after meeting with Congressman Skaggs's office, it became clear that there was an opportunity here. There were some very fine people at the Department of Energy and Kaiser-Hill, the contractor. There were some fine people

in the community that were committed to turning this from a negative into a positive. People at the Department of Energy started to catch fire with the community. We started to separate the real concerned citizens—the ones that really cared deeply—from the ones that just wanted to throw rocks at the site. It was real easy for politicians to take shots and echo the citizens' concerns about what was left here and what we had to deal with in the future. So, it took a tremendous effort and a sense of alignment with the politicians, the site, and the community to make this something positive to be involved in. It became a positive experience for me.

Contributor 32—Staff member, U.S. Congress

At the congressional level, a great deal of dissatisfaction was associated with Rocky Flats as well as the other DOE cleanup sites. One member of Congress described his displeasure at the lack of a motivating and clarifying vision.

I visited Rocky Flats, I think it was 1996 or 1997. That was after we determined that there were some problems, not just with Rocky Flats but with Hanford and with Savannah [other DOE nuclear sites] in terms of their how their personnel were being utilized. The first thing that struck me when I got involved with the Energy Committee was that environmental management was begin-

> ning to eat up the entire bill. In time all the funds would be gone. That bothered me. What bothered me also was that there were more employees in 1995 than there were in 1989. That was true throughout the whole DOE complex. That bothered me. I asked questions at a hearing about that issue but didn't get any good answers. I went back the next year and asked the same questions again, with a similar answer. Then I got tough. I said, "You know, I'm going to help you." I want you to categorize how your people are being utilized—the cleanup people, the administrative people, and the lab coats. The numbers were ghastly. Two and a half people, two and a half times the [number of] cleanup people were involved as "business suits," as we called them. That bothered me. That forced us to come back to them and say that this is not even acceptable. I won't accept it.
>
> Contributor 31—U.S. Congressman

The transformation from a negative project to a positive vision was a critical one. Adopting an abundance approach in contrast to a deficit approach was the key. Looking for possibilities, crafting an optimistic future, and assuming a positive stance toward the task were essential prerequisites.

> The challenge here was to get people to buy into the vision of a closure and how it benefited

everyone. At Rocky, everyone had been aligned about how horrible this was—how horrible this waste was here, we were never getting rid of it, it was going to contaminate our water systems, and it was going to imperil a city the size of Denver for the next hundred years. Everyone felt good about throwing rocks, but, in the end, the best you can achieve is the absence of something. The shift that took place was the vision of a closure project. Imagine these workers who had been working for the goals of the Cold War: to give the Americans a deterrent to Soviet aggression. Now they had to shift their thinking to "I'm working myself out of a job. If we're successful, I don't have a job." The only way that could really take place was for [the leadership at Rocky Flats] to convince people that they were part of something really big—something that would be the highlight of their career and highlight of their life. That worked.

Contributor 32—Staff member, U.S. Congress

In other words, a clear, positive vision of the future was a prerequisite for making any progress at Rocky Flats. But the vision went beyond just accomplishing a task. It was an abundance vision, a vision with profound purpose, a vision larger than individual benefit. Unfortunately, when the project began, no such vision existed, at least not in the minds of individuals associated with the project.

> When we got here, the Baseline Management Report said it would take 70 years and some 36 or more billion dollars to clean this place up. Well, first of all, I don't know about you, but I can't see out that far. 70 years? I'll be dead by then. So I'm working toward a job that's beyond my lifetime? No, that doesn't give me satisfaction. And 36 billion dollars? That's a lot of money by anybody's definition. There was no real vision. We just said, "We're going to clean the place up and shut down in 70 years." That wasn't exciting to me, and it wasn't exciting for the employees.

Contributor 21—Manager, DOE

From the federal government's perspective, the absence of a clear or compelling vision was just as obvious.

> In 1995 we knew we weren't in production. We knew we needed to be in cleanup. But no one could articulate what that meant. There was still a notion that Rocky Flats would be here forever. This project would outlast all of us. Changing that mind-set to a notion that this is a finite project that's going to come to an end was a very important change in the overall culture. Getting the community to understand that, getting all of the

> people who interact with the site from the outside to understand that, was hard. It took time.
>
> Contributor 16—Manager, DOE

To be fair, debates had occurred regarding what kind of end state should be achieved at Rocky Flats. Two primary alternatives were considered, although no consensus existed as to which was the better or the more feasible alternative to pursue.

> The public wanted to see how much it would cost to clean up the site to where you would leave essentially no contamination. Other people wanted to see what it would look like and how long it would take to leave a bunch of facilities still standing with everything cleaned up inside—kind of a mothball approach. This was the approach the Nuclear Regulatory Commission was using for a lot of the reactors. Then there was a wide range of different options in between those two bounding conditions—one being a total cleanup and one being a kind of a mothball.
>
> Contributor 7—Manager, Kaiser-Hill

Controversy continues to the present day, in fact, regarding what constitutes adequate completion of the project and the ideal end state. The extent to which extraordinary performance was achieved is still not universally applauded. For example, one representative of the Peace and Justice Center stated:

> A Washington-area think tank, the Institute for Energy and Environmental Research (IEER), proposed cleaning Rocky Flats to a level at which a subsistence farmer could occupy the site and eat food grown there—10 picocuries of plutonium per gram of soil or less. IEER recommended using these standards "even if the site is designated as a wildlife refuge, since it is not reasonable to assume that such a designation will endure for hundreds of years." DOE and the regulators dismissed IEER's proposal in favor of the revised RFCA (50 picocuries), which will rely on institutional and engineered controls to contain the long-lived contaminants left in the environment at Rocky Flats. A National Academy of Sciences study calls such controls "inherently failure prone."
>
> Contributor 25—Community Representative

In the absence of a consensual vision to guide the project prior to 1995, little progress had been made. In fact, years had passed prior to Kaiser-Hill's acceptance of the project with no measurable success because a clear and consensual vision had not been accepted by the various constituencies. As a vision began to be formulated, it was not immediately accepted by all relevant constituencies. A magical process did not occur in which a single vision was designated which created unambiguous goals for the project.

> At the very beginning, Kaiser-Hill came up with some ideas that tried to change too much too quickly.... it was a result of a brain-storming session—how fast can we do it? how much can we achieve? how many current barriers could we break? how could we radically change the path to be able to go forward? It went too far ... and it got shot down by DOE and the regulators and the state and the activists. But that was great, because it broke open the box ... everybody came together to find ways of doing something that were, perhaps, slightly less radical but that got us toward a desirable end point. So, while it was an enormous failure at the time, I think it paved the way for taking the less radical steps.

Contributor 5—Manager, Kaiser-Hill

The initial attempts at vision creation, in other words, initiated a process that led to the formation of a vision that could be accepted consensually. One DOE executive assigned to the Rocky Flats at the outset of the cleanup project identified the central role that this vision played:

> We had to establish something that was real, that you could touch. So we initially said, "Okay, we're going to shut this place down in ten years for about ten billion dollars." That was our first

> goal. That would be 55 years earlier than anyone had projected before, and it would be for 25 billion dollars less than anybody had said they could do it before. I think that was a major breakthrough. That allowed us to focus and identify priorities. We could say, "You will be here for that closing. You can bring your children here for that closing ceremony." People could relate to that. They could say, "Now I can see where that's a mission. I can see where I can play a role in that."
>
> Contributor 21—Manager, DOE

Importantly, the vision was articulated not only by leaders at the project site but also in the federal government and at DOE. The vision had to be explained and shared by individuals at the federal level as well as at the local level.

> Back here in Washington, we had some very insightful folks who started to realize that 70 years and hundreds of billions of dollars to complete the cleanup of the complex was unacceptable. I think the first ray of light we saw back here was the former assistant secretary, who came out with the 10-year plan. A lot of people balked at the 10-year plan, thinking that there's no way we can ever complete this mission in 10 years. But there were a couple of us in the field who took that challenge and said,

> "Yes, we can." That was the catalyzing event at headquarters here. We said, "Yes, we can make a difference; yes, we can do something different; and no, we don't have to accept the fate of hundreds of billions of dollars and decades and generations to complete the cleanup here." Those kinds of things got us started.
>
> Contributor 14—Manager, DOE

Although various attributions have been made regarding where the aggressive cleanup vision originated, the most important fact is that it was shared and articulated by leaders in several critical organizations—at Rocky Flats, in Congress, at DOE, in the state of Colorado, and by community groups surrounding the Rocky Flats site.

Of course, every organization argues that it has a vision or a specified mission to accomplish. This enabler of success is commonly identified as being critical for success in most organizations—average performers as well as spectacular performers. The difference between normal organizational visions and the one that was articulated for Rocky Flats, however, concerns its abundance focus and revolutionary nature. The Rocky Flats vision identified a target that extended well beyond anything that almost anyone had imagined. One Rocky Flats CEO described it in this way:

> To change the place, we had to create a vision and mission that the old culture and the old work processes could not achieve. We had to bring the place to its knees. We could not just do incremental change, so we needed a revolutionary vision.
>
> Contributor 9—Senior Executive, Kaiser-Hill

To make a revolutionary vision real—that is, to make it more than hyperbole or an exaggerated aspiration that no one took seriously—visual images that supported a bold new vision were needed. That is, both right brain elements (e.g., visual imagery) and left brain elements (e.g., targets and benchmarks) were necessary parts of the vision. Importantly, visual images were created as part of the articulation process that made the vision come alive in the eyes of important constituencies.

> In thinking through how to do an accelerated approach to cleanup, Kaiser-Hill produced a visual image. They had a "before" image and an "after" image of when they were finished with their contract, what the site might look like. The "after" image is a prairie. It is back to its prairie ecosystem, and it has a boundary of where the former industrial site was. You can actually see this blueprint idea of a construction site where buildings, telephone poles, water towers, and stacks were brought down, and it is back to its original prairie. When you visually see that, it has

a huge impact on not only the workers but on the community as well. We all galvanized around that image, and we were hoping to see that image made real.

Contributor 33—Assistant to a U.S. Congressman

The [Boulder] *Daily Camera* had gotten a copy of a picture that we had kind of fabricated with a company in Boulder called Pixel Kitchen. They had taken an overhead picture of the site and put together an artist's rendition of what the site could look like following closure. The *Daily Camera* had actually published that picture on the front page of the newspaper with the question, "Is this what Rocky Flats will look like?" Well, as you can imagine, it caused quite a stir in the community. A lot of people were just completely caught off guard, because the government had been talking about taking 50 or 60 years to perform cleanup. Now there was actual talk about cleaning up in our lifetime. It was quite an interesting time.

Contributor 7—Manager, Kaiser-Hill

This actual visual image of what the end state would look like was enormously important in helping various constituencies come to consensus about what the outcomes would be. One Rocky Flats manager stated:

Figure 9: Rocky Flats before and after cleanup: a comparison of the Rocky Flats site in 1995 with what was envisioned at the completion of the project

Our greatest ally in our cleanup and closure of Rocky Flats has been to form cohesion within our community. When I first began working in Rocky Flats in 1990, there were so many different elements of the community. There were local governments. There were economic development interests. There were people that were antinuclear. There were people concerned about the environment. They were all in separate groups, and they were all trying to approach Rocky Flats from different angles. It was in the mid1990s [after the visual images were disseminated] when the groups began to coalesce ... and began to work together. I think that that was probably the greatest event that could have happened in terms of helping us understand this problem—hearing the other perspectives in the community and then realizing that we all share the common vision for Rocky Flats. It was through that shared vision that we began to work together.

Contributor 36—Manager, Kaiser-Hill

A congressional staff member reached the same conclusion:

We had an actual visual image of what we wanted this place to be.... I think once we got that in place, the contractor, the DOE, and the community all rallied and galvanized interest to see this project through.

Contributor 33—Assistant to a U.S. Congressman

Other project staff noted that visual images helped remind employees of the purpose, importance, and value of this new vision:

> At Rocky Flats the effort to preserve a piece of land became the Rock Creek Reserve. It was about 800 acres. It is a beautiful parcel of land. What happened, I think, was that with the creation of this one reserve, people really began to focus on the fact that there was untouched prairie. There was an old homestead house that was a beautiful symbol of what the Front Range had been. It really opened the door for a much broader discussion of land preservation and, ultimately, led to the designation of the entire Rocky Flats site as a candidate for a wildlife reserve. As a result, I think that Rocky Flats will have served two purposes: it will have helped do its part to win the Cold War, and it will also help preserve a beautiful part of the Front Range for Denver and the other communities in that area.

Contributor 18—Manager, DOE

The result of a clear vision was the alignment and the motivation of multiple groups to believe that achieving something previously thought to be impossible was actually possible.

First of all, we have to have a vision of an end state for the site. We're building more of a consensus here. We have a cleanup agreement that's aligned with the vision. We believe that we have a project closure baseline that actually describes how we could achieve closure of the site. These are some of the key elements that began to set the stage for people really beginning to believe in their hearts and minds that achieving closure of the site could happen in our lifetime.

Contributor 7—Manager, Kaiser-Hill

Symbolic Leadership Activities

As illustrated above, the effective articulation of a motivating and inspiring vision is always dependent on visual images and symbols. An important part of helping Rocky Flats employees capture a new vision of what the future could hold was the demonstration of several symbolic events that represented and reinforced the new future. Some of these symbolic events were planned, but some ended up being serendipitous.

For example, one of the key messages associated with the vision for Rocky Flats' future was that the site would really be demolished. Meanwhile, it was to be a temporary facility. This contrasted with the long-held belief of many employees that the federal government would never really close the facility and that eventually it would begin production again. Despite the announcements that production would be discontinued, a residue of disbelief remained, especially among union members and those whose parents and grandparents had worked at Rocky Flats in the past. Hence, several actions were taken by Kaiser-Hill leaders to symbolically change the image of Rocky Flats' future. One was a name change.

> Early on, the name was Rocky Flats Plant. That had a close identification with production and had a closer identification with the FBI raid. Plus, it was looking backward more than looking forward. We decided that we needed to change the name to create a new image of what we wanted to do and what we wanted to be. So we basically had a contest, an open invitation to everyone—the employees and the community citizens groups—to tell us what they thought the name ought to be. I don't remember exactly where the name came from, but we settled on changing the name to Rocky Flats Environmental Technology Site, which has a vision for the future.
>
> Contributor 21—Manager, DOE

Several other events were described by unionized workers and supervisors that also led to altered images of the facility. Each was symbolic, communicating the new vision in vivid ways.

We closed the cafeterias. We closed the fitness facilities. All for symbolic reasons, not because it would save us money. They weren't on the priority list.... If this place is going to close in a couple of years, it should feel more and look more like a construction site. At a construction site, you eat off a lunch truck.

Contributor 10—Senior Executive, Kaiser-Hill

We ripped out the ceiling in the administration building just to send a message to the workforce. It was symbolic message. Kaiser-Hill then got rid of the administration building so that all VPs have to work at the site.

Contributor 11—Supervisors, Kaiser-Hill

Sometimes symbolic gestures were not planned as proactive strategies but were reactions to arising circumstances. For example, one senior executive at Rocky Flats described another symbolic gesture associated with the new vision.

We had another situation where we had a bunch of empty trailers as we downsized from 7,000 employees to 3,000 employees. We didn't need all of these trailers anymore, so we started moving people out of them. But you put gas in a vacuum, and what happens? It expands. So we had the smaller workforce expanding into all of

> these other trailers so people could have their own trailer. We went out with padlocks and started locking the trailers so that they couldn't use them. They got the message that you can't use those trailers. We're going to take those trailers down at some point.
>
> Contributor 21—Manager, DOE

The rationale for these symbolic activities—which were not part of the work plan—was to make it clear to Rocky Flats employees that Rocky Flats was now a site characterized by temporariness and transition. The actual work of cleanup and closure also created several important events that were interpreted as symbolic and meaningful. Inasmuch as many of the employees had worked at Rocky Flats for decades, and in some cases they were the second or third generation in a family to be employed there, tearing down buildings offered a dramatic example of symbolic change.

> Building 779 was the first plutonium building in the world to be taken down. No matter how difficult, we were committed to do that. It was an important initial symbolic move. The 779 crew provided the energy for the whole project. They burned their ship. They were the wrecking crew. It became the symbol of what we were going to accomplish.

Contributor 10—Senior Executive, Kaiser-Hill

The destruction of these buildings, of course, often had a dramatic impact on those who worked in them. Destruction of buildings provided significant events in motivating the process of culture change.

> There were very hard and discrete points of cultural change. One that I remember very, very well was the demolition and destruction of building 886. I was the manager.... Up until that point there had been structures taken down, but this was a process building that had specific meaning and value to a lot of people on the site. They had been working for months to remove equipment from the building and decontaminate the building. It was time to start, with the "jaws of life," to take bites out of the building. It was kind of a rainy morning, but it wasn't raining. We hadn't planned anything big, although we did have a few members of the press that wanted to see it.... We walked over to the building, and it was really mostly a lot of workers standing there watching. I walked up and stood behind two of our workers, and there were tears rolling down the cheeks of one of the workers. I looked at him and I said, "Are you okay?" He looked at me and said, "I can't believe they're taking that building down. I worked there. I don't think

> people realize how much of us went into the operation here." That was a very important symbol. Even the workforce saw how real this was. So this was a very specific turning point that symbolized what happened at the site.
>
> Contributor 20—Senior Executive, DOE

Leaders at Rocky Flats also used unplanned events to create visible messages associated with the vision. For example, among the most visible features of the Rocky Flats site were guard towers and miles of razor wire along the perimeter.

Figure 10: The jaws of life

> When I got on site as the manager, the first thing I did was to establish trust and credibility. The site was surrounded by miles and miles of barbed wire and guards were posted.... So we did a number of things. We took down fences—miles

> and miles of fences. We took down guard posts so that when citizens wanted to come see me, they only had to go to one checkpoint. They didn't have to be escorted past that point. They could come directly to my office. I had an open door policy with the media and with the employees, whether they were DOE employees, site employees, contract employees, or citizen groups.
>
> Contributor 21—Manager, DOE

The seemingly simple symbolic action of removing guard towers, however, encountered unexpected opposition. It illustrates the principle that positively deviant actions almost always encounter the same kind of resistance as negative deviance. Symbolically, however, positively deviant actions are critical for fostering success.

> One of the first things that we came up against in wanting to take down these guard posts was rules. [One employee], who worked for Kaiser-Hill, came to work and said, "You told us to take down the guard post, but I can't take it down." I said, "Well, why not?" "Because the regulations require that before you take down a federal building, a public building, you must first offer it to the homeless." And I said, "Wait a minute. We're inside a protected area. There are signs on this building saying *Danger Radiation*. And before you can tear that down, we have to get some

Figure 11: Bringing down a guard tower

ruling from somebody that we've offered it to the public?" I said, "That's crazy. Get a bulldozer and knock it down. I'll take the flak." And he did. He went and got a bulldozer and knocked them down. We established very quickly that we were going to work by different rules now. Not that we were going to violate rules, but that we were going to use some common sense. We were going to stand up for what made sense and do what was right if there was a rule that was stupid.

Contributor 21—Manager, DOE

Still another example of how a symbolic event reinforced the vision of the future occurred unexpectedly. Working at Rocky Flats were lifelong employees, union members, and Kaiser-Hill managers and supervisors. There was also a substantial number of employees from the Department of Energy. Some of the stereotypes that were perpetuated both in Washington and onsite were not particularly favorable to the federal government or to the protesters, environmentalists, and adversaries in the local area. An adversarial climate had long existed between these various groups and the Rocky Flats facility. One event highlights the way in which those stereotypes began to be broken down and, symbolically, replaced by a sense of partnership and goodwill.

> [A senior DOE official] really focused on the community, and taught us all the importance of being good neighbors. One example was that there were some of the environmental groups and nuclear opponents that had planted what they called a peace garden outside the main gates of Rocky Flats. After several weeks, some DOE employees went out and wrecked the garden. What [this senior official] did was ask for volunteers to help him go out and replant the garden. It was a symbol, basically, of the department's commitment to the local community to be a good neighbor, to respect other views, to do our best to listen to other people's views, and to come up with a plan that even if we didn't get agreement, we could explain to folks why we weren't taking their suggestions.

Contributor 20—Senior Executive, DOE

Of course, one of the most important symbolic events was the announcement that a substantial portion of the profits earned from a rapid cleanup and closure would be shared with the workforce. Management would not become wealthy at the expense of the workforce. Not only was commitment enhanced by such an announcement, but the vision of cooperation, teamwork, mutual respect, and objective performance outcomes was reinforced.

> CH2MHill announced immediately that they would share 20 percent of earnings. The top 100 performers got $35,000 in bonuses. The mid group got $15,000. The lower group got $5,000 to $10,000. We did this for visibility. We wanted to communicate that there were no teachers' pets. Performance evaluations would be objective and would drive bonuses.

Contributor 9—Senior Executive, Kaiser-Hill

These examples of symbolic activities illustrate the importance of having both right brain and left brain aspects of the vision. Establishing specific objectives, goals, standards, and processes (left brain elements) is not enough to capture the dedication and positive energy of a workforce. The symbolic activities and events that reinforced the vision (right brain elements) were a necessary component of a successful strategy.

The leadership at Rocky Flats had to capture both the hearts and the minds of various constituencies, and symbolic events were an effective way to initiate emotional and cultural changes.

Innovation and Creativity

Another set of enablers for making the impossible possible was the inclination toward, and multiple activities centered on, innovation and creativity. The CEO of CH2MHill, the parent company of Kaiser-Hill, attributed success at Rocky Flats, at least partly, to the innovation and learning that characterized the leadership and workforce.

> A key is innovation, technical innovation, and contractual innovation, and incentive innovation.... Our incentive was to learn how to lower our costs as we went through continuous learning and innovation.
>
> Contributor 1—Senior Executive, CH2MHill

One conducive factor was an environment that was fast moving, challenging, and conducive to experimentation. This kind of environment can create defensiveness and a hunkering down mentality, or it can stimulate innovation and learning. One state government manager likened the climate to "a bit like drinking from a fire hose. There's so much going on at this site" (Contributor 27—Senior Manager, CDPHE). The demands of this project made innovativeness a prerequisite for success. According to one Rocky Flats manager:

> One of the things that's so fun about Rocky Flats, and I think the regulators would probably tell you the same thing, is that every day you get sort of a new twist and a new issue and another opportunity to make something happen by solving a problem. If you don't like problem-solving, you won't like working here; but if you like to solve problems and you like to see progress, this is a really exciting place to be.
>
> Contributor 8—Manager, Kaiser-Hill

It was not the environmental conditions that led to dramatic success, of course, but an orientation toward innovation that characterized the company itself. That is, DOE had usually been the director of initiatives with most contractors, and innovation, speed, and experimentation were not typical of those relationships. Kaiser-Hill, on the other hand, entered the Rocky Flats project with a completely different approach.

> The other thing that made a huge difference was that we had the very good fortune of partnering with a contractor—Kaiser-Hill—that was willing to really be innovative and creative and come to us with ideas of how they could accelerate cleanup. It was basically a new experience for the department. Most of our contractors were very

> careful to wait for the Department of Energy to give them guidance, and then they would work and let us know what problems they were having. It was a new experience for us to have a contractor come in and tell us they could do the job faster, and cheaper, and that they would deliver a plan on how to do it.
>
> Contributor 18—Manager, DOE

Kaiser-Hill approached the Rocky Flats project with an attitude of try it, find a way, and learn from mistakes. The CEO exemplified and modeled this attitude.

> One of the great things about [the CEO] is that he was able to hear someone say "no" and respond, "Okay, we can't do that, so let's find a new baseline. We'll do something else." Even if it was his idea, he was fine with being told "no," moving on, and coming up with another idea. That's basically what we did. Being told "no" opened a door so that we could do something else that would be successful.
>
> Contributor 5—Manager, Kaiser-Hill

This innovative attitude carried over throughout the project, even in subsequent years when new CEOs were appointed. The statement of one subsequent CEO illustrates the continuity of this innovative attitude.

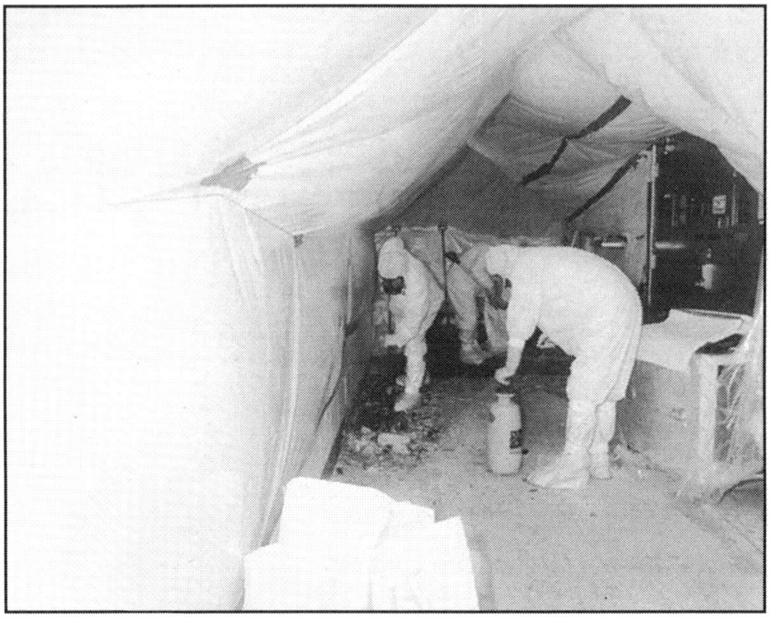

Figure 12: Cleaning asbestos

There is a lot of shared attitude that goes like this: "I don't know how to do this, and here is the limited set of time and money I have, but I'll get it done." There was no actual critical path in this project from the outset. Innovation and the combination of art and science helped make it successful.... We engage in lots of small trials. The example of taking apart glove boxes is an example. We use a variety of procedures now in taking apart a glove box: cutting, intracoating, and so on, all of which we invented. A lot of entrepreneurship exists because we reward people, we have created a good environment, we encourage people, and there is a lot of positive energy.

Contributor 9—Senior Executive, Kaiser-Hill

One way in which innovation occurred was simply challenging existing rules and regulations that seemed to slow the process. Questioning red tape and bureaucracy was one of the most fruitful areas for confronting existing procedures and creating innovation. One executive described the approach to innovation adopted by Kaiser-Hill.

> One of the challenges of working at a site like Rocky Flats was that there was a lot of bureaucracy and a lot of red tape. The contractor realized when they came in that they had to find a way to cut through some of this bureaucracy and red tape. One of the best examples I can think of is the demolition of building 111, which was the administration building for the site contractor. This was one of the original buildings that was built at Rocky Flats when it first began operations in the early '50s. It was a building that had the typical asbestos contamination and other things that you would think about for a building its age. Because it was on a nuclear weapons site, and because of the concerns with radiation, there were a lot of rules and regulations that the site contractor was faced with in trying to demolish this building. Many of those rules and regulations didn't make sense for an administration building that never was involved in nuclear operations. By asking those questions, they were able to come up with a better way, a smarter way, of doing the demolition of that building. They were able to

> save a substantial amount of money, which then was put into other projects. It helped speed them along.
>
> Contributor 36—Manager, Kaiser-Hill

As might be expected, Kaiser-Hill's approach to innovation and experimentation was not always successful. Fits and starts, failures and overreaching, disappointments and resistance were part of the learning process. For example:

> We invested about $20 million in a "robotic size-reduction" process which was supposed to tear apart a glove box in about a week. It was a big technological bust. We just abandoned it and sold the technology. It was neat technology ... but with decontamination and "instacoat," we got it down to a day anyway, so we don't need that anymore.
>
> Contributor 9—Senior Executive, Kaiser-Hill

Despite failures and missteps, however, over 200 innovations were created by the workforce at Rocky Flats in the service of a faster, more efficient, and safer cleanup and closure. The development of a highly innovative culture allowed for experiments with hundreds of potential solutions to difficult problems rather than searching for the one right way to approach the tasks. Examples of innovations include the development of a special container for plutonium shipments ("pipe and go") which saved an estimated $100 million; a cerium nitrate solution that allowed radioactive pollution to be wiped off contaminated containers and glove boxes, which saved an estimated $50 million; a coating solution ("instacoat") for sealing large pieces of polluted equipment, which saved an estimated $10 to $20 million; and a process for changing the gloves in glove boxes, which increased output from two or three per shift to 20 per shift.

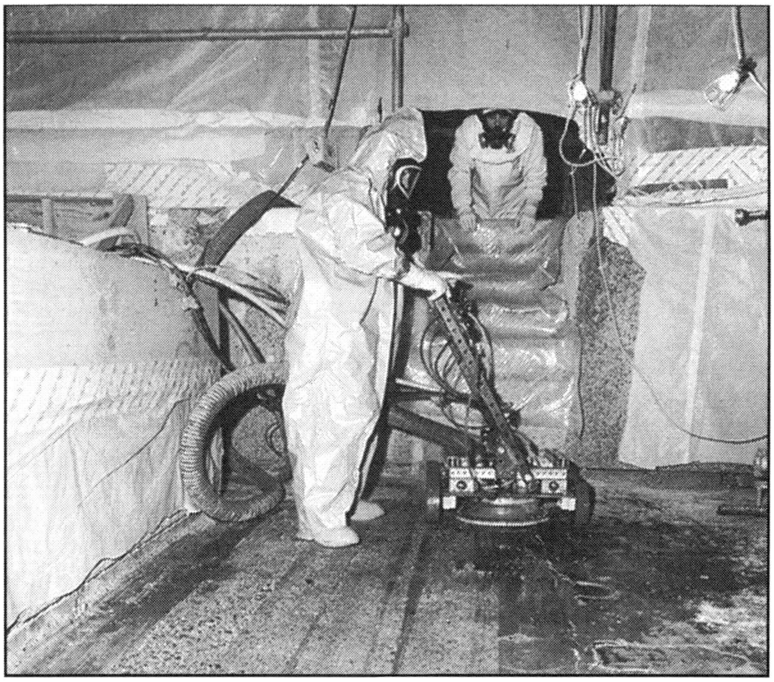

Figure 13: Hydroplaning and stripping concrete

One example, in particular, illustrates the innovation process at Rocky Flats as it unfolded in the glove box removal process.

Rocky Flats used to be able to dismantle a single glove box in a year. A glove box is a con-

Figure 14: Removing a glove box

tainment vessel where we actually took plutonium out and worked with it. These things are highly contaminated. They're lead lined. They are very complicated in the way the gloves, the ventilation system, and the safety systems are situated. We felt real good if we could get one of these glove boxes out a year. Well, Rocky Flats owns over a thousand contaminated glove boxes, so at that rate it would take us a thousand years to finish. In the 1996 and 1997 time frame, we said we don't have to take these apart bolt by bolt. So we gave the workers these big machines with sharp saws at the end, and we started cutting them up. We were able to get out about one box a week. We said, "Man, major breakthrough. We were able to increase our productivity by a factor of 50." Then we said, "Wait. We don't have to give workers sharp saws. We can give them plasma cutting torches, and we can take them one step away from the glove boxes where they're not exposed to so much contamination and radiation." Now we're getting out two or three a week. Then one of the workers said, "Why are we cutting these things up in the first place?" "Well, we need to fit them into this box." And he says, "Why don't we get a bigger box?" So we went from taking apart bolt by bolt, to finding innovative ways to cut these apart, to finally saying, "We don't need to cut these things up to dismantle them." Right now, what we do is decontaminate them, separate them into pieces, put them into boxes, and ship them out as low level waste. We're doing two and three a day. So, from one a year to two or three a day, from taking apart piece by piece to not bothering take them apart—that's the innovation that I'm talking about. When you have a motivated contractor, a motivated regulatory community, motivated local governments, and motivated workers, that's the kind of innovation that we expect to see.

Contributor 14—Manager, DOE

One factor that makes this innovation story even more impressive is that the workers employed to do this job were not experts trained in taking apart glove boxes or tearing down radioactively contaminated buildings. They were the same people who had built the buildings and operated the equipment. They were builders, not demolishers; operators, not obliterators. They had to be trained to do a new set of tasks and to take on a new set of work challenges. Task requirements and measures of success were completely different in a shutdown environment.

> The workforce had to know the work; they had to be experts; but we had to use the same workforce. We had to transform the workforce because they didn't know how to do the work they were tasked to do. People didn't choose to work for CH2MHill. They were drafted. They had to learn to use their know-how in a different way.... The workforce was proud of its production records, but it had to gain a whole new set of goals, standards, and rewards.
>
> Contributor 1—Senior Executive, CH2MHill

In sum, innovation at Rocky Flats capitalized on a fast-paced environment that demanded new approaches to accomplishing work, coupled with a "can do" attitude among the workforce that produced continuous learning, trial-and-error attempts, and creative experiments. It might be described as a learn-as-you-go approach rather than a well-designed-procedures approach to cleanup and closure—an evolution of learning rather than a carefully planned transformation. Both failure and success served as an incentive for learning and measurable progress.

Figure 15: Shipping a coated and sealed glove box

We didn't really know what we were doing. We just knew that we were going in the right direction, and that it was okay to fail. There were a lot of things that didn't work out. On the other hand, there were even more things that either worked or worked the second or third time, because we figured it out. If you look at some of the early incentives we placed in the contract, we were still incentivizing process and not product. It was an evolutionary process. The important thing is that we were measuring things, and we were learning. From 1995 to when we put the closure contract in place in 2000, you'll see

> very methodical series of improvements—three steps forward, one step back.
>
> Contributor 14—Manager, DOE

Meaningful Work

The difficulty, of course, was that all this success began with a workforce that was unmotivated, discouraged, and without purpose and meaning. Upon arrival, Kaiser-Hill and DOE encountered an environment characterized by loss of focus, lack of meaning, and absence of purpose.

> How are we going to get motivated again? How are we going to start this place back up? How are we going to get people excited about their work? How are they going to know what their job is? These became the most important things. Most of us, when we get up in the morning, want to do a job where we feel like we've accomplished something. These people didn't know what they were supposed to be doing every day. They had spent 50 years of their lives defending our country, and they were excited about what they had accomplished. They felt very patriotic. Yet, the news media, and all of these other forces working against them, made them feel very bad about their work. They didn't know what their work was anymore. So what we tried to do was develop a vision for what they should be doing

> and how they could feel good again about themselves and their work.

Contributor 21—Manager, DOE

The leadership challenge involved identifying a profound new purpose and motivating meaningfulness associated with the new objectives. Both Kaiser-Hill and DOE leaders were confident that if the workforce captured a sense of the importance of the scope of this new work, dramatic progress could be made.

> Almost anything we did would be an improvement. That's not because the people here before weren't competent. They were very competent, but they had no focus. They had no mission. Once we gave them a mission, a vision, then we could be open, teach people ... and make things happen. We made a lot of changes in a short period of time. It was all to make it safe—safe for the employees, safe for the people who live off this site, and to save the taxpayers some money. We gave them meaning, and it was very gratifying.

Contributor 21—Manager, DOE

Floor supervisors echoed the notion that a profound purpose—a purpose associated with core values, attached to outcomes larger than an individual's benefit, and producing results that would last over a long period of time—made a powerful difference in the work.

> People want to work, so you need to give them direction, purpose, and the tools. When people don't have anything to do, they don't want to do anything when asked.
>
> Contributor 11—Supervisors, Kaiser-Hill

That sense of meaning and profound purpose was articulated by different individuals in slightly different ways, but each perspective provided resonance and direction. One congressional leader articulated the significance of the project this way:

> I went into this with a lot of concern about being assigned to Rocky Flats. I came away thinking this is one of Governor Owens's and one of Senator Allard's greatest achievements. You know, 2 million people live close to this site. Cleaning up Rocky Flats means we will have really achieved something that protects people in Colorado for the future. When this is a wildlife refuge in the future, it's going to be a wonderful thing for the people of Colorado. If you've looked down the Front Range, that's a vast habitat for wildlife, for birds, and for all kinds of species and animals—endangered animals. You're looking at something that doesn't exist on the Front Range anymore. It has disappeared pretty much everywhere else. So, it's a lasting achievement and a

tribute to everyone who has worked on it. It really has made a difference in the way Colorado will look in the future, and you don't get that very often.

Contributor 32—Staff member, U.S. Congress

Congressman Knollenberg referred to this purpose as "catch the fever":

We call it "catch the fever" because you are actually becoming part of something historical. Most everyone now is very proud of the work they do, even the steelworkers union, the trade unions, the guards union. They are proud of what they do, and they are proud to be able to achieve something special. Everyone wants meaning in their job. Now they are back to work and the buildings are going away. Building 771 was the most dangerous building in the world, and now it's not. It's going to come down shortly. We are proud of our achievements, and they are, too.

Contributor 31—U.S. Congressman

One key DOE leader assigned to the Rocky Flats project described his motivation for tackling what seemed to be a daunting assignment with a low probability of success.

The other reason for my getting involved was that it was important. It was doing something

> meaningful. I feel very fortunate to live in this country, and I have always wanted to serve this country as a way of saying thank you. I went to West Point; then I served in the army for a while; and then I worked for the federal government. That was my way of saying thank you for allowing me to live in this great country. It was a way to do something, hopefully, that would make a difference and be meaningful. So I wanted to try it.
>
> Contributor 21—Manager, DOE

Of course, providing a meaningful purpose in work requires more than just mentioning it, or ascribing an outcome that might resonate with people. Trying to identify meaningful outcomes faces the danger of seeming like Pollyanna or like inauthentic manipulation. In the case of Rocky Flats, the meaningful purpose was reinforced in a powerful way, using the incentive system as a key lever.

> One of the first things we tried to do was change the type of contract from an award fee—cost-plus contract—to an incentive-based project management type of contact in which they could only get paid for accomplishing real things. Part of the problem with DOE was, when it came time to award the fee, a contractor would submit all the things that they thought they had done well. DOE, depending how they woke up

> that morning, would make a judgment as to whether that was good, bad, or how much they deserved—70 percent or 90 percent or whatever amount. During the first two six-month periods, I gave the contractors zero fee. Zero fee! Well, the contractor went ballistic. It had never happened with DOE before. Never had a DOE manager anywhere ever given anyone zero fee. So we raised the level of expectation. I said, "You want to get paid. We're going to pay you. But you have to earn it. And it's going to be objective." That was the approach we took—make it so you got paid for performance. The idea was that you showed up and you did something useful and meaningful. And guess what happened? Everyone went home feeling good about themselves: "I went to work." I had a mission. I accomplished that mission. And I got recognized. So I have a purpose again.
>
> Contributor 21—Manager, DOE

In other words, meaningful work and the creation of a profound purpose was another of the key enablers for achieving dramatic success at Rocky Flats. One senior DOE official who had worked at Rocky Flats during the 1995 contract period returned to the site after having been employed elsewhere. The impact of the meaningful purpose associated with the cleanup and closure tasks was obvious.

> To be able to come back now, five years later, and see the progress that we've made is just so rewarding. It reinforced what I believed all along. The employees, the workers, could do it if we just gave them the vision, gave them the tools, and then got out of the way. Give them the rules, tell them the envelope in which they have to work, and then stand back and let them do it. By golly, they're good people. They can do it. They're competent. They're skilled. They want to do good work. Most of us don't wake up in the morning and say, "I want to go to work and do a lousy job today." We want to go home at night saying, "I feel like I've accomplished something." I believe that. That's what I've seen here at Rocky Flats, whether it be the guards, the fire department, the ambulance drivers, DOE, or the steelworkers. Give them a purpose, give them a mission, give them the tools, give them the training, and they'll do it.
>
> Contributor 21—Manager, DOE

Summary

Enablers of extraordinary success in the Adhocracy or Create quadrant emphasized an abundance vision of the future, typified by profound meaning and outcomes that would provide benefit well beyond the needs of the workforce or the financial return to the organization itself. Multiple symbolic activities were required to reinforce that meaningful vision, as well as opportunities for innovativeness and creativity in addressing problems and obstacles. This inspiring vision and its meaningfulness provided a foundation upon which other key enablers were based. Figure 5.1 summarizes the theme and the key enablers.

Theme:
Innovation, risk-taking, visionary thinking, and symbolic leadership

Key Enablers:
Clear, shared vision
Symbolic leadership
Activities
Innovation and creativity
Meaningful work

Figure 5.1 KEY ENABLERS IN THE ADHOCRACY OR CREATE QUADRANT

Among the conclusions to be drawn from these enablers are the following:

- ***A positive vision of abundance must replace a problem-centered or deficit-based vision.***
- ***The vision must not be espoused by only the senior leader; it must be created by and shared among all relevant constituencies.***
- ***Effective visions must have more emphasis on right brain elements than on left brain elements, so that imagery provides inspiration.***
- ***Leaders must strive for positive deviance, so that aspirations represent revolutionary, not merely successful, performance.***

- ***The objective must include a profound purpose, or meaningfulness beyond personal benefit and immediate outcomes.***
- ***Leaders must institute symbolic events that signal the ideal future.***
- ***Employees must share in the risk of failure, so that the financial burden of missteps and mistakes is not borne entirely by the organization.***

6

Key Enablers—Stability, Discipline, and Process Control

This is the second of four chapters that address the question *What levers can leaders use to produce similar results?* This chapter addresses the enablers that relate specifically to the careful, clear, and controlled leadership themes.

In direct contrast to the Adhocracy or Create quadrant in the Competing Values Framework, the Hierarchy or Control quadrant focuses on stability, control, measurement, clarity of objectives, discipline, and detailed planning and processes in organizations. These factors are often criticized as inhibiting and sabotaging spectacular performance, yet it is clear from our analysis that they were prerequisites for extraordinary success at Rocky Flats. Whereas the Adhocracy or Create quadrant highlights symbolism, vision, and challenging the rules in the pursuit of innovation, enablers in the Hierarchy or Control quadrant emphasize efficiency, smooth functioning, predictability, and standardized procedures. They focus on the tight control of internal activities. Consistency and dependability are emphasized in contrast to innovation and dynamism.

This is not to say, however, that the key enablers in this quadrant are contrary to an overall abundance philosophy. As illustrated below, the approach to successful completion of the project was still grounded in virtuousness, extending beyond doing well to doing spectacularly well, and developing mechanisms to produce extraordinary results. Positive deviance, not just achieving a condition as successful or healthy, was the objective. In particular, among the key enablers of the spectacular success of the Rocky Flats project were (1) *goal clarity;* (2) *a new type of agreement with the federal government, in the form of the contract and an interagency agreement;* (3) *detailed planning and specific, objective performance measures, milestones, and accountability; and* (4) *an assurance of stable funding.* This chapter describes each of these four enablers.

Goal Clarity

A definite and often mentioned enabler of success at Rocky Flats was the specificity and clarity of the goal. For example, statements by senior officials in the Department of Energy, in the union, and by senior executives at Rocky Flats all reinforce the importance of a clear target and goal.

> *From a DOE official:* We had an objective. We had to close Rocky Flats. We had to be able to define what that meant as completely as possible

and as succinctly as possible. We couldn't take the Sears catalog to describe what we wanted. The elegance of it was, we described what we wanted in six lines. There are six criteria in our contract that say here are the six things that we're going to measure against. They're all single lines that say what is going to be done.

Contributor 15—Senior Executive, DOE

From the union: Now we have a clearly identified goal. Everyone knows exactly what we are to do and is aware of our visible progress. The main message is: This place will close with or without you. You may as well get on board and earn some money in the process.

Contributor 11—Supervisors, Kaiser-Hill

From a senior executive at Rocky Flats: Before I interviewed for the job, I ... came to the site and talked to people here at Rocky Flats about what the problems were and what the issues were. So when I went in for an interview for the job, I had developed a 30day plan, a 60-day plan, a 90-day plan, a 180-day plan, and then a one-year plan. I used that as part of my interview process. When I came to Rocky Flats, I brought that same plan with me. The very first thing on that plan was to regain trust and establish credibility with

> the workers, with the state, with the elected officials, with the public community, and with the news media. My job as manager was to take the site from a shutdown-do-nothing-spend-lots-of-money culture to something else. We were spending almost a billion dollars a year doing paper studies. We were being fined by the EPA and by the state because we were missing all these milestones. The basic thing was to get us back on mode in developing a vision for where we wanted to go and how we were going to get there.
>
> Contributor 7—Manager, Kaiser-Hill

Creating and communicating a clear target and an unambiguous goal was an effort that required the involvement of a variety of individuals. No single person—CEO, secretary of the Department of Energy, or governor of Colorado—could be the heroic figure who marshaled all the required forces purely on the basis of charisma or dynamic leadership. Multiple parties were engaged in establishing and articulating a consistent, clear goal for the project. Even a U.S. senator was engaged in setting goals and clarifying key objectives.

> We set up some clearly defined goals. The most obvious one was By what date do you want to have cleanup occur? Then, set that date and stick to it. Make everybody understand that if you don't stick to that cleanup date, the funnel is not

> going to continue to flow forever. There has to be a commitment from the elected officials from the area, so you have to pull together the elected officials with the workers and the management of the plant. Once you set these common goals, get affected communities together also.
>
> Contributor 30—U.S. Senator

In addition to members of the U.S. Senate, the state of Colorado played a key role in clarifying the goal. Although this was not a simple or straightforward task—otherwise, it would have been done by this group long before 1995—identifying an unambiguous and circumscribed goal was made possible because the overall project was not so complex as to be undefinable or unbounded. One state official put it this way:

> First, there was recognition that the traditional way of doing business hadn't worked here. Almost everyone who looked at Rocky Flats from, say, 1989 on, came away feeling that this place was not working and that not enough work was being accomplished. Morale was bad, and something different had to be tried. We had an approach that said we're going to try to do something different here. Second, even though the site is large by conventional standards, it is small by nuclear weapons plant standards. So the department felt that we could really get our arms around it. It

> was possible to go from beginning to end and potentially close the site in some reasonable period of time. Third, I would reiterate that the governor telling the Department of Energy that not only could we go fast, but if that resulted in people being relocated or being put out of work, that was tolerable in this area because the economic growth in this part of Colorado had the ability to absorb the losses. Pushing forward, getting results, and making things happen was perceived very strongly in Washington as something that people wanted. As a result, we could make it happen politically.
>
> Contributor 15—Senior Executive, DOE

When the project was undertaken in 1995, the goals were not nearly as clear as they became over time, and it was the constant clarifying of goals that enabled success. The project, in other words, did not begin with distinct and straightforward objectives that never varied. Precision and clarity had to be pursued constantly as the project unfolded over time. In fact, the completion goal itself evolved so that the target date for closure in 1995 was 2010, in2000 it was 2006, and in 2003 it was 2005. This transition toward goal clarity was explained by a senior DOE official:

> 1995 was a period of chaos at Rocky Flats, and that chaos pervaded virtually every aspect of the organization. It was true with the federal or-

ganization, with the contractors, and with the regulators. It was true in our relationship with the community organizations and with the media. We didn't have a clear message. We didn't have a clear plan as to where we were going. We didn't have clarity as to how to organize ourselves to achieve a clear set of objectives. Understand that 1995 was not the Dark Ages. We understood that our mission was cleanup. We knew that the production days were over, and this was the initiative of Secretary O'Leary. There was an understanding that we had to share information with the public. There was an understanding that we had to have a public process, but we didn't have sharing of information or a public process. We had processes that we were attempting to put into place, but the processes did not have any specific goals. There were very general goals or no goals at all. That's one important feature that characterized what life was like in 1995 compared to 2002. Now, we still have openness. We still have the commitment to cleanup, but it is openness and cleanup with the goal of closure. And closure isn't an abstract goal. It's a goal that has a specific schedule, a specific set of activities, and a specific set of requirements that need to be achieved by certain dates within certain cost parameters. It is possible to understand the transition from 1995 to 2002 as the development of greater and greater clarity in every important aspect of the

> organization, in the contract, in the safety organization, in our regulatory work, and in our community work.
>
> Contributor 16—Manager, DOE

The existence of clearly articulated, shared goals and targets provided two further benefits, in addition to giving the workforce a target with which they could identify. First, it allowed the establishment of straightforward and unambiguous priorities. Consensual goals helped determine the parameters within which priorities could be established. These priorities became another key enabler in the pursuit of spectacular performance.

> There were a number of basic strategies that [the CEO] had set for this group. Cleanup should focus first on early risk reduction, such as draining the plutonium liquid, stabilization of plutonium materials, and those types of things. Second, after risk reduction, look for opportunities to generate money to accomplish more risk reduction through mortgage reduction. That is, look for opportunities to save money on activities that were costing a lot of money. The strategy for accelerated closure was really to go after the plutonium and the enriched uranium risk first, and find ways to save money through innovation, find ways to identify money, and do more risk reduction through good business practices. After we got the major risks

> taken care of, then we would begin to focus on the other activities, such as building demolition, environmental restoration, and waste management. That sequencing really describes the way we approached the closure project.
>
> Contributor 7—Manager, Kaiser-Hill

A second consequence of clear goals was the ability to create partnerships with external stakeholders. That is, clear goals helped relationships with outside entities become smoother, more efficient, and more consensual. Agreement was made possible, and joint efforts focused on the same outcome ensued. For example, one DOE official stated:

> What was missing in the beginning was any notion of what, exactly, we wanted from the public. We didn't even know what we were trying to achieve ourselves. The public had a vague sense of values, concerns, and issues, and we had a vague agenda. If you take those two pieces together and impose lots of process, you get lots of meetings, lots of minutes, lots of recommendations, and lots of reports, but you don't necessarily achieve a partnership. There is no agreement on what you are trying to partner on. You can't partner on process by itself. You have to partner on a shared notion of an outcome. The clearer that shared notion of an outcome, the more effective your partnership will be. If the two parties

> only have a vague idea of what they're trying to achieve, all the meetings in the world won't achieve a partnership.
>
> Contributor 16—Manager, DOE

The New Contract—1995

In addition to the clarity of goals, success in the Rocky Flats project would not have been possible had the nature of the contract with DOE not been changed. A critical success factor was the development of an enabling government contract. It was widely recognized that the form of the past contracts for federal projects was inadequate for CH2MHill's approach to the Rocky Flats cleanup. Previous contracts had been created to support ongoing operations, not decommissioning and decontamination. One federal government official outlined the general problem:

> There was wide recognition that the traditional form of contracting in the Department of Energy wasn't working. It was costing too much, and things were taking too long. In addition, Rocky Flats had been a very difficult site for almost everybody who had been involved. Roy Romer, the governor of Colorado ... in 1993, made it clear to me and to Secretary O'Leary that he was very anxious to see strong measures taken to clean this site up. The combination of wanting to do some different things in contracting plus the gov-

ernor's clear signal to go ahead and make things happen, kind of gave us the impetus to move toward a performance-based contract.

Contributor 15—Senior Executive, DOE

A senior CH2MHill executive agreed on the inadequacy of past contract provisions:

It became clear that the past contract was overrun with regulations that were outdated and in the way. That motivated us to redo the contract. We have been able to waive DOE regulations for demolishing buildings, for example. CH2MHill took a lot of risk in order to keep the costs down, but it is one tenth the cost compared to having to confirm with DOE on every single request.

Contributor 1—Senior Executive, CH2MHill

The goal at Rocky Flats, therefore, was to foster enough confidence on the part of DOE that a new contract could be negotiated. This philosophy was articulated by a senior Kaiser-Hill executive:

Our strategy under the closure contract was to demonstrate to DOE that although we didn't have all the answers at the time, we could close this project by 2006 for $3.963 billion. If we didn't have the answer, we would figure it out and get it done. We were willing to take risks. The risk in the contract based on a contingent fee is that we

> wouldn't be paid until the job was complete. So we demonstrated that we would take those risks.
>
> Contributor 6—Senior Executive, Kaiser-Hill

The differences between the traditional contracts with DOE and the new agreement for Rocky Flats in 1995 provide a glimpse into why the contracting process was such a key enabler of success. These descriptions of distinctive features of the contract highlight dissimilarities between typical contracts with DOE and the new contract with Kaiser-Hill. The first account is from a senior Kaiser-Hill executive, and the second is from a senior DOE official.

> *From Kaiser-Hill:* There were a number of key elements that were unique for DOE contracts. For the first time, the government acknowledged in the contract that they were responsible to provide certain items that were their responsibility—items such as receiver sites for certain kinds of wastes like plutonium and enriched uranium. They agreed to take on some significant risks from a contract perspective. Similarly, Kaiser-Hill agreed to take all the risks associated with the unknowns—such as any of the ... plutonium- or uranium-contaminated buildings. So, essentially, if we found something in one of these buildings that we did not know about, we were responsible to figure it out. One of the unique things about this closure contract is there is a lot of risk-taking by both

the Department of Energy and Kaiser-Hill, and risk-sharing going on between them.... A key feature of this contract was that the Department of Energy took an unprecedented risk with these government-furnished services—receiver sites and pack vessels. I think it was the right thing for the Department of Energy to do, and it showed real leadership in the Department. Similarly, Kaiser-Hill took a lot of risks in this contract. For example, Kaiser-Hill assumed all risks associated with the demolition of all the nuclear facilities. If we discovered contamination that exceeded our wildest dreams or plans, if we found unique features about a building that we didn't know existed, we were responsible to figure it out and get it done for the price that we gave the Department of Energy. That's one of the things that make this contract unique.

Contributor 7—Manager, Kaiser-Hill

From the DOE perspective: As we put the closure contract in place, it represented a number of major differences in how the Department of Energy approached work at Rocky Flats. First, rather than telling the contractor day in and day out, minute by minute, what the expectations were, we set a single performance expectation at the end of a period of time, in this case December 15, 2006. We measured variance on whether or

> not the contractor was meeting the schedule and cost requirements of a baseline that would get them to 2006. The other major institutional change in the contract was a concept called "government-furnished equipment and services," or GFS&I. The contractor was responsible and accountable for delivering performance. The government was accountable and responsible for delivering to the contractor, on a schedule, the things the contractor needed to complete its work—such things as a waste receiver site, a waste isolation pilot plant, and a container to transport nuclear material from Rocky Flats to a receiver site. Those were government-furnished items. This contract held the government liable for providing the services in the contract. If we, the government, didn't provide those services, then we would pay for the delay.... Nobody wants to go back to Congress and say, "Look, the Rocky contract just increased by a hundred million dollars because we didn't do our job." So, it provides an extraordinary amount of motivation.
>
> Contributor 14—Manager, DOE

A traditional contract with DOE was based on specific goals, prescribed work rules, carefully crafted and monitored procedures, and frequent reporting of progress. The new contract contained more discretion, more risk, and a higher potential reward. The differences between the new contract and the more traditional contract were described succinctly by a senior Kaiser-Hill official, specifically as they relate to the way in which work was done:

> Under an M&O contract, the Department of Energy tells the contractor what to do and how to do it. Under a closure contract the Department of Energy says, "Here is what I want done: close Rocky Flats." We figure out the how. We figure out the work logic. We get the work done. Those are the differences between the two types of contracts. The risk under an M&O contract to a contractor is very low. The risk under a closure contract is very high. The rewards under an M&O contract are low, and they should be, because the risk is low. The rewards under a closure contract are much higher, and they should be, because risk and reward are balanced.... Under the integrating management contract, we did not own work logic. The Department of Energy owned work logic. So, if we wanted to change work logic, we had to go to DOE and ask permission to change work logic. If we want to change work logic under our closure contract, we just change it.
>
> Contributor 6—Senior Executive, Kaiser-Hill

The efficiencies that were created by this new alternative contract were desirable both for DOE and for Rocky Flats employees. One DOE official highlighted a key advantage:

> When the contractor had an equipment problem that caused a shutdown or project delay, they didn't need the Department of Energy to take a couple of weeks or months to transfer money from project A to project B. We gave the contractor responsibility for executing their baseline. We basically said, "You're responsible for all of this. You're going to be held accountable at the end. You don't have to come back and ask us for resources." So it removed an internal impediment.
>
> Contributor 14—Manager, DOE

One of the most important features of the new contract was the involvement of the unions at Rocky Flats. The contract produced key advantages for union employees that had never been present before, especially as they related to the connection between incentives and performance outcomes.

> In the first union contract bargained in 1996, $1,000 in incentive pay was negotiated with the union. This was a breakthrough, because unions traditionally are not connected to organizational performance. Because employment was lifelong, they didn't care about performance. This was a major shift. This convinced us that incentive pay was a key driver. The union really responded to incentive pay and was very appreciative.

Union officials especially noted several benefits of the contract inasmuch as these features had never been a part of their employment agreement before. These benefits included the creation of a matching 401 (k) plan for union employees, a one-time payment of $5,000 for laid-off employees along with an additional $3,000 completion bonus, severance pay of 20 weeks, voluntary separation pay that matched the involuntary payments, the ability of employees targeted for layoffs to keep all their vacation days, and an agreement that Kaiser-Hill would donate $100,000 for research on lung disease.

In sum, the 1995 contract between DOE and Kaiser-Hill was an important enabler of achieving extraordinary performance and was considered the benchmark for the way contracts should be formulated. It provided appropriate structure and controls as well as sufficient flexibility to adjust as circumstances changed.

> I've been around this business for over 30 years, and the contract that we had with the Department of Energy [in 1995] was the best contract of its day. What I liked about the contract, and the way we operated, was that we recognized the contract would evolve. We built the contract so we could evolve. There is enough structure in the contract to provide flexibility while not getting out of bounds. The closure contract was the same

> in 2000. It is the first of its kind. It's on the leading edge.
>
> Contributor 6—Senior Executive, Kaiser-Hill

A Revised Contract—2000

The contract signed between DOE and Kaiser-Hill in 1995 created the opportunity to change the nature of the work being done and the processes used to accomplish the work—from top-down, bureaucratically controlled work activities to the empowerment of Kaiser-Hill to accept the risks associated with closure. However, the extraordinary success that has been achieved would still not have been possible without a second, more enabling contract in 2000. The 1995 competitive contract had had only a five-year life span. A new contract was needed in 2000. The key feature of that new contract was that it was a "sole source" contract. That is, Kaiser-Hill was awarded the contract without having to enter into a traditional competitive bidding process; in addition, Kaiser-Hill was given the opportunity to manage all subcontractors associated with the site. One DOE manager stated:

> We felt that Kaiser-Hill knew the site the best of any contractor. They'd been on this site for approximately three and a half years. They had developed an accelerated closure plan that was credible. The regulators thought it was credible.

> The stakeholders thought it was credible. It would be very difficult for a new contractor to come on-site and gain the same type of experience that Kaiser-Hill had. On the other side was the challenge of getting the best deal for the government. That is not necessarily the best deal in terms of cost. It's the best deal in ensuring that the contractor will be finished within the time frame. On that basis we thought that the sole source was the right way to go.
>
> Contributor 19—Senior Executive, DOE

Countering the pressure to put the 2000 contract up for bid was the argument that the traditional bidding process would cost the federal government money, time, and, potentially, safety concerns. It was argued that taxpayers would be placed at a distinct disadvantage if traditional procedures were followed.

> Well, probably the critical part of the discussion was Should we compete this contract, or should we go with the sole source contract? The case that we made to the Secretary for a sole source contract was that the security cost to maintain the plutonium materials was roughly $100 million a year. For each year we delayed getting the materials off Rocky Flats, it would cost us another $100 million. That's when the Secretary agreed that we should sole source the contract.

Contributor 19—Senior Executive, DOE

One of the CEOs at Rocky Flats identified the importance of this new contract arrangement.

> Between 1995 and 2000, Kaiser-Hill managed only four major subcontractors. Kaiser-Hill managed the overall contract. But after 2000 Kaiser-Hill took over all project management. Everyone working on the Rocky Flats project is now under our control. This is important because the subcontractors do not care as much as we do. They still do not perform at the standard of excellence we expect and adhere to. They are good but not excellent, so we need to have responsibility to oversee all of them. What would we do differently if we could do it again? We would do the 2000 contract earlier. We would manage the whole project earlier—that is, the frontline supervision would be Kaiser-Hill.

Contributor 9—Senior Executive, Kaiser-Hill

The sole source contract was made possible by the collaborative and trusting relationship that had been formed between personnel at Rocky Flats and the various federal agencies. Trust replaced hierarchical controls, so that the formal contract could be written in such as way as to produce time and cost savings. A DOE executive interpreted the process this way:

We knew that it could not be an adversarial relationship. It had not been adversarial until that time. We certainly didn't want to have the contract set up where it would be adversarial into the future. We also had to have the appropriate roles and responsibilities for the federal employees who are responsible for overseeing that the funds are appropriately spent as well as the contractor in executing the contract. We formed a partnering agreement where the federal workforce and the contract workforce came together and agreed on what we were about in closing Rocky Flats. The emphasis during the negotiations, as well as here at headquarters, for approving the contract was for the contractor to make a lot of money. If they were making a lot of money, then the government was saving an awful lot of money—in fact, more than double the amount of money, when you consider the fee they were getting. Some folks looked at it and said, "But that is an awful large fee." But look at the money that we were saving from what we had planned at the time.

Contributor 19—Senior Executive, DOE

Despite its unique and clear advantages in terms of flexibility, cost savings, and speed, however, the new contract was a necessary but not a sufficient enabler. This was highlighted by one senior DOE official.

> We can turn all the contracts in the DOE complex into Rocky Flats-type contracts, but it wouldn't change a thing. Success is not based on the contract. It's the other enablers that make the difference.
>
> Contributor 23—Senior Executive, DOE

Interagency Agreement

In addition to the contract at Rocky Flats, in July 1995 the Department of Energy, the EPA, and the state of Colorado signed a new interagency agreement called the Rocky Flats Cleanup Agreement (RFCA). This agreement articulated an accelerated cleanup goal for the first time. It contained language and targets that had been developed by CH2MHill personnel in their planning process but had never been adopted outside the company until RFCA was signed. RFCA was an agreement to organize and align the oversight and coordination efforts of these government agencies.

> The other thing we had to change was the basic interagency agreement. It was based on some 200 paper milestones. When I got here, we were late on more than half of the 200 milestones, and we looked ahead and we said, "We're going to be late on the remaining milestones also." The paper studies were subjective. DOE would look at it and say, "No, it needs more work, go back to the contractor." The contractor and DOE

> would agree to send something to EPA, and EPA would look at it and say, "No, I think you need to do a little more work," so it would come back. It was exchanging paper all the time. We had to agree with the regulators on what those few concrete milestones were, and when they wanted them to be accomplished, and to what standards. That whole agreement had to be renegotiated. That was unheard-of before also.
>
> Contributor 21—Manager, DOE

Kaiser-Hill, the primary contractor of the site, demonstrated its recognition of the need to ensure vastly improved communication, coordination, and trust between regulators by hiring a full-time employee to help manage the coordination between the interagency agreement and the DOE contract, mainly to ensure efficiency and alignment.

> I was very aware of what hadn't worked. I had been involved with the site at a period when the site was highly combative, saw the regulators and the activist community as enemies, where they had 43 people doing community relations to try to spin things, and they were failing at an alarming rate.... One of the things that we talked about was the need to change the relationship with the regulators. That was clearly why I was hired—change the relationship with the community, consolidate the environmental requirements,

> and create a framework for regulatory compliance and cleanup that broke things down into smaller pieces. Make sure we didn't have milestones that were out five years or ten years in the future that were really meaningless. We talked about trying to get the regulators on the same page—combining the Superfund law and the hazardous waste law. The strategy was to create a situation where one agency was making decisions on a particular issue, so you didn't have to go through double review every time there was a decision to be made. We were basically aligning the contractor's needs and expectations with the regulators' needs and expectations.
>
> Contributor 5—Manager, Kaiser-Hill

The alignment of this interagency agreement with the contract between DOE and Kaiser-Hill was identified by one DOE manager as a key to project success.

> What the regulatory agreement and the new contract had in common is that they both emphasized giving the responsible people more authority to achieve the broad goals that everybody agreed upon. They tried to minimize the extent to which there was micromanagement or intervention on the details. And the political community was looking for a success, any success. If Rocky Flats could produce a credible success, it made these politicians look good.

Contributor 16—Manager, DOE

In other words, the formal agreements between DOE and Kaiser-Hill, as well as among the relevant government agencies, were key enablers for the spectacular success of the Rocky Flats project. By providing a means for politicians to look good, for goals to be clarified, and for a coordinated effort to occur which led to achievement of objectives, the interagency agreement served as a key enabler of goal accomplishment. Governmental agencies needed to coordinate efforts, pursue the same target, and clarify who was responsible for which part of the project in order for success to be achieved. This interagency agreement accomplished those purposes.

In addition to contracts and agreements, several additional control-oriented enablers proved to be critical for achieving the extraordinary results—detailed planning, careful measurements, clear milestones, "projectizing" the work, and stable funding. Most of these factors relate to the *processes* by which the project was organized, and each is illustrated with quotations below.

Detailed Planning

Even before securing the contract for the cleanup and closure of Rocky Flats, individuals at Kaiser-Hill were earnestly engaged in determining what to do with the radioactive material, how to stabilize it, where it would go, and what processes would be required.

This analysis produced an extremely large variety of activities, all of which were critical in the process of cleanup and closure.

> We identified the 400 or 500 key activities that would result in the closure of Rocky Flats. We developed a unique work breakdown structure that allowed for the sequencing and cost estimating of these activities. We came up with a credible cost estimate, a work logic, and a sequence that would result in closure of the site. This work structure, consisting of about 500 activities, became very important as we began developing the closure project baseline.

Contributor 7—Manager, Kaiser-Hill

One important element in the detailed planning process was simplifying the list of 500 tasks into a smaller number of key activities. Providing clarity in the process for addressing these myriad activities is illustrated by a senior Rocky Flats executive:

> The closure project baseline really comprises three major elements. The first is a detailed description of the various scopes of work that must be accomplished to achieve closure. That is described in great detail on an almost activity-by-activity basis. The second element is the cost estimates of the same activities that you now define in the scope of work. You prepare a cost estimate for each of these activities. The third

> element is the scheduled duration of each of these activities. It was a fairly significant activity not only to do it, but to bring the rest of the site into doing this type of planning.
>
> Contributor 7—Manager, Kaiser-Hill

The complex project, in other words, was organized into three simple activities—a detailed description of the work scope, estimates of costs, and a time line. A key aspect of this detailed planning was involving external constituency groups in the process. Community groups, regulators, environmentalists, and state officials were all engaged in the detailed planning.

> We put on 3×5 cards all the things that had to be done and how much it would cost to do each one of them. We had a whole wall about the size of one of these rooms covered with 3×5 cards. We had based them on our priorities. We established priorities: safety was first; complying with regulatory agreements was second; third was cleaning the site up; I forget what the fourth and fifth were. We could then shift cards around, based on priorities. You could see if you only had $500 million a year, then we could only do, say, 20 items, 20 tasks. So which task do you want done first? People saw that we couldn't do everything with $500 million. So one of the things we got the community to agree to was to help us go lobby for more money. It wasn't just lobbying for

> jobs. It was lobbying for money to make it safe and clean it up. It was not just to make the communities feel good. It was something really important to them, to the workers, and to the site.
>
> Contributor 21—Manager, DOE

These detailed plans were an important prerequisite to obtaining the needed support from Congress. Communicating the detailed planning process and the specific activities to be achieved helped ensure an adequate resource base.

> We also developed a good management [plan] when Federico Peña was Secretary of Energy. It was a detailed plan as to how we could accelerate the cleanup. At the time the projection was 2010, but there was a commitment to try to accelerate it even further. By having a well-written and detailed management plan, we were successful in convincing Congress that we did have a viable plan and that we would use the funding wisely. Up until that point, we had an enforceable agreement that didn't have the same type of vision and the same types of details as to how we could do the job differently and really speed things up. With the first management plan I think we got Congress's attention that we were serious and that we had done a careful job of thinking through the job. There was a much, much greater willing-

> ness, I think, to provide the funding needed to support the cleanup.
>
> Contributor 20—Senior Executive, DOE

"Projectizing"

Identifying and prioritizing activities was an important first step, but a process had to be put into place that allowed the organization to systematically address these activities. The organization had a long history of ongoing operations in which major work assignments were approached as projects with distinct beginnings, middles, and ends. Two managers, one working at DOE in Washington and one working onsite at Rocky Flats, explained why this mind-set was so important.

> I was spending all of my time telling DOE that these are projects. It's not a long-term program. It's a series of projects. They have a beginning, a middle, and an end—a cost, scope, and a schedule. They will all be completed. That was kind of new to DOE, to think of everything as projects, because they were still in their program mentality. Neither the contractors nor the federal employees had changed their thinking about what we do with cleanup sites. They were really bureaucratic. They were all focused on the process rather than the end result. The DOE cleanup program was viewed by people in Congress and in the

> communities as a large jobs program. That takes away the incentive to close down sites quickly and cheaply.
>
> Contributor 22—Manager, DOE

> We said we were going to "projectize" a site. So everything we do is going to have cost, scope, and schedule. We're going to manage using project management. It's no longer subjective, it's objective. You either make the date or you don't make the date. You drain the number of tanks you were going to drain, you ship the amount of tonnage you were going to ship, or you don't. You either spend the money or you don't. It's measurable. It's no longer "How do I feel?" or "Do I feel good about this person?" or "They didn't show me enough respect, and so I'm going to get back at them." Now it's to establish this site as a project. Then you develop projects within the project, and each one of them has measurable milestones. That was it.
>
> Contributor 21—Manager, DOE

The importance of viewing this work as a project—as opposed to, say, a large-scale transformation, restructuring, or downsizing—was aptly pointed out in the following statement by a senior Rocky Flats executive.

I cannot overemphasize the importance of having a senior leadership both from Kaiser-Hill and DOE become very knowledgeable about project management principles, continue to drive the organization day in and day out to think about this as a project, to report measurable progress, and to talk to each other about this as a project. The senior management and the leadership must be significant champions of project management and project management approaches.

Contributor 7—Manager, Kaiser-Hill

Measurement

Projectizing not only meant defining the Rocky Flats cleanup and closure task as a set of finite and definable projects it also emphasized objective measurement. As implied in the quotation above, measures in previous years had been subjective or absent altogether.

Before 1995 it was a very subjective way to evaluate performance. The way we evaluated performance was based on a personal relationship rather than a business relationship. In 1995 we started changing that set of relationships. Instead of managing the contractor, we managed the contract. Instead of establishing personal relationships, it was based on business relationships. Instead of relying on subjective evaluation, it was

> objective evaluation—things that we had to measure, things that were real, and things that were meaningful. The first contract in 1995 started to establish that.
>
> Contributor 14—Manager, DOE

The Kaiser-Hill approach to projectizing was to establish measures for everything important—that is, for all desired outcomes. Assessment of activities and efforts was less essential because they were not as important as end results. Outcomes were the focus of the objective measurement system.

> Projectizing management is probably the most helpful concept that Kaiser-Hill employed through the contract. I don't think any of us instantly came into this. One of my favorite quotes from [a former Rocky Flats CEO] is "If you want to affect performance, measure it." Even if you don't define the right measure, whatever you measure will cause a change in performance. So we identified what we called the purple chart, which was an identification of the actual physical work that had to occur in the cleanup—how many grams of this, how many metric tons of this, how many linear feet of this, how many facilities, and so on. I think we may have had 10 or 12 specific measures, and we spent the time to actually quantify those. The project was actually projectized around those. The contract incentives were focused

> around those. The cleanup agreement was focused around those. We didn't have to measure how many documents were produced. It really was how much material was disposed of? How much square footage was decontaminated? How many linear feet were free released? I mean, we really measured the things that demonstrated what got done. And we projectized all of our activities around that. Our budget, our contract payments, and our regulatory commitments all focused on the same physical measures of progress.
>
> Contributor 20—Senior Executive, DOE

The purple chart referred to above was an important measuring device for determining progress. It served as a standard against which success could be determined. It specified exact measures and outcomes. As stated by a senior executive at Rocky Flats, it was one of the most important keys to the spectacular success achieved at Rocky Flats.

> I was talking about some of the key enablers for making this whole project go. One of the things that was really important at this period of time was the development of performance measures. This idea began focusing on outcome-based work at the site rather than on paperwork and reports. We actually had something we fondly called the green chart or the purple chart. This was a very detailed listing of all of the many ac-

> tivities that are required in order for you to close a site. It was actually a table. For instance, it had the number of kilograms of plutonium that had to be processed in order for us to be complete, the amount of the low level waste that had to be shipped offsite in order for us to be complete, and the number of individual hazardous substance sites that had to be cleaned up. It became a very important management tool.
>
> Contributor 7—Manager, Kaiser-Hill

These charts also served another critical function, and that was to communicate progress to external constituencies—Congress, community members, state government officials, regulators, and employees. It helped maintain trust and credibility associated with the project. At any given moment, anyone could know the score or the progress being made on key objectives.

> The institution of these green charts and purple charts with all of these performance metrics and the regular tracking of ourselves against them became important not only for measuring our own progress, but it became very important to share with our stakeholders, members of Congress, and others—to talk about how we were doing. That is an important facet of our communication strategy. We are talking about what we had in front of us, what we were accomplishing, and reporting back,

> "Yes, we accomplished it," or "No, we didn't," and what we were going to do to make sure that we fixed it. So consistent and regular reporting of our accomplishments was very important.
>
> Contributor 7—Manager, Kaiser-Hill

Determining criteria, measuring objective performance, and maintaining accountability for outcomes were not merely the responsibilities of senior executives and managers. Rather, multiple employee groups were engaged in the process of record keeping, accountability, and information exchange. In contrast to normal practice, in which accountability for assessment resides at the top, responsibility at Rocky Flats was distributed throughout the organization.

> We have tried to find ways to streamline the red tape process. We still are obligated to make certain we have the administrative records and the data. That is as essential as the cleanup of Rocky Flats. We have to have good, solid, and detailed records as to how that cleanup was accomplished. But we do need to find ways to simplify and streamline the red tape. The best way to do that is by open dialogue, complete access to information, technical staff sitting in on meetings with site staff as decisions are being made, talking about things early in the scoping process so we know what's coming. That way we don't get something that's a complete surprise to us.

Contributor 27—Senior Manager, CDPHE

In establishing an effective measurement system, of course, it was necessary for a baseline or a beginning point to be established from which progress could be measured. It is difficult to know if improvement is occurring without knowing the starting point. The baselines produced at Rocky Flats were so shocking to the various internal and external constituencies that they also served as incentives toward high performance.

> We thought it was extremely important to try to get a baseline, so that as we made improvements from that baseline, we would really be able to tell the Congress and the American people how much progress we were making. When we produced the baselines, people were shocked at the amount of money that it looked like it was going to cost. It was going to cost more money to actually clean up the sites than it did to produce all of the nuclear weapons in the first place. I think that took people aback and got a lot of people thinking about how we could do this faster and cheaper so that it didn't cost the entire U.S. treasury.

Contributor 15—Senior Executive, DOE

One result associated with these projectizing and measurement activities was an improvement on each shift of from 45 percent efficiency to 70 percent efficiency, and when activities arose that represented risk factors—for example, factors that could compromise safety, slow down the project, miss budget targets—a vice president was personally assigned to maintain accountability for that issue.

Moreover, the focused concentration on safety produced additional, unexpected benefits. Savings in workers' compensation premiums were marked as a result of the extraordinary emphasis on safety and the dramatically improved safety record:

> We got a rebate on our workers' comp insurance this year, a $300,000 rebate. You give me any other major project anywhere in the country that is seeing a decrease in workers' comp as people go away.
>
> Contributor 9—Senior Executive, Kaiser-Hill

Milestones and Accountability

Multiple tasks and responsibilities, of course, can quickly overwhelm a system, and even though the 500 or more activities were prioritized and measured, accomplishing them was quite a different matter. A key success factor, therefore, was the reduction of those myriad activities into a few key targets or goals. One Rocky Flats executive stated:

> The biggest lesson that I learned was that it is important to specify big objectives that the

contractor would be rewarded for achieving. It was counterproductive to have hundreds of little objectives, even though they might be worthy. It was important to keep your eye on the ball, and the ball is four or five major issues. One of the other things that I learned was just how important it was to have disciplined operations here. It was extremely important for people who worked here to know what they were going to try to achieve on a daily, weekly, monthly, quarterly, annual basis. Then, develop the appropriate safety envelope around them so that they could actually do the work. Some people had to be moved out of the way so that you could create the kind of environment that people could really work in. Those were a couple of major lessons that I learned in the process.

Contributor 15—Senior Executive, DOE

A similar observation was offered by a DOE manager.

We have hundreds of DOE orders. We felt it our obligation at the beginning of every fiscal year to tell the contractor what it needed to do. We provided a phone book, literally a phone book, of detailed instructions on what they could do and what they couldn't do—basically a day-in-and-day-out, minute-by-minute list of expectations. Around 1997, we said, "That's going to go away." This was a frustration because everybody expected to get their 5, 10, 15, 20 pages in the program execution guidebook. So in 1999 we had one sentence, essentially "Execute the contract for the year." We don't have a program execution guide, because it is just to execute the contract. We have to give the contractor the responsibility, accountability, and authority to figure out how best to work. For instance, suppose there are two projects and all of a sudden one runs into an equipment failure. Before, the contractor would have to come back to the Department of Energy and say, "May I take money from this project and put it on that project?" Sometimes it would take months to get the permission, and those workers just sat there idle. So we made the contractor accountable and responsible for that project, and we gave them control to move resources within projects.

Contributor 14—Manager, DOE

In other words, both detailed microprocess and broad macrotargets were necessary for performance to occur. Individual activities had to be identified, prioritized, and budgeted, and clustering them into a few clear objectives and milestones was a means by which workers, managers, and external observers could ensure progress. These milestones served a focusing function in aligning the efforts of various interest groups.

Stable Funding

A final Hierarchy quadrant enabler of spectacular success at Rocky Flats was the guarantee of stable funding—a secure resource base—from the federal government. That is, once key objectives and milestones were in place, what enabled work to move forward was the assurance that attention would not need to be diverted into politicking activities or lobbying Congress for support. A representative of DOE explained the importance of secure funding guarantees.

> Once the project baseline was established for Rocky Flats—the new, improved, and faster baseline—our part of the bargain was to ensure that that we would give you a consistent level of funding. If you say you have a 10-year plan, and you need X amount of dollars every year, we can't make guarantees on the appropriations process, but we can certainly do our best to give you constant levels of funding. Otherwise they'll spend 90 percent of their time worried about next year's funding instead of spending 90 percent of their time executing the program really well. We wanted them to focus on executing the program and meeting all their milestones, and we'd worry about trying to get you level funding. I give them the money, and they need to execute the sched-

> ule. If the schedule then slips, or if the project overruns, they can't blame Congress, which is one of the things agencies really like to do. They say, "The project slipped because we asked for $100,000 and Congress only gave us $90,000, so it's your fault." That was a common strategy to place blame if the project didn't stay on schedule.
>
> Contributor 22—Manager, DOE

The way in which stable funding could be ensured was by establishing a "closure account" at the federal level. A closure account was essentially a fund into which monies were placed, and was designed to cover the duration of the project. A budget was established to cover costs until the end of the project, and those funds could not be reallocated to another project or arbitrarily taken away.

> When sites get put into the closure account, it is a commitment by the Department of Energy and Congress that these sites will be completed. And if the sites aren't done, Congress isn't going to come back and have a sympathetic ear to hear that Rocky Flats is going to take another three or four years. That was a challenge Congress put on us. Guaranteed funding on the way up also means guaranteed funding on the way down. Now why was it important to segregate closure funds? There are statutory requirements that prevent taking money out of Rocky Flats and funding a nonclo-

> sure site. So, if at the end of a year Savannah River or Hanford or Idaho needed money, they couldn't come to Rocky Flats and take it. When DOE was looking for money, they really couldn't go back to the closure account.
>
> Contributor 14—Manager, DOE

The importance of the closure account is hard to underestimate. A guarantee of consistent funding enabled efficiency, focus, and security at the Rocky Flats facility. At the same time, it also established an expectation and a deadline which eliminated funding after a certain point in time. Strict accountability was associated with stable funding.

> There is something important about consistent funding that's worth emphasizing. Being able to say to Congress, "We need this amount of money each year, and we know with clarity that if you give it for this number of years, we'll be done." It's a unique thing that is different from normal. Usually it is an endless negotiation every year. It became a one-year snapshot of a multiyear project. It allowed for a certain consistency of message, a certain clarity, and a certain dependability. If something happened and we needed to come back to the appropriators to ask for a different amount of money than last year, we knew we had better have a good story to tell. We'd better really mean it. It imposed a certain discipline on

> us. Congress was saying, "We'll give you consistent funding, but you can't be like every other DOE project, where the shelf life of your commitment is a few weeks or a few months. If you want us to treat you like a project, you'd better behave like a project." We took that very seriously.
>
> Contributor 16—Manager, DOE

By way of contrast, the alternative to stable funding by means of a closure account is highlighted by the description of one senior executive at Rocky Flats. This description of the normal way of funding DOE projects highlights the importance of an alternative way to control project funding.

> The funding was subject to multiple micromanagements, multiple checks, and annual deviations based on factors beyond our control. That was exactly what we faced in the middle of the 1990s. We had this complex, multibillion-dollar project, but the funding framework said that the funds would be spoon-fed through hundreds of different sources. We had a situation where we didn't really have the authority to control or spend money. It was completely untenable. It could not succeed. It had to change. There were several things we tried to do. First, we tried to reduce the extent to which there was micromanagement from DOE headquarters, especially regarding the control of the funds. When I arrived at Rocky Flats, the

> funds that came to the site were divided into four or five discrete categories. We had to ask for the money in those categories. We got it in those categories. The officials responsible for those programs had another level of oversight. If we wanted to move money from one account to another, we had to go all the way up the chain and get it approved. So we worked with DOE headquarters and with Congress because we wanted it to be statutory. We wanted it to be law that we had one source of funds. We achieved that.
>
> Contributor 16—Manager, DOE

Summary

Enablers of exceptional success in the Hierarchy or Control quadrant exceptional success in the Hierarchy or Control quadrant emphasize efficiency, smooth functioning, predictability, and standardized procedures. Internal processes had to be carefully and competently managed, deadlines had to be established and monitored, and rigid accountability had to be maintained in order for the Rocky Flats success to be produced. In particular, the key enablers that explain the spectacular success of the Rocky Flats project include clear goals that were continually being clarified and modified as the project progressed; a new type of agreement with the federal government, in the form of a contract and an interagency agreement that offered empowerment and discretion never before experienced by a government contractor; detailed planning and carefully designed processes that were associated with specific, objective performance measures, milestones, and accountability; and an assurance of a stable and consistent resource base. Figure 6.1 summarizes the theme and key enablers.

Theme:
Maintaining stability, carefully controlling processes, precise objectives, and financial discipline

Key Enablers:
Goal clarity
New contracts and interagency agreement
Detailed planning, projectizing, measurement, milestones, and accountability
Stable funding

Figure 6.1 KEY ENABLERS IN THE HIERARCHY OR CONTROL QUADRANT

Among the conclusions to be drawn from these enablers are the following:

- ***Positively deviant goals guiding organizational performance must come from multiple sources, not just from the top of the organization.***
- ***Downsizing of the workforce must provide advantages and benefits rather than displacement and harm.***

- ***Contracts—or governing entities—must focus on outcomes, not effort, and must offer broad discretion regarding means and methods.***
- ***The source of the contract—or the governing entity—and the recipient of the contract must share equal risk.***
- ***Multiple stakeholders must share equal responsibility and accountability for extraordinary performance.***
- ***The contract—or the expectations, vision, and goals standards—and not the contractor or the workers and managers—should be carefully managed.***
- ***Every value-adding activity should be planned, budgeted, and measured, and nonvalue-adding activities should be avoided.***
- ***The myriad activities and targets should be consolidated into a few key success factors.***
- ***Stable resources must be ensured for those engaged in the pursuit of positive deviance.***
- ***Leaders must never compromise the integrity and trustworthiness of the organization, or of themselves, for any reason.***

7

Key Enablers—Relationships, Human Capital, and Collaborative Culture

This is the third of four chapters that address the question *What levers can leaders use to produce similar results?* This chapter addresses the enablers that relate specifically to the collaborative, engagement, and participative leadership themes.

Success at Rocky Flats can be explained by another set of factors—the development and coordination of human capital and the nurturing of a collaborative culture inside the organization. As pointed out in the previous two chapters, the organization's culture had to be changed in order for success to be achieved. The organizational culture that had been perpetuated over the decades since the founding of Rocky Flats was very strong and was distinguished by pride in the workforce. However, it was also highly secretive and insular. Such a culture made sense during an era of production, but it made much less sense in an era requiring public collaboration while working toward site closure. Furthermore, with the loss of mission at Rocky Flats, the site had endured years of low morale, aimlessness, and a distinct loss of pride and meaningful work. Addressing the "broken" culture was an obvious lever for change.

The innovative vision (Adhocracy or Create quadrant) and the specific goals and measures (Hierarchy or Control quadrant) could not substitute for the need to pay attention to people and culture (Clan or Collaborate quadrant). In addition to culture, however, establishing credibility among various constituencies and fostering collaborative relationships were key enablers carried out by the organization's new leadership team. Hiring and developing the requisite talent, building strong relationships among them, and fostering trust were also keys to successful performance. This chapter highlights and illustrates four leadership enablers, all consistent with the Clan or Collaborate quadrant activities typical of effective organizations—(1) culture, (2) collaboration, (3) trust and credibility, and (4) human capital and social relationships.

Organizational Culture

One key to the successful transformation at Rocky Flats was addressing the need to change the culture of the organization. The effectiveness of strategic plans, political support, financial resources, and dynamic leadership can be thwarted in the absence of fundamental culture change. In fact, it is estimated that between half and three quarters of change efforts in organizations fail as a result of cultural resistance.

Culture is the single biggest obstacle to successful organizational change (Cameron & Quinn, 2006).

Organizational culture refers to the values, assumptions, underlying beliefs, and ways of doing things that are typical of an organization and its members. At Rocky Flats, a strong and recognizable culture had developed over nearly half a century of operation. This traditional culture valued pride in craftsmanship and a strong belief in the organization's patriotic purpose. Both were necessary to achieve the highest consistency and productivity in output of any of the DOE nuclear facilities, as well as to sustain a willingness of workers to engage in dangerous work. The historic culture also prioritized exceptionally high secrecy; members of the same family might not even discuss their work with one another. Such insularity was understandable in an era of weapons production. When the mission of the organization changed abruptly, when external entities became more and more hostile and imposing, and when a new contractor took command of the facility, the old culture had to change or risk complete failure. One former CEO at Rocky Flats highlighted several aspects of the Rocky Flats culture in describing the change that occurred:

> We transformed the culture of the workforce from "I worked here for 25 years"; "My dad worked here"; "People call us criminals"; "We have no real tasks left"; "They are trying to

> eliminate my job" to a culture of excitement, positive energy, innovation.
>
> Contributor 10—Senior Executive, Kaiser-Hill

Culture is taken for granted and seldom recognized by people immersed within it. According to an ancient proverb, "Fish discover water last." Therefore, changing culture requires that basic assumptions be challenged and ways of thinking confronted. Changing culture is especially difficult because people's lives, families, and values are under attack. Culture change at Rocky Flats required a change not only in the way employees accomplished tasks and worked together but also in their ways of thinking. One senior strategic planning officer at Rocky Flats indicated the extent of the challenge:

> One cannot underestimate the amount of time and the cultural changes that have to be implemented in order to get large groups of people in various organizations to think about their work in a project fashion.... There was a significant cultural change that needed to take place. It was a very difficult change, especially for people who had been planning to work the same year in and year out. It required people to begin thinking about what it was going to be like when their jobs were done. It began getting people thinking about what the end looked like.

Contributor 7—Manager, Kaiser-Hill

At first, challenges to the existing organizational culture came not from a clear strategic plan or a well-outlined architecture of change but from a variety of uncoordinated elements that challenged the status quo. The success of the culture change effort, in fact, was at least partially dependent on having a variety of factors imposed simultaneously on the existing system. One senior Kaiser-Hill manager enumerated several of these factors:

> When Kaiser-Hill came in 1995, you had a new management team of 50 people who were imposed on the existing structure. The existing organization had its own culture, and they had been told that it was going to take 75 years to clean up the site. It was going to cost 40, 50, 60 billion dollars. They and their children would be able to work at Rocky Flats forever. All the employees—union members—had been working for companies that built weapons. And here you have an environmental company come in to head a new contract. There was an enormous amount of distrust. The relationship between DOE and the contractor had to be completely reimagined and reenvisioned. The Department of Energy also was going through an enormous transition as the environmental management budget overtook the weapons part of the DOE budget. So you had a federal agency that was

> undergoing enormous change, and you had the contractor coming in and trying to impose a whole new set of values and a whole new vision for the site. It was incredibly exciting for the management team, but it was clear that there was a lot of hostility among the ranks.
>
> Contributor 5—Manager, Kaiser-Hill

Confronting the status quo at Rocky Flats occurred almost immediately upon the arrival of Kaiser-Hill, with the announcement of a large downsizing in the workforce as well as a change in the way work was to be done. A former CEO at Rocky Flats described the first few weeks:

> I think it would be fair to say that the workforce viewed us with enormous trepidation. They were very nervous about the change to come. They knew that our job was to get work done, and they were very concerned about that. They also knew that it was our job to put the plant on more of a commercial basis. That meant everything from changing vacation schedules to reducing benefits to placing expectations on the schedule. Many of them were really, really angry. One of the first things we were asked to do was lay off 2,000 people, which we did in the first eight weeks. That was an enormous shock to the system. I think many of us would probably characterize that first year as a pretty ugly time.

> We were disrupting a culture that was fairly set in its ways. It was a real tough place to be for the first year. Compare that to how it is today, and what a phenomenal change. You compare that with how it is today, and I think the change is just incredible.
>
> Contributor 9—Senior Executive, Kaiser-Hill

One key to initiating culture change at Rocky Flats was to create a picture of a desired future that made it obvious the current culture could not succeed. The culture of the present had to be seen as inadequate and in need of change in order to achieve success in the future. A former Rocky Flats CEO stated:

> The only way we would be able to accomplish what we wanted was to create a vision for the site that the old culture couldn't deliver. That old culture was a production culture. Not only did we have to have a vision for what the outcome would be, but we had to attack every piece of the management and delivery systems, whether that was how work was planned, how work was executed, the labor agreements, the stakeholder relationships, or the relationship with the client. Every part of it was not functioning in a way that would get us to where we needed to be.
>
> Contributor 9—Senior Executive, Kaiser-Hill

In other words, culture change required attacking almost every part of the existing system—from work processes to relationships to ways of thinking about careers. The success of this change effort was described by a former CEO at Rocky Flats a year before the facility closed.

> The biggest difference I see between now and 1995 is that if we went into a building or went around the plant site, nobody talked to you. Nobody looked you in the face. They really didn't want to know you. They weren't proud of what they were doing. They didn't care. You go into the buildings now, and it's a totally different feeling. The energy that people put into their work is obvious. The involvement, the pride, the humor—you wouldn't even know this was the same place it was in 1995.
>
> Contributor 9—Senior Executive, Kaiser-Hill

Of course, a complete culture change at Rocky Flats cannot be accounted for simply by announcing a layoff, the arrival of a new contractor, a change in friendliness and positive energy, the signing of a new contract, or a different labor agreement, although each of these factors certainly played an important role. Rather, a variety of other enablers worked in association with culture change efforts to produce the dramatic change. In particular, collaboration, trust-building, and nurturing human relationships were key elements in supporting and enabling this culture change—factors all located in the Clan or Collaborate quadrant.

Collaboration

The variety of constituencies with vested interests in Rocky Flats served to mitigate a common vision and strategy for decontaminating and decommissioning the facility. Each of these constituencies had its own view of the problems, and proposed solutions were nonconsensual, unclear, and frequently changing. Communities worried about air emissions, polluted groundwater, and the impact of job loss; environmentalists viewed Rocky Flats as a threat to the safety of the entire region; federal regulatory agencies (e.g., EPA) regarded the Rocky Flats project as an intractable problem with little evidence of progress; the Colorado state government (e.g., governor's office, state Department of Public Health and Environment [CDPHE]) worried about the continued presence of an unpopular nuclear site characterized by many unknowns and possible radioactive emissions; union workers were interested in preserving employment as well as in personal safety; and Kaiser-Hill management wanted to develop credibility and commitment from federal funders by closing the facility quickly and cleaning up the residual pollution.

Without generating some synergy and collaboration among these various groups, it would have been impossible for progress to be made at Rocky Flats. One of the first initiatives undertaken by Kaiser-Hill was to convene a task force to determine whether the project could be achieved at all and, if so, in what time frame.

> The idea was to have a mix of both new people and old people to serve on this team to develop this proof of concept. It was probably the hardest I've ever worked here. We worked day and night, weekends, and holidays to begin putting together this proof of concept. By about August of 1995, after about a month or six weeks, we had produced a draft document called the Interim End State. It was a possible approach about how we could achieve accelerated cleanup of the site by 2003.... We had demonstrated in this proof of concept that you could do something like this for about $5 billion by about 2003. What's interesting to note is that at the same time, the government in March of 1995 had published a $36 billion estimate taking 70 years to do a similar kind of job.
>
> Contributor 7—Manager, Kaiser-Hill

This task force recommended an extremely aggressive schedule and proposed a strategy of "mothballing" the site, essentially consolidating and entombing the nuclear waste for long-term storage onsite. This approach was subsequently rejected as unrealistic by both DOE and Kaiser-Hill. Moreover, when the broader community heard of this option, it was strongly criticized as maintaining a nuclear waste threat on the site in perpetuity. On the other hand, the fact that an aggressive vision was proposed, coupled with the commitment to work with the various constituencies, provided the first inkling that an accelerated time frame and a dramatically reduced budget might be within the realm of possibility. It began the momentum toward change.

Three major collaborations were required: collaboration with and among government officials, collaboration with and among community officials, and collaboration with union members and site workers.

> The climate changed to one of working together. Instead of working against each other, people started working together. That was the shift that really allowed this to become a real closure site and to make progress. It isn't much more magical than people sitting down at the table and actually solving problems as opposed to fighting about problems.
>
> Contributor 8—Manager, Kaiser-Hill

Government. One challenge was lining up federal and state agencies to share the goals and vision of Kaiser-Hill. For example, collaboration among DOE, EPA, and the CDPHE was an important first step—changing adversaries into collaborators.

> Historically you think of the Department of Energy and the regulatory agencies as having very different interests. Well, it turned out when we actually sat down to the table, the interests really weren't that different. Once we understood that, and once we knew we were going to put the regulatory pieces in place, it wasn't that hard. But we had to get over the first hump.
>
> Contributor 8—Manager, Kaiser-Hill

Key staff members in both state and federal government positions were vital to the success of the endeavor. Though they were not the visible players in the process, they often served as the instigators and catalysts to get different agencies working together.

> The governor empowered Lieutenant Governor Schoettler to work with us. Secretary O'Leary, who was my boss, basically said, "Go make it happen. Do what you have to do. Just get it done." She stood behind me. Also, the House Appropriations Committee, and particularly its chief clerk, Jeanne Wilson, was extremely supportive of the budgetary moves that were necessary to make things happen. Inside the department, just a ton of people really saw the opportunity from a contracting perspective to do

> something new and different and to break out of old molds. They were empowered to do that in an interesting way, not only by the Appropriations Committee but also by the House Energy and Commerce Committee, which was chaired by Congressman John Dingle. He had been a longtime critic of the Department of Energy. He really pushed us to develop a new contracting mechanism that would put a premium on action and would hold contractors more accountable for what they did. These were the prime supporters in the process.
>
> Contributor 15—Senior Executive, DOE

In other words, a wide variety of individuals and government agencies needed to collaborate in their efforts to pursue a single goal. The traditional disagreements and adversarial positions on matters of environmental cleanup had to be changed into coordinated efforts.

> Once you get some synergy among the elected officials and the agencies on what ought to happen, and you have a number of elected officials and leaders that want to make that happen, and you have a community that is willing to accept and adopt the vision—all of those elements need to work together to have success. They have worked for us since we got that Rocky Flats cleanup agreement in place.

Contributor 33—Assistant to U.S. Congressman

Communities. The role of the communities was crucial. In addition to the Denver metropolitan area 16 miles to the east, the Rocky Flats site is surrounded by four affected counties, multiple cities and small towns up and down the Front Range, and a large number of independent civic, educational, and environmental groups. Getting those various groups together, sharing collective goals, and working toward a common resolution was a key enabler of success.

The trust that was developed with the community was very important. That involved nothing more than spending a lot of time with the communities, educating them, bringing them onsite, making them part of the decision process. It didn't mean that the communities always got what they wanted. It means that they had input regarding where Rocky Flats was going. Without bringing the community in, we would be unable to do the things that we're doing today, whether it's the onsite disposal of the building rubble or some of the work we're doing with the soil action levels. Without bringing the community in and having them part of that decision process, we would not be in the condition we're in today.

Contributor 14—Manager, DOE

Convincing community groups to become engaged was not an easy task, of course. Adversarial and distrustful relationships had existed for decades. One key was sharing information openly and honestly with community groups for the first time.

> When I first began my work with Rocky Flats in the 1990s, there was a very formal relationship between the Department of Energy, the people who worked at the site, and the community. Most of the interactions with the community were around things that you would find required by law.... Over the years we have evolved into different types of public participation and public opportunities. There are focus groups, or technical review groups, or various committees where the site has worked with us on a very specific issue, not only to provide us with the information, but to help us understand what was happening with the particular plan or proposal for the site. It has been these very focused activities, versus a focus on only what was required in the past, that has been a very good benefit for us.
>
> Contributor 36—Manager, Kaiser-Hill

One senior DOE official described a turning point in the relationships with community groups, in which individuals first connected emotionally and culturally—in terms of common values and concerns—and then, finally, on strategies, goals, and a vision.

> I think the biggest turn for us was a public meeting we held. We probably had 200 people in the room. We asked the community leaders to help us identify the top ten priorities and to establish principles for the cleanup. It was a brutal meeting. Most of us walked out with tears in our eyes because we really felt like failures. There seemed to be no alignment. However, we eventually reached an emotional accord, and even though it was a very painful session, it was a very discrete turning point culturally for this site. In the next session we actually were able to start to align on priorities, how to approach the work, and the value of approaching it in a certain way.
>
> Contributor 20—Senior Executive, DOE

Not only were these collaborative relationships useful to overcome resistance to progress, but they also led to better performance than would have occurred in their absence. For example, one community group was asked to help establish cleanup standards, even though the federal government standards were clear and publicly available. The result of that collaborative process was a more rigorous standard for cleanup than that in federal standards.

> A group of community members had expressed concern about the original soil action levels that

were established in 1996. After some negotiation, the Department of Energy agreed to provide the funds to help establish the soil action level oversight panel. This group worked diligently for 18 months. They hired a contractor, and the contractor conducted an independent assessment. I think that a lot of interesting questions were raised during that process that helped the community better understand all of the technical issues that are involved in establishing cleanup levels. We provided the forum where they could express their concern about how the levels were established. The end result was that we had our own set of cleanup levels that were significantly lower than those originally established by the Department of Energy and the regulators.

Contributor 36—Manager, Kaiser-Hill

Collaboration, of course, was not a product of friends or trusted advisers getting together, but the product of adversaries and antagonists being able and willing to work together. For example:

When our board was first formed in 1994, we brought together people that, at one time, had sat on opposite sides of the room and argued different positions about Rocky Flats. These people were now sitting at a common table. They had to come together, and they had to talk with one another, and they had to be civil to one another.

> It was very interesting to see these former adversaries coming together.... One of them was a site worker. He was a site manager. He had been working on nuclear issues or ... nuclear weapons for most of his career. Another gentleman was a member of a peace and justice organization who had been one of the original activists ... protesting out at the gates of Rocky Flats.... But here they were, chairs of one of our committees. They were asked to work together, and they did so marvelously over the years. They were able to come together and share a common vision.

Contributor 36—Manager, Kaiser-Hill

One community activist described his own engagement in the collaborative processes initiated at Rocky Flats.

> The whole activity of a person like myself changed very, very drastically. Very soon I found myself sitting at the table with the Rocky Flats management, with people from the EPA, and with the Colorado Department of Public Health, and from the Department of Energy. We were talking about what to do about Rocky Flats—what were the dangers? What can we what do? What do we need to do to try to clean up this very contaminated site? I must say that that has been far more difficult than sitting on the tracks, coming to a legal demonstration like we had here, or standing

> and holding hands while people encircled the Rocky Flats site.
>
> Contributor 25—Community Representative

Workforce. Another key to closure and cleanup at Rocky Flats was the willingness of the workforce to adopt a new mission, to work in ways that contradicted their previous culture, and to demonstrate integrity in the process. Subversive and defiant behavior on the part of the unionized workforce could have completely destroyed any hope of success at Rocky Flats. After all, unions exist at least partly to ensure jobs, yet at Rocky Flats, the task was clearly to eliminate jobs as quickly as possible. Collaborative relationships were critical, and they were facilitated by engagement and involvement activities.

> An extremely important and often overlooked major sea change had to do with our relationship with the workforce, and specifically with the steelworkers, the guards' unions, and the trade unions. They're the ones who do the work, and they're the ones who built up the nuclear weapons arsenal. They're the ones who for 40 years served a very patriotic purpose. In the early part of the 1990s they were kind of cast off as having very little value in the whole process. In the mid-1990s we started to bring them back in and made them part of the process. This was through the integrated safety management program (the ISMS pro-

gram), the new contracts, and the work planning. To have them part of that process and to tailor the contracts, the work agreements, and to make them part of the success was absolutely essential.

Contributor 14—Manager, DOE

Since Kaiser-Hill took over the management of Rocky Flats in 1995, three CEOs have served. Each has been explicit in articulating the need to have good relationships with the unionized workforce. One CEO stated:

It took years to change the attitude of the workforce. They hated us at first. But new union leadership occurred in 2000. Now there is more engagement and planning. The philosophy is "They will exceed our plan every time if they are involved. The union helped us with discipline problems. They have now become advocates. They want good work as much as we do." They changed their message to the workers and gave them pride again. The union head said: "You are being too lenient on workers." You have to come down harder on poor performers. Get tough.

Contributor 9—Senior Executive, Kaiser-Hill

Other CEOs put it this way:

We have intentionally focused on good labor relations. We have improved the relationship with the unions, and the unions have become part of our vision.

Contributor 10—Senior Executive, Kaiser-Hill

We got workers on board by interviewing and listening to them. We tried to take action on their suggestions, and that unleashed their desire to do good work.

Contributor 1—Senior Executive, CH2MHill

Among the strategies used for encouraging worker collaboration was getting management and union members working in the same facilities.

We were slow in engaging the workforce until we got management on the floor with the workers. In building 779, we finally got managers and workers engaged together. We got managers on the floor in a protective suit. Workers were involved in the planning process.

Contributor 9—Senior Executive, Kaiser-Hill

We now keep teams together. Before, people changed jobs almost every day and no continuity existed. Now teams remain together and work together. You always have a partner who will know your job.

Contributor 11—Supervisors, Kaiser-Hill

In other words, collaboration was facilitated among the workforce by means of co-location, working together on the same tasks, and structuring work so that teams and partnerships replaced individual assignments.

Of course, constituencies were not at all in agreement when Kaiser-Hill took over the Rocky Flats project. A key enabler of their successful performance was fostering collaboration among the various constituencies that had interest in the site—the workforce, the communities, the state of Colorado, environmental groups, the federal regulators, and the Congress. Providing various groups with opportunities for face-to-face meetings, chances to express opinions and viewpoints, involvement in setting standards, and engagement in strategy sessions in collaboration with the other groups led each constituency to gain clarity about the overall objective and to buy into a common vision.

You've got to gain credibility and trust. You've got to involve people. When I say involve people, that doesn't mean they make the decisions. It means you listen to them. You get their input early on and frequently, and you

> provide feedback to them. An important part of what I need to do is to involve other people, whether it be the workers, the employees, the unions, the contractor, the citizen groups, the elected officials, or the news media. Go to them frequently. Be open and honest with them. If you don't know something, tell them, "I don't know the answer to that, but I'll get back to you." If you don't agree with them, tell them why. Not everyone is going to stand up and salute. But most of the time, if I feel like I'm being heard, I can go along with a lot of things. One of the most important things is to give people the opportunity to be heard.
>
> Contributor 21—Manager, DOE

Trust and Credibility

Collaborative work arrangements and relationships were dependent on a sense of trust among those required to work together. A key foundation stone in the success of the Rocky Flats project was the establishment of trust among the various constituencies who were initially divided regarding their goals for the Rocky Flats site. If groups believed that they were being deceived or manipulated, no amount of persuasion, publicity, or promotion would lead to effective cooperation. As one Kaiser-Hill board member and senior CH2MHill executive put it:

> We had big obstacles to overcome, since there was a culture of secrecy at the site. Trust is the key. The community didn't trust us. The government didn't trust us. The union didn't trust us. We had to make sure that we always told the truth.

Contributor 1—Senior Executive, CH2MHill

In an atmosphere of distrust, skepticism, and cynicism, trust became a crucial ingredient in making progress at Rocky Flats. However, establishing trust was neither quick nor easy, and the building of trusting relationships was a long and slow process.

> I think the turning point was not something that you can put your finger on. I think it took years and years of hard work, and the efforts of a tremendous number of people all working together to do the best they could, to be honest about the problems they were having. I don't see it as a problem that we overcame overnight, or that there was a definite turning point. I think it was incremental. And I think that the trust we gained was something that we had to earn, and it took a long time to earn it. I think it was very much a group effort, and it took the efforts of a huge number of people at the site; the Department of Energy, here at headquarters; all levels within the state of Colorado; and Congress. So it's hard

> to say that there was ever a definite turning point. I think it was very much an incremental effort.

Contributor 20—Senior Executive, DOE

In previous years Rocky Flats had been governed by the Atomic Energy Commission (AEC) rather than the Environmental Protection Administration (EPA), and EPA access had been severely limited. A publicized accident at Rocky Flats in the late 1960s led to speculation of widespread pollution and radioactive leaks, creating a hostile and skeptical climate. In 1995, local environmentalists, the Colorado Department of Public Health and Environment, the Department of Energy, and the press all began with antagonistic positions toward the Rocky Flats project. Initial levels of trust were built on following through on commitments. One former CEO stated flat out:

> You have to nail nine out of ten promises when you work with DOE and other constituencies to maintain credibility.

Contributor 10—Senior Executive, Kaiser-Hill

An important ingredient of trust-building was achieving promised results.

> These sites in most cases have been around half a century. Given the fact that they operated for many years in secrecy, there has been great distrust. Firm beliefs have been established. Trying

> to break through that is a difficult process. It is not something that just happens overnight. It's something that takes a lot of work, a lot of time, a lot of years, and a lot of meetings. It's not easy.... Some of that trust and credibility has to be based on results.... You could not have done this in 1996. There wasn't enough trust that any work could be done. We didn't know how Rocky Flats would be closed. We couldn't do what we're doing now six years ago. You have to see some results; you have to develop credibility; the site has to make some progress; you also have to have a clear picture of how something is going to get done.
>
> Contributor 27—Senior Manager, CDPHE

The results that were created were sometimes achieved with the specific goal of establishing a baseline of trust. Performance objectives were aimed more at building credibility than at producing an outcome for which incentives would be paid.

> When I came to Rocky Flats, we were on the cusp of negotiating our first set of rolling milestones under the new agreement—commitments such as tearing down a building, shipping quantities of waste. We had to set a milestone that was challenging but was achievable. The first step we made in building trust was to set a milestone to get approximately 15,000 thousand cubic meters

> of mixed waste offsite. It was pondcrete and saltcrete. It was stored in tents, and the regulators were very uncomfortable about it. It was something we had a trust issue about.... So, one of our very first milestones, our commitment to the regulators, was to get this material offsite. We achieved that ahead of schedule. I think that was a very important first step to making the commitments, showing progress, and building trust.
>
> Contributor 17—Regulator, DOE

The idea of following through on commitments—at almost any cost—was driven by top management from the very outset of the project.

> I feel very strongly that whenever we make a commitment, we need to demonstrate that we're going to follow through on that commitment. Quite frankly, it's probably the area in which I had the biggest impact on Rocky Flats. In my first six months at the site, it became very clear that there really had been years of disappointment because commitments were made and not kept. Nobody actually felt like anyone else was taking responsibility for following through on commitments to carry out the environmental cleanup agreement, the regulatory agreement. There is no way you can do it unless you really are driven to fulfill the commitments you make. Especially when we work

> for the federal government and represent the interest of the public, they are trusting in us to do that. They're counting on us to follow through.... If I say something, the only way that it won't get done is if something dramatic gets in the way. I will move mountains if I say I'm going to do it. I'll move mountains to try to do it.

Contributor 20—Senior Executive, DOE

The visible commitment by senior executives in Kaiser-Hill and in DOE helped produce a culture of openness and honesty. It was readily observable by those who were hired at Rocky Flats when the new contract was signed in 1995.

> When I arrived in 1995, there was a commitment to work with the community. There was a commitment to openness. There was a commitment to share information and to get feedback. There were processes in place. There was a series of public meetings. There were focus groups. The Department of Energy recognized in 1995 that the days of secrecy were over. If you were not going to present information or not bring the public in, there had better be a serious national security reason, or serious procurement sensitivity reason, or a privacy reason. Otherwise, the presumption was that public interaction was the norm.

Contributor 16—Manager, DOE

One constituency that was crucial to the success of the Rocky Flats project was the state and federal regulators. Starting from a history of exclusion, adversarial relationships, and distrust, changing the relationships with regulatory agencies was important in order to eliminate useless paper studies and other non-work-related activities. For progress to be made in cleanup and closure, regulators from both the state of Colorado and the federal government had to be brought into the fold.

> One of the things that has been vital to our success in implementing [the contract] is having good relationships with the regulators, the state health department, and the EPA. We've been able to discuss, to debate, to argue about issues, but then understand and trust that we had the best interest of closure and the local communities at heart. We've been able to go through those meetings, come out sometimes agreeing and sometimes disagreeing, but as a consequence of each one, to build a trust and build an alliance. The alliance was based on having a common interest in closure and in safely implementing [the contract].

Contributor 17—Regulator, DOE

Honesty and openness were, unsurprisingly, the key to trust-building.

> You start demonstrating you can walk the talk. You recognize as you're moving forward that you're not going to be perfect. You're going to make mistakes. Things are going to happen. But if you've developed a relationship that's built on honesty and trust with the regulators, they're going to continue trusting you. We notified the regulators when we made a mistake, and we said, "Geez, we made a mistake. Here's what we did. Here's what we're going to do to fix it. We promise we're going to make our commitment." And we made our commitment. Then what you do is build that trust. They learn to trust you, and you can continue moving forward in getting the project done. That was one of our strategies.
>
> Contributor 6—Senior Executive, Kaiser-Hill

Being proactive in publishing information, making it available to all interested constituencies before they requested it, and providing needed education about progress at the site also were critical enablers of success. Proactive openness assisted in building the foundation of confidence among multiple constituencies.

> We have a Web page that we keep up to date. We also have a quarterly newsletter that we send out to try to provide information to the

community about many of the activities that are happening at Rocky Flats. By taking the information and bringing it down just a little bit to a level that the average citizen can understand, we provide a valuable bridge to help people understand what's happening at the site. One of the things that we have found successful is to hold specialized workshops where we can take an afternoon, an evening, or a full day if it's necessary, to bring people in and to bring experts in. They may be experts who aren't members of the Department of Energy, who don't work at the site, but who are outside people from academia or from private contractors who can shed some light on the technical issue that we're working on. It's hearing these people come and explain things that provides a little bit more credibility, or it provides a backup for what we're hearing from the site. So we've found these types of workshops to be quite successful in bringing out information and helping us understand the issues that we are faced with at this site.

Contributor 36—Manager, Kaiser-Hill

Of course, most information about Rocky Flats was shared through the media, so what people read in the press was often the single most important source in helping them form opinions and perspectives. Special attention was paid at Rocky Flats, therefore, to the relationship with the press.

> There was another thing that we did in terms of building trust and credibility with the public. Whenever there was a problem, we put out a news release before anyone could report it in the media. They had developed their own lines of communication in the site, so they were getting calls from the employees all the time about this problem and that problem. So we set up a system of immediate news. We had fax machine numbers, and we pushed a button and the news release would go out to 20, 30, 40 people as soon as we knew something. Even if we didn't know what was really going on, even if we didn't know the answers to what happened, but we knew that something happened, we would put out a release saying something like this: "There is a jumping can of plutonium, and here is what we know." And that's how we established credibility. We weren't hiding behind anything. We weren't waiting until we knew all of the answers. We were telling people up front, "We have a problem, and we're working in it." Then we would follow up, and then tell them what we found. That worked pretty effectively for us in terms of regaining trust.
>
> Contributor 21—Manager, DOE

From the standpoint of regulators and the media, this honesty and openness was a refreshing and welcome change from past practice. One staff member of an elected official summarized the consequences of adopting a trustworthy stance by Rocky Flats managers and the Department of Energy personnel on site.

> When you're in a political office, what you need is the truth from DOE and from the regulators. You need to know what's going on. In the past, the department had always been secret regarding what took place at Rocky Flats, and for good reason. It was something that was essential to winning the Cold War, where secrecy was essential. Now it was a closure site where you needed to trust that what you were being told about what was taking place out there was accurate. When an obstacle or a problem popped up, the Department was always forthcoming with what the real story was. It allowed us to remain confident in their ability to close the site, to meet these obstacles, to treat the public appropriately, and to be forthcoming with the public. The vision was established, but trust came later. I can tell you that in the whole time of my association, no official from the Department of Energy ever fed me a line that wasn't accurate. They didn't always tell me everything, because I wasn't cleared for sensitive information. But everything they told

> me was accurate. It allowed me to do my job, and it allowed me to talk to the community and reassure them at different points of this process that this was trustworthy. As you know, politicians have to run for office, and if they get caught in a situation where they've given out information and it's not accurate, it will come back to haunt us when we run for election. So, a relationship of trust was essential to moving forward. [One senior DOE official at the site], in particular, insisted upon being honest with the citizenry, telling them when there were difficulties, and admitting the problems. It gave people confidence.
>
> Contributor 32—Staff member, U.S. Congress

Articulating the need for trust, honesty, and openness is important, of course, as is sharing information as widely and as quickly as possible, but actually being able to follow through is quite a challenge. Enormous pressures exist in almost all organizations to interpret the numbers positively, to reinterpret the facts optimistically, or to withhold unfavorable information. Such was certainly the case at Rocky Flats. Since everything wasn't good news all the time, the question was, What should be shared and what should be kept secret?

> It is easy in this room to say what the right thing to do is—put the information out there, be forthright, be honest, be out there, virtue is its

own award. But when there's a committee vote coming up, your sponsors in Congress are saying, "For a week or so, give us no bad news." Or when there is an important public event coming up where we need support from some important public official, negative press will make them less likely to support us. Or, when we need DOE Secretarial approval right away to waive a process, that Secretary might give us that waiver only if we can avoid controversy. In those situations, we are deciding if we can we keep this thing quiet for just a few more days. Every time we tried to do that, we ended up getting burned. The smart thing was always to put the information out there first. We tried to live by that. I don't want to say we always succeeded, but we tried to live by that. We tried to always be proactive, with the understanding that our friends would rather hear the information from us than hear it from one of our critics or from a news reporter. So, that was one obstacle we faced—just the management of the inevitable bad news.

Contributor 16—Manager, DOE

Maintaining openness, honesty, and transparency was especially challenging because the work being accomplished had never been done before. Processes didn't exist for demolishing a plutonium-polluted building. No manuals exist for how to do that job.

Hence, trial-and-error learning was required, and, by definition, that produces mistakes and missteps. A basic foundation of trust had to be present initially to accomplish such challenging work, and by maintaining a commitment to trustworthiness, the work could progress effectively.

> The workers in the buildings have gotten comfortable with the regulatory person who is assigned to those buildings, and vice versa. It has been a long, slow process to establish some trust and some credibility, setting aside some fear and reservation.... The first big, serious plutonium building that involved decommissioning was building 779. That had some plutonium contamination, and there were some fits and starts in trying to figure out how this was best done. This was not taken from a cookbook. There was a lot of trial and error in getting used to how to do this and how to sort it out. The players started getting more comfortable with it, but there had to be some trust and credibility. When we tackled other buildings, the bigger plutonium buildings, we went through some of the same adjustment ... getting the level of trust, getting the system down, doing some trial and error, having some sessions where we hash out how it is going to be done.

Contributor 27—Senior Manager, CDPHE

Human Capital and Social Relationships

Trust is always a product of human relationships, and the management of Rocky Flats took great care to identify and select the team of people they felt could successfully achieve the objectives. As discussed in chapter 6, and consistent with Collins (2001) and others, "getting the right people on the bus" was a prerequisite to successful performance. At Rocky Flats, initial successes were dependent on having the best people doing the work. This entailed both bringing in new people—especially in managerial ranks—and keeping the best of the unionized workforce. A rule of thumb is that

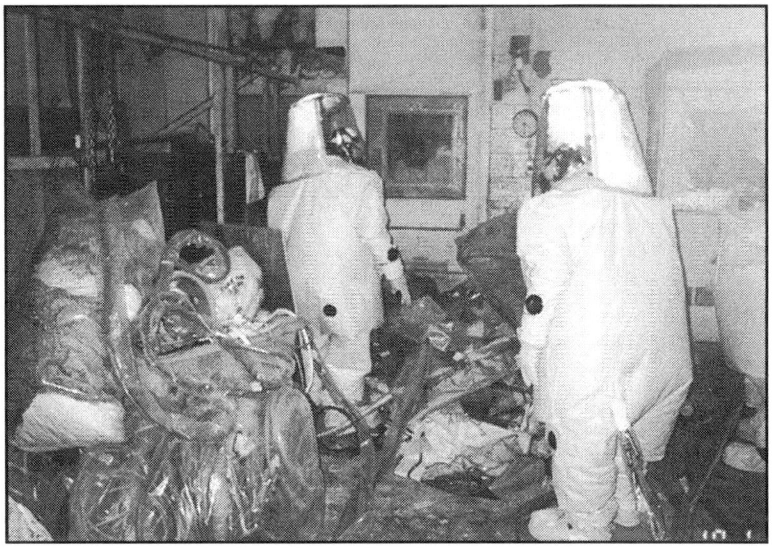

Figure 16: Gathering radioactive trash

> You cannot take a building down with the same people who built it and operated it. You

> also can't put trades and union members in the same space. But both are happening at Rocky Flats.
>
> Contributor 9—Senior Executive, Kaiser-Hill

In other words, you don't hire builders to demolish buildings, or developers to destroy their own handiwork. But at Rocky Flats, the best people—those who knew the equipment, the facilities, and the work that had been accomplished onsite—were the unionized workforce. Although they had to learn an entirely new set of tasks and objectives, a former Rocky Flats CEO stated:

> We decided that this workforce would be kept and that they would do the closure. We wanted to give them a chance. We brought in 25 salaried people in all areas of the organization, and we challenged the salaried people as well.
>
> Contributor 10—Senior Executive, Kaiser-Hill

In the senior ranks, the CH2MHill team identified new managerial employees and focused on bringing in knowledgeable people who shared the vision and the culture of the CH2MHill organization. One senior executive described his management team this way:

> I had to completely revamp my whole team and my organization to make sure that I had the talent that was up to the challenge that we had

> in front of us. I said the very first day when I arrived at Rocky Flats, "This is the best team I've ever worked with," and I say that today. It is the best team I've ever worked with, because the team has changed over time, and as the team has changed, we've always added higher quality people than we had before. That isn't to say the people we had before weren't good. It's just that we've had to get folks that are really, really good, and I think we have the best in the industry now.
>
> Contributor 6—Senior Executive, Kaiser-Hill

Another senior manager reinforced the idea that the right people were required to achieve the closure and cleanup objectives. The right people are willing to engage, to work consensually, and to support one another.

> In the end this is a people business, and while you may be technically right about something, or you may be legally right about something, if you don't have people pulling in the same direction it's going to be very hard to get it done. So the first thing that sites need to realize is that you have to have the right people on the job, and you have to develop the relationships so that the real discussion and communication can begin. Until you have some relationships and some trust, it's going to be very frustrating.

Contributor 8—Manager, Kaiser-Hill

The relationships among employees served as a significant enabler of spectacular performance at Rocky Flats. Cooperative interactions, employee involvement, and sharing a common mission all have been mentioned as critical components of success at Rocky Flats. Adopting a philosophy that employees want to do the right thing, make a contribution, and work harmoniously together was one key to healthy social relationships. This philosophy was shared by a senior elected state official. The involvement and participation of the workforce was an important key to success.

> I think there are some general principles here that are really important. One is, you can't make decisions in secret when people's future and their welfare are involved. They want to know what is going on, they want to have some kind of say, and they want to know that they're being heard. So being open in public is very important. Second is bringing in the leadership of all of the local communities as well as the state and the federal leadership. Ultimately the money is going to come from the federal government, so they need to be involved. Nothing was going to get done if we had people filing lawsuits, or if you had local communities saying "Not in my backyard." A third thing is that people will focus on solving problems if you empower them to do it, if you entrust them to solve it. They may fight bitterly, but if some-

body is standing there saying, "Solve the problem, I know you can do it," they'll do it. People really do rise to the occasion. A fourth factor is to make sure it's funded. We were really motivated to come up with the solutions to the problems here because we knew that the only way we could get Congress to fund a cleanup agreement was to go as a united front. So, my top advice is to make sure that your various constituencies are heard. Make sure they have a say in what is in their best interest.

Contributor 29—Senior Executive, state of Colorado

The development of social capital—networks of people working in cooperative relationships with one another—was not an automatic outcome of the announcement that Rocky Flats would transition from a production site to a closure and cleanup project. The antagonism and distrust of the unionized workforce was a potentially insurmountable obstacle to achieving the vision at Rocky Flats. Investment in social capital—building strong interpersonal relationships and trustworthy dealings with workers—was a prerequisite to addressing these initial barriers. The challenge was to reignite the motivation and unleash the latent social capital that existed among the workforce.

I think back on our relationship with the United Steel Workers of America when we first arrived here at Rocky Flats. It was not a good relationship. It was an adversarial relationship that had no trust between the parties involved. Contrast that with what's going on now with us and the steelworkers. We've tried to do the same thing with the guards and with the building trades. It is our job to figure out how to get the obstacles out of the way of the workers so they can get their work done and do it safely. We solicit their assistance and their help. They didn't have that trust with us in the beginning, and we had to build that over time. It takes a while to do that. But now, and I'll quote Dave Kins, who last Saturday at the steelworkers' golf tournament stood up in front of the membership of the steelworkers and said, "This is the best relationship that I have ever seen in the 40 years that I've been in this business and been a labor person. The relationship between Kaiser-Hill and the United Steel Workers of America is the best relationship I've ever seen. It's based on trust and honesty and integrity." You can't get it any better than that. That's what we believe in, and we're doing the same thing with the building trades. By having that trust and that cooperative partnership, we're able to do things that other companies who don't have that kind of a relationship could not do. Our steelworkers and our building trades give us ideas on how to do things better. They give us ideas on how to do things safer. They know. They do the work every single day. It's our job to listen to them and help them.

Contributor 6—Senior Executive, Kaiser-Hill

Rocky Flats became unique in developing a unionized workforce that was enthusiastically working itself out of a job as quickly as possible. Several factors explain this counterintuitive and positively deviant phenomenon, one of which was the care that was provided to individuals whose jobs were eliminated as part of the closure and cleanup. A group of union supervisors described the Rocky Flats approach to downsizing:

> The scope of work is disappearing, so we now have monthly layoffs. We never take out jobs unless the work is gone, too. We lose work first. We try to give four months' notice, and in the meantime, we train them, provide job fairs, and so on. There will be waves of downsizing as the project closes. We have a career transition center. We provide four months' notice for all employees who will be displaced. We then track these employees to ensure job placement. Every person in Security who wanted a job, got a job in a DOE site when they were laid off here. We had 26 shipping people who had been laid off. All of them now have a job. One major challenge is keeping the right people as we downsize, so

we are using incentives and retention bonuses to do that.

Contributor 11—Supervisors, Kaiser-Hill

A senior DOE official promised:

When people leave Rocky Flats, they are placed somewhere else in DOE if at all possible.

Contributor 23—Senior Executive, DOE

Whereas in a large majority of downsizing cases, the results are deteriorating performance, subversive behavior, and loss of morale and productivity within the organization (Cameron, 1998), the Rocky Flats story is dramatically different. Another of the key enablers was a focus on helping employees develop loyalty to the company rather than to the site. An executive officer at CH2MHill described this orientation:

Another key to our success has been that we are a main source for career planning. We will become these Rocky Flats employees' parent company. So, loyalty is building to the *company* and not just to the *site.* People are willing to work themselves out of a job because CH2MHill will take care of them.

Contributor 1—Senior Executive, CH2MHill

And that promise was trusted by the workforce. Supervisors and midlevel managers at Rocky Flats affirmed:

> We have had a chance to move up in this firm. Because of the good job we're doing, we know we will get a job when this place closes and we leave here. So we have a desire to succeed.
>
> Contributor 11—Supervisors, Kaiser-Hill

Thus, providing safety nets for employees, and even chances for promotion as a result of their spectacular performance at Rocky Flats, removed an incentive to the more usual consequences of downsizing, such as drops in morale, commitment, trust, communication, and loyalty. Human capital was being developed at the same time it was being eliminated. Cross-training, skill-building, and outplacement support were all coupled with job elimination.

> Of course, not every employee has been enthusiastic and supportive of the new direction at Rocky Flats, and the continual restructuring has certainly been a dramatic disruption from past practice. For example, in 1995 the steelworkers' contract contained 56 separate job classifications, but in the latest contract, only seven still exist. This restructuring of work provides a great deal more flexibility ... among

> workers to engage in a variety of tasks, but it also produces more ambiguity. Specialty skills have been replaced by workers who can do a variety of jobs, and employees are frequently required to take on work that requires learning and stretching. For those who resist such changes, a group of managers and supervisors described their strategy: "We had resisters. We just mixed them in with the others, and social pressure took care of them."
>
> Contributor 11—Supervisors, Kaiser-Hill

In other words, the more typical strategies of punishment, isolation, blackballing, reprimand, and other negative reinforcers were not a part of Rocky Flats' approach to its human capital development. Creating conditions where employees were exposed to positive social pressure to do the right thing, to accomplish objectives, and to work harmoniously were substituted instead.

Summary

In summary, an important cluster of factors that enabled positive deviance at Rocky Flats relates to the Clan or Collaborate quadrant in the Competing Values Framework. Enabling collaboration among a variety of disparate constituencies; building trust and credibility among these various groups, especially for the leaders of the closure and cleanup effort; and nurturing the development of human capital by providing empowered and engaged workers served as crucial building blocks for the trust and confidence needed to accomplish extraordinary results. The human side of the strategy—a focus on culture and values, collaboration, and credibility—was an important precondition for the success at Rocky Flats. On the other hand, just being nice, taking care of the people, remaining optimistic, and displaying caring and sensitivity to employee concerns is obviously not sufficient for spectacular success. Many of these factors can be interpreted as syrupy and saccharine in the absence of firm pressure to get the work done. Figure 7.1 summarizes the theme and the key enablers.

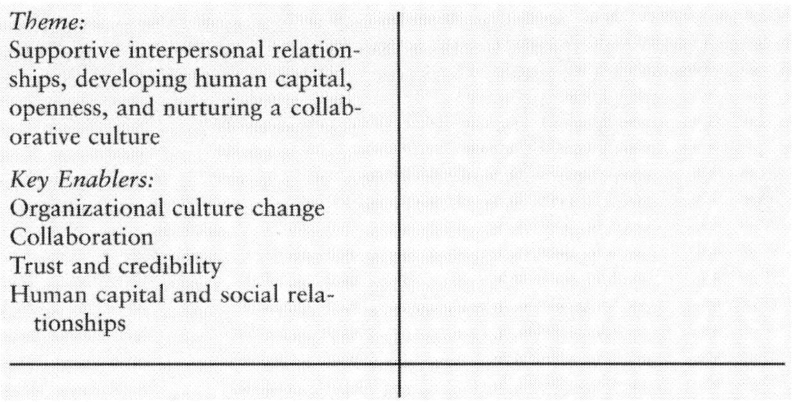

Figure 7.1 KEY ENABLERS IN THE CLAN OR COLLABORATE QUADRANT

Among the conclusions to be drawn from this quadrant are the following:

- ***Successful leaders create challenges and opportunities that make the current (traditional) culture appear inadequate and incapable.***

- ***Extraordinary success emerges from generating collaboration among adversaries.***
- ***The abundance approach must be fostered among antagonists.***
- ***Managers and workers must be co-located to enhance collaboration.***
- ***Ensuring trust trumps measurement, control, plans, or communication strategies, so maintain integrity at all costs.***
- ***Positive safety nets must be provided for at-risk employees.***
- ***Overcommunication and preemptive information-sharing should be the norm.***
- ***Use social pressure to manage resistors.***

8

Key Enablers—Politics, Incentives, and Rigorous Performance Standards

This is the fourth of the four chapters that address the question: *What levers can leaders use to produce similar results?* This chapter addresses the enablers that relate specifically to the rigorous, uncompromising, and results-oriented leadership themes.

In contrast to the focus on internal dynamics—culture, collaboration, credibility, and trust—another critical cluster of enablers relates to the Market or Compete quadrant in the Competing Values Framework. Rather than emphasizing cohesion-building activities, this quadrant emphasizes aggressive actions, external constituencies, market forces, performance incentives, and obtaining measurable results. The focus is on hard-driving management, achieving performance, and accomplishing goals—an obvious prerequisite in the Rocky Flats success story. The Market or Compete quadrant is so named because of its focus on competitive dynamics in the marketplace and on managing external stakeholder relationships. More attention is paid to constituencies outside the organization than to employees and managers inside the organization. In contrast to Clan or Collaborate quadrant activities, these enablers target (1) external stakeholder engagement, (2) managing political relationships, (3) taking bold action, and (4) providing incentives for measurable progress to facilitate positive deviance.

External Political Strategies

It should be emphasized that the Rocky Flats project started in a deficit condition. That is, little support for the project existed at any level—especially at the federal level, among regulators and members of Congress—and resistance to the project and skepticism that progress could be achieved was widespread.

> In the grand scheme of DOE, Rocky Flats had never been a favored site. It had never been a site that got a lot of money. That was because it was a steelworkers' site, not a lab. It was blue collar, not Ph.D. The site had never gotten the kind of money some of the other sites had. We went to Washington, D.C., to create a positive presence in the minds of the Hill staff for Rocky Flats.
>
> Contributor 5—Manager, Kaiser-Hill

In light of the rising concern and the possibility of major resistance at the federal and state levels, an external political strategy was required. Effectively managing the power dynamics among various external entities proved to be crucial to the success of the project. Creating a positive political strategy turned out to be a major challenge.

> There is still this notion that Rocky Flats is a horrible, contaminated nuclear site where bad things happen. Even after seven years of success we've not really overcome that. Similarly, when you get to Washington, the number of members of Congress who care about the environmental cleanup of the nuclear complex is very small. There are many priorities for this nation that come far ahead of this. Typically the only members who care are the members who have sites in their own districts. For that reason the support for the complex is very narrow. That means support for any one project is even narrower. These are all things we've tried to overcome. Let me anticipate your next question. What do we do to try to overcome them? We tried very hard to build support among nontraditional sectors. We tried in small ways to get members who didn't have a transparent interest in the project to become interested. One of the principal arguments we used was the sooner Rocky Flats gets closed down, the sooner there's money freed up for other projects. It was a struggle, because convincing a member from, say, Indiana that he should care about a site in Colorado, because five years from now there will be $600 million that will no longer be

> needed to be spent there, isn't always an easy sell. We had some success, but it wasn't easy.

Contributor 16—Manager, DOE

Even when a plan was created for closing and cleaning up the site, there was resistance. Outside entities did not line up in support and, in fact, were inclined to oppose it.

> When that document [the plan for closure and cleanup] got published, it began to get a lot of people excited. Remember, the Department of Energy had just issued a report on one side of the house saying it was going to take 70 years to clean up and about $36 billion. And here we have a group of people on the site, almost in parallel, saying that cleanup could be achieved for tens of billions of dollars less and decades sooner. This, I think, created some difficulties for [the DOE field manager]. It created upset and consternation up at headquarters and other places when this document got published.

Contributor 7—Manager, Kaiser-Hill

Not only was resistance from the Department of Energy and from Congress a strong possibility, but the governors of surrounding states also were potential roadblocks.

There were a number of people from the Department of Energy who were protective of their own sites, and accelerated closure was a new concept. It meant that other sites got less funding. During my time in the governor's office in particular, when we were successful at Rocky, we couldn't be too joyful about it because it meant that another site wasn't getting funding. We had to be careful not to take credit for things that the site had achieved at the expense of South Carolina, or Washington state, or Idaho, or any of the other sites.

Contributor 32—Staff member, U.S. Congress

Building political support required a long-term strategy based on humility:

It looks like when you support accelerated closure at Rocky Flats, the sites at New Mexico would be hurt by accelerated closure in Colorado. Certainly we've had difficulties with South Carolina regarding shipping. You need to have a complexwide concern. We were very good in governors' meetings at not bragging about our success at Rocky Flats, because in the early days it was at the expense of the other sites in the short run. Short-term thinking is a way of life in Congress. So maintaining a long-term vision is difficult in those circumstances, but it's a necessity to the closure of these sites.

Figure 17: Radioactive waste containers being shipped to permanent storage facilities

Contributor 32—Staff member, U.S. Congress

One key enabler for success at Rocky Flats, therefore, was garnering the support of other state governors. In addition to active political leadership by individuals within Kaiser-Hill and in the DOE, the governor's office in Colorado played a key leadership role in exerting a great deal of political influence on several other states in order for the Rocky Flats project to succeed. Among the reasons this was necessary were the necessity of crossing state lines in shipping material offsite, competing with other states with DOE sites for federal funds, and the politically sensitive issue of disposing of radioactive waste in designated sites in other states.

> One of the major issues is the idea of removing the plutonium and shipping it to offsite locations. The lieutenant governor realized that to do this, you've got to ship the material through a number of different states. Those states are going to have political dynamics as well. So she wanted to gather those communities around Rocky Flats together to have them work together with their counterparts across the country, to help them feel comfortable about receiving Rocky Flats wastes and materials. We worked on trying to deal with the transportation corridor issues politically.
>
> Contributor 33—Assistant to a U.S. Congressman

Governor-to-governor discussions were imperative, so active support from the governor of the state of Colorado became key. A senior congressional staff member commented:

> It was essential that Governor Owens work with those other governors whose sites weren't moving forward in the 1999 to 2001 time frame. The personal relationship of governors—Governor Owens, Governor Geringer in Wyoming, Governor Kempthorne in Idaho, the governor of Nevada, and others—was essential. I invested an enormous amount of my personal time working with each one of those governors' staffs, so that when we

> got the okay to ship, we had worked out all those shipping difficulties between the states. I know the Department of Energy invested a lot of money in funding the Western Governors Association so we could have those discussions.... We got governors thinking in terms of, "Hey, if we can close Rocky, that means something good for Idaho or Nevada or Washington state or Savannah River in South Carolina." So a tremendous amount of effort went into maintaining those relationships.
>
> Contributor 32—Staff member, U.S. Congress

In addition to political support at the state level, Rocky Flats' success was dependent on political support from the House and the Senate. Senator Allard was one of the strong public advocates who helped enable the Rocky Flats success.

> I think my getting involved certainly helped as far as the Senate side is concerned.... They needed to have an advocate in the Senate, so I sat down with my colleagues—for example, Senator Domenici from New Mexico—and talked to him about the importance of moving forward with Rocky Flats in Colorado as a cleanup. I told him that this could be a great opportunity to at least clean up one site and set a standard for the rest of the country. So my colleagues began to think, here is an opportunity to clean up the former nuclear weapons site and to set a standard for

cleanup for the rest of the country.... Among the factors that favored congressional support were that other senators began to realize that Rocky Flats could be held up as an example of the way cleanup could occur throughout the country. We were doing some unique things with Rocky Flats as far as motivating the contractor, working with the workers in the unions, and working with the local community. That, I think, tweaked their interest and their imagination enough that they thought there was perhaps a future for cleanup in their own states.

Contributor 30—U.S. Senator

Not surprisingly, political support was not always dependent on formal meetings or achieved through rational persuasion. Coalition-building and personal relationships played a significant role in the management of the political agenda. One senator described this process.

We had staff meetings with Congressman Skaggs, who represented that district at that time. We saw the common ground and found out that we could work together in a bipartisan way. We had an opportunity to sit down with the administrator out there.... We visited with the representatives from the contractor. Obviously we had to get the Secretary of Energy at that time, Bill Richardson, who I played basketball with on the

> House basketball team. We had established camaraderie there, and we had a lot of confidence in each other. He said that he would help out even though he was from the other side of the aisle. So we had Democrats and Republicans working together. His successor, Secretary of Energy Spencer Abraham, was also a good friend of mine who was willing to make as strong a commitment as Secretary Richardson. I continued to work with the local politicians, particularly the governors in the state, Governor Romer and Governor Owens. We had very good liaison work between the workers themselves and my office. Meeting together as a group, meeting with each other, all this communication began to solidify confidence in one another, and that helped things move forward.
>
> Contributor 30—U.S. Senator

The behind-the-scenes political support-building process, in other words, became an important enabler of continuing progress at Rocky Flats. This kind of invisible support—not usually identified as a critical factor in transformational change—was as critical as the Adhocracy, Hierarchy, and Clan enablers. In addition to Senate support, House backing was necessary and was markedly enhanced by a congressman from Michigan who did not have a DOE site in his district, had no formal ties to Colorado or Rocky Flats, and was a relatively new member of Congress.

> There were members of Congress who really stand out, and one of them was Congressman Joe Knollenberg of Michigan. He was a new member of the subcommittee back in 1995. He looked at the whole cleanup program, and he began to say, "Why aren't we talking about closing these sites? Let's just close the sites." He's actually the first one who started to push for closure. "I want to know when you're going to close these sites. We're not just going to run programs forever." He was really forceful on this, and he actually took the time to go visit the cleanup sites and spend a lot of time on them. So he was a good proponent.
>
> Contributor 22—Manager, DOE

It should be reemphasized that the political strategies surrounding Rocky Flats were produced by multiple leaders, not just a single visionary. Multiple sources of political leadership operated simultaneously, and successive leaders in DOE, at Rocky Flats, and in Congress maintained the momentum. Blockages at a variety of points in the process and by any number of individuals could have curtailed success. One reason that resistance seemed to dissipate rather than grow was that the political strategy was positive in its orientation. Rather than relying on threats and arm-twisting, a vision of abundance, setting a new standard, freeing up resources, decreasing harm, and enhancing a previously unachieved extraordinary level of performance all created positive energy and support rather than resistance. A positive political strategy was the key.

> I don't think the message here is "Do it the Rocky Flats way." That is absolutely not the message. Everyone has to find his or her own way. If there is a message here, it is that there cannot be success without an affirmative political strategy. I think future managers cannot be afraid of the political arena, because the political arena is real. It's there. It's part of your life. The question is, what is your political strategy? Who has bought into that strategy? Is there an understanding of what the strategy is? Is there a plan for how to maintain progress with that strategy for accountability? No site can be affective without a conscious political strategy. Ultimately, decisions about who gets funded, what laws are made, and regulatory relief involve public policy trade-offs. Those public policy trade-offs are made in the political arena. So if there is any closing word of advice, I would say, take the politics seriously and make them work for you. It's not easy, but it's possible, even at the sites that start out in the worst posture. Who would have thought in 1995 that Rocky Flats would be the site where members of Congress from other states are tripping over each other to throw money at it? Who would have thought in 1995 that Rocky Flats is

> the site that is so privileged by Congress that other sites are trying to figure out ways to hide their activities in our scope? It wasn't easy. It wasn't a slam dunk. It didn't have to be this way. But one of the lessons is that a political strategy is critical to the success of a project like this.
>
> Contributor 16—Manager, DOE

A key to maintaining a positive political strategy and to maintaining the political support required at the congressional level was the ability to perform, to achieve results, and to allay concerns about mistakes and safety violations. That is, Rocky Flats leaders felt a need to support the external political leaders whose own credibility and reputations were on the line.

> Folks were supporting us on the Hill. They were putting some of their credibility on the line in our behalf. We owed it to them to support them. What supporting them meant was success. It meant getting the job done. It meant accountability. It meant being able to project scope for this year very clearly. This is what our projected scope is for next year, and we will come back a year from now so you can tell whether or not we accomplished the scope we said we would. It also meant being able to maintain a very solid record in safety and a very solid record with the community. If we were going to be a site that Congress was going to take a risk on and fund ahead of

> other sites, we really needed to be ahead of the class.
>
> Contributor 16—Manager, DOE

In other words, the principle of generalized reciprocity was at work. Because a variety of external entities put reputations on the line, provided special support, and went the extra mile in garnering resources, individuals at Rocky Flats, in turn, responded by extending themselves to an extraordinary degree to ensure that this support was reciprocated. One congressional staff member identified achieving early tangible results as his most important piece of advice for enabling high performance.

> When the public saw that we were really cleaning the site up, we got the kind of alignment and support from the citizenry that was lacking prior to that. That is probably my most important piece of advice to the other DOE sites.
>
> Contributor 32—Staff member, U.S. Congress

External Stakeholder Connections

In addition to political support, other explanations for the dramatic success at Rocky Flats included the capability with which Market or Compete quadrant dynamics were managed—in particular, external political relationships, stakeholder engagement, the incentive system, a bold action orientation, and an emphasis on measurable progress. For example, one senior manager admitted:

> There was never a period of time when I worked at Rocky Flats when we didn't have one or another serious controversy with the community.
>
> Contributor 16—Manager, DOE

Nevertheless, the relationships with external constituencies changed markedly over the years. Gradually, those who lacked a critical vested interest in Rocky Flats lost interest, and only those representing important external interests stayed involved. These groups and individuals, however, were demanding in their expectations and firm in their convictions that Rocky Flats would be dismantled and decontaminated. They escalated the pressure for solid performance.

> As there was more and more distance from the days of production and from the FBI raid, the large number of people who wanted to be involved in Rocky Flats activities for the purpose of protesting or criticizing what we were doing, dwindled. There even became a sense that "Rocky Flats is becoming boring." You were sitting there debating where to install the passive reactive barrier, not whether or not the Cold War is a good thing or not. We were no longer debating whether Rocky or the DOE should comply with the law.

> The issues became more minute and more specialized, so we found that the casual people dropped off. We were left with folks who were very focused, very smart, very informed, and who had the time to really drill in. The good news is that it makes a partnership a lot easier because you're dealing with people who really understand what's going on. On the other hand, they kept us on our toes a lot better. We couldn't smoke them. We couldn't get anything past them. When you have full-time people who have been at it for years, who studied the documents, if you make a mistake or have an oversight, they're going to catch it. I think that knowing they were out there made us smarter. It made us better. It made us do better staff work. We knew we were going to have to get it past them before we could go public on it.
>
> Contributor 16—Manager, DOE

A senior DOE official described the incremental improvement that occurred with the community and other external constituencies over time.

> I don't remember the day that I saw the change. We started making some progress on the cleanup agreement with the regulators. I knew we had made a breakthrough because we had involved the state. In order to do that, we had to get the public citizen groups together—the Rocky

> Mountain Peace Center and all of these other peace groups. We had to get the five city mayors and the two county commissioners all saying that they supported this thing. That was the real evidence that we were making some progress and changing the culture. I wish I could think of the incident at the time. It was over several years, and it took work.
>
> Contributor 21—Manager, DOE

Coordination among the various external stakeholders relied on two key strategies: (1) increasing dialogue with stakeholders to learn about and address their concerns and to increase the transparency of activities at Rock Flats, and (2) consolidating the disparate entities. For more than 40 years Rocky Flats had been immersed in a culture of secrecy, insularity, and confidentiality. Outsiders could not be allowed into the facility without careful screening because of security concerns, and workers were not allowed to talk about their work with outsiders, even neighbors and friends. Hence, anyone not a part of Rocky Flats became viewed as a potential risk to national security, and the last thing managers at the facility would do is initiate dialogue or information-sharing sessions with members of external groups. This changed, however, after Kaiser-Hill took over the facility in 1995. In addition to the change in orientation initiated by Kaiser-Hill, DOE also became a champion of openness and constituency involvement. One senior DOE official stated:

> I went to a lot of meetings. I went offsite to places like the Peace Center. The Peace Center is in the basement of a church. We sat down on couches and just talked about the issues and the problems. I made the rounds. I went to all five city mayors. I went to two counties' commissioners. We tried to listen mainly to what they wanted. I met with the unions and tried to discern what their issues were. I also met with the guards. You know, we had three unions on site, each with their own agenda. The first thing I did was just to listen, learn, talk to people, and try to hear what they had to say, so I could figure out how we were going to do this thing.
>
> Contributor 21—Manager, DOE

Initiating these kinds of meetings just to listen and discuss issues does not seem to be a radically different thing to do. Yet it represented a substantial departure from the kinds of meetings that were held prior to 1995 when Kaiser-Hill took over.

> In the early 1990s it was very interesting to go to a public meeting related to Rocky Flats. These meetings would be focused on a specific plan or document. It would be a very formal setting, and they would say, "We're here to hear the public comments on this document." So the people

> would be called one by one to come up to the microphone and express their comments about whatever plan or document was being discussed. There was no dialogue between the people sitting in the front of the room and the people in the audience. That has been a dramatic change from where we were in the early 1990s to where we are today. There is a very intense and robust dialogue between the site representatives, members of the regulating community, members of the state government, and the general community around Rocky Flats. We actually sit around the table, all are equal, and we discuss the ideas about the cleanup and closure of Rocky Flats. That has been a really dramatic change for me.
>
> Contributor 36—Manager, Kaiser-Hill

By and large, the meetings held with these multiple constituencies were conducted in the facilities and offices of the community groups. In a gesture aimed at reaching out to the community and demonstrating openness to the desires and concerns of external groups, Rocky Flats and DOE leaders visited a large number of constituencies on their home turf. Two senior leaders described their experience as follows:

> During this period of time there were a lot of public meetings and stakeholder conversations. There was at least one summit that included many, many stakeholders talking about this idea

> of accelerated closure of Rocky Flats, with [the CEO at Rocky Flats and the DOE director] taking particularly significant leadership roles.
>
> Contributor 7—Manager, Kaiser-Hill

> ...we began to engage the communities more and more. The communities of Arvada, Broomfield, Boulder, and others began to play much more significant roles in addition to the Citizens Advisory Board. [We] were making monthly presentations and having monthly conversations with community leaders. At the same time we began to have a lot of conversations with key folks from the state of Colorado and from the EPA who are involved not only as key architects of the cleanup agreement, but who also continue to stay very involved with our planning and thinking processes as we go through these iterations.
>
> Contributor 7—Manager, Kaiser-Hill

Reaching agreement among disparate groups was not automatically accomplished, of course. The coordination and motivational roles played by the governor's office in the state of Colorado were critical.

> We had working committees that met weekly. We discovered that we needed some additional assistance, to be honest, because the three parties were so entrenched in their positions, based on

past experience. We needed some help, and we were lucky that Governor Romer identified Lieutenant Governor Gail Schoettler as the point person on behalf of the governor's office. She was very effective in sitting the three parties down and saying, "Come on, guys, we need to work this out." Just the mere fact of having to go to the lieutenant governor's office and explain your position, or explain why you couldn't work this out, was very instrumental in getting the job done.

Contributor 21—Manager, DOE

The ultimate goal of these meetings with external constituencies was not just to mitigate the antagonism and animosity of these groups, of course; it was also to foster common ground and a shared agenda and vision among these groups. The meetings were meant to build support and political capital. One senior-level elected official explained her role in this transformation.

Rocky Flats for some time had had community meetings of interested citizens. The taxpayers were supporting a lot of that effort, but the decision makers had not been involved. I got all of the local communities together. We usually got Jefferson County Courthouse and all of the local communities were represented, as well as anybody else who was interested. The various citizens'

> groups participated as well. We had the EPA there. We had the State Health Department there. We always tried to have the representatives from the congressional offices there as well. The purpose was to share information and, above all, to share people's fears and their worries about it. So things came out like, "We're really worried about the water. Is the water going to be clean?" or "Are people going to be endangered by contaminated water?" There was a lot of discussion. That was really valuable for people to have a forum where they could air their concerns and talk about solutions. It did another thing as well. It got people politically motivated. The local government people were fabulous about lobbying in Washington. They made a lot of trips there. Once we had a plan in place, and they knew they had something that they could sell, they really worked hard to get our members of Congress to push this in Congress. They were fantastic.

Contributor 29—Senior Executive, state of Colorado

Another important objective of these meetings was to go beyond mere persuasion or public relations. An abundance objective was demonstrated, stretching well beyond acceptable outcomes to extraordinary outcomes. The external constituency meetings served the purpose of clarifying this vision for Rocky Flats and identifying common desirable outcomes. Multiple groups had input into the vision, as is described by both a DOE manager.

> We got together with the citizen groups like the Rocky Mountain Peace Center, and we said, "What do you want?" They said: "We want it safe." We formed a citizen committee, and we asked them to tell us what they wanted this site to look like after it's safe and after it's cleaned up. We took these inputs and we then developed a vision that said, "Make it safe and clean it up." We used that as a baseline, so when we started with that vision, it gave us focus. When we sat down with the regulators and started to renegotiate this agreement, it always came back to what this vision was—make it safe and clean it up. But then they added, "Shut it down." But it started with making it safe and cleaning it up, and we could then relate everything we did to "was it safe and was it cleaning the site up?" And if it wasn't contributing to making it safe and cleaning it up, then it didn't belong as a milestone, and we had to get it out of the existing agreement and develop a new agreement.
>
> Contributor 21—Manager, DOE

Of course, not every group was pleased with the resulting decisions, particularly as they related to the level of radioactive pollution in the remaining soil. Several community groups sought an RSAL (residual soil action level) of 35 instead of the agreed-upon level of 50. One community activist related how the compromise was reached.

> Because the price of the cleanup and closure had been fixed, the plan mandated by the revised RFCA [Rocky Flats Cleanup Agreement] had to be done for no more than would have been spent under the original 1996 RFCA. Energy, Kaiser-Hill, and the regulators had to decide how they could provide the cleanup the public wanted without spending more. They came up with a trade-off. Their plan proposed a better surface cleanup in exchange for a less thorough subsurface cleanup. Kaiser-Hill would clean the surface enough to protect a wildlife refuge worker and put controls in place to contain the contamination left below the surface.
>
> Contributor 25—Community Representative

To be clear, the RSAL level was established on the basis of risk reduction. Because no standard level of pollution has been established for any area in the country, the levels established at each cleanup site were negotiated on the basis of how much residual risk remained. At Rocky Flats, the level of remaining pollution was established at a level that would provide safety for almost any long-term use. (For alternative viewpoints, see appendix 1.)

Leadership at the local and state levels was matched by leadership at the federal level. Various individuals took leadership roles aimed at helping to foster support and agreement. To repeat, no single leader was responsible for the success of the project, and it took multiple leaders in multiple agencies working in cooperation with one another to create a supportive external environment.

> When we first started the contract in 1995, we didn't have friends or allies. We had to make our own friends and allies through performance. In the beginning the lieutenant governor of the state of Colorado really took Rocky Flats under her wing. She saw the vision that we saw, and she really started supporting us. From a political standpoint, she was the first heavyweight politician that supported us. Over time, Congressman Udall, Senator Allard, Governor Romer, and now Governor Bill Owens have all seen what we're trying to do at Rocky Flats and have supported us. Now, from a DOE standpoint, Jessie Roberson was one of our greatest allies in the beginning with the vision she saw, with what ASAP meant in closing Rocky Flats, and how to do it on an accelerated basis. Paul Golan, who is now at headquarters, was also a tremendous supporter for us. Now the stakeholders and even the regulators support what we're trying to do at Rocky Flats. They are working with us to help us figure out the best way to do what meets

> the regulatory requirements or meets the community needs that surround Rocky Flats. So I think this has really become a very cooperative effort from all parties concerned in getting this project finished.
>
> Contributor 6—Senior Executive, Kaiser-Hill

Of course, one formula for ensuring failure in any change effort is death by meetings. A common resistance tactic is to hold multiple meetings in order to ensure that discussion replaces action. Convening groups merely to express opinions, expectations, and frustrations blocks progress unless specific actions, goals, and execution steps are identified. Consolidating these disparate perspectives was an especially important strategy for turning discussions into activity. This occurred by creating representative advisory groups to amalgamate issues.

> One of the frustrations I had when I first got into Governor Romer's office was the plethora of public groups and committees and task forces and review commissions. It was death by a thousand meetings. It was a great opportunity for us to develop a site-specific advisory board that would collapse a lot of these disparate types of public involvement groups into one focused group. That way we would all know where the action was. It would

be very efficient. We could deal with all the different issues in that one setting. That ultimately became the Rocky Flats Citizens Advisory Board. So today we have the Citizens Advisory Board, which focuses on cleanup issues. We also have the Rocky Flats Local Impacts Initiative, which is the office for transitioning the workers who are outplaced. I think they function pretty well together.

Contributor 33—Assistant to U.S. Congressman

A key indicator of the success of this consolidation of perspectives was that even without ongoing leadership from the state of Colorado or from Rocky Flats leaders, the Citizens Advisory Board and the Rocky Flats Local Impacts Initiative continued to stay actively involved and supportive. Adversaries were transformed into advocates, supporters, and team players.

Unfortunately, the lieutenant governor ran for governor in 1998 but did not win. The local governments around Rocky Flats decided to keep those kinds of meetings going anyway. That evolved into the RFCLOG—Rocky Flats Coalition of Local Governments. That group is still functioning today. It is still performing the function of helping to make sure that this project actually is implemented and realized.

Bold Action and Pressure to Succeed

Maintaining pressure to perform was a key part of the positive strategy adopted at Rocky Flats. In order to maintain support and garner resources from political leaders and other external stakeholders, dogged determinism and an uncompromising approach to performance were necessary. Demanding timely results, expecting performance, and requiring measurable outcomes were prerequisites for achieving extraordinary success. Establishing rigorous goals, not becoming dissuaded or deflected from the targets, and pressing ahead in spite of contrarians were key enablers.

> The most difficult party in the cleanup strategy was [DOE] headquarters. They had 20 sites and 20 different kinds of interests at every site. We popped up out of the blue with this approach that didn't fit in. The strategy in the past had been to "levelize"—to have everything kind of move along together. Communities had been built up around the DOE's projects, and so the financial investment was really what supported the local economy around the sites. Because of that, there was a levelizing approach—nobody could get ahead of anybody. No change in funding. Nobody got too excited. Everything moved together. We showed up and said, "We think we can do this quicker,

sooner, better, and wouldn't that be a great model?" It was, like, "No! No!" They would push us back down and say, "Get back in line." But we'd always pop back up. Well, it took about two years of us demonstrating that we could do it. Everybody had to be convinced—Congress, DOE, the government auditors. The GAO came out and looked and said, "They can't do it." They came back in another year or two and said, "Well, maybe." They were here just a year ago, and they said, "Looking pretty good." It is looking good. To convince people that you are capable of doing something that has never been done—you have ten other sites where they don't see a thing being done—you have to actually withstand the pressure of people saying "No." Just keep pressing ahead, show them, and accept that it will take time for them to believe it. But we now have a new standard.

Contributor 20—Senior Executive, DOE

Resistance came not only from federal agencies but also from local community groups. In 1992, when President George H.W. Bush announced the closure of the Rocky Flats production activities,

People were satisfied. They said, "Our mission has been completed. We've seen the closure of Rocky Flats." We had to remind individuals in the community that the mission wasn't complete.

> There was still a long road of cleanup ahead of them.

Contributor 36—Manager, Kaiser-Hill

The continuing threat of resistance, in other words, was never removed. The fear was that success would breed failure—that is, seeing a remarkable amount of success would result in people becoming lackadaisical or careless. In fact, one senior executive in the Department of Energy indicated that

> Our biggest fear is that they will spike the ball on the five-yard line ... that they'll celebrate before they've finished the job.

Contributor 23—Senior Executive, DOE

A former CEO at Rocky Flats cautioned that complacency remained a major threat:

> Our major threats for the future are complacency, stopping doing what we're doing, and not offloading people in the right way.

Contributor 10—Senior Executive, Kaiser-Hill

A DOE officer cautioned:

> One thing I would say is, be careful. People get overconfident. I had the honor of serving in the military at one point. They used to say that people either got killed right off the bat when

> they went into things, or they got killed right at the end because they would take their eye off the ball. They would lose their focus and concentration. Don't lose your focus and concentration here. You've still got a ways to go.
>
> Contributor 15—Senior Executive, DOE

It is one thing to caution against overconfidence, of course, and quite another thing to keep up the pressure and the drive. The difficulty of maintaining momentum until the end was emphasized by a senior manager at Rocky Flats:

> I would just say the only easy day was yesterday, and that it's going to continue to be a difficult project until the day it's done. I will be very worried that everybody thinks Rocky Flats is finished. It's over the hump. All the hard stuff is done. Every day between now and the time we're done is going to be very hard. Every day there are trucks rolling. There is energized electrical equipment. There are radiological materials that are still clear and present dangers. The minute we forget that we're in a very hazardous, difficult environment, the minute we forget that we earn public trust, that we earn regulator trust, is the day Rocky Flats goes off track. So, if there are any parting words, they are that we need to keep our eye on the ball. We need to realize that if we don't, Rocky Flats

> will go off track faster than it ever came on track.
>
> Contributor 14—Manager, DOE

In other words, pressure for continuing performance remained intense at Rocky Flats until the last day of operation. Successful performance was expected, and penalties were given to those who did not perform. One of the most dramatic examples of high performance requirements was the removal of supervisors who were not performing up to expectations. In certain instances, union employees provided feedback on supervisors' performance, and when performance was rated poorly by those with whom they worked, these supervisors were removed.

> We eliminated all supervisors that were rated by workers as resistive, treated employees poorly, were obstacles, and were not performing. Employees actually rated their supervisors and sent in the ratings. [One of my staff member's] checked on the accuracy of the data, then we removed the poor performers.
>
> Contributor 10—Senior Executive, Kaiser-Hill

One particularly vivid example of the abundance approach to performance at Rocky Flats—emphasizing spectacular performance in contrast to merely acceptable or good performance—relates to glove boxes. Bold action, "extra mile" effort, and responding to pressures to perform at extraordinarily high levels are illustrated by the establishment of almost unreasonably high performance goals for removing radioactively contaminated glove boxes.

Glove boxes are the structures inside certain buildings at Rocky Flats in which radioactive materials were machined and manufactured. Workers put their hands into thick rubber gloves that were attached to the walls of a large box in order to handle radioactive material without being exposed to radiation. Inside these boxes, radioactive levels were extremely high, so dismantling and disposing of them was a dangerous task that required great care. Glove boxes had been periodically dismantled and disposed of during the operational phase at Rocky Flats as a regular part of maintenance and repair. Because of the complexity and safety concerns associated with this task, approximately one glove box per year could be dismantled. With more than 1,000 glove boxes existing at Rocky Flats, a thousand years would be required for Kaiser-Hill to complete the task of removing all contaminated glove boxes unless extraordinary measures were taken.

> We were doing glove box removal in building 779. [Our CEO] proposed that we would do 25 glove boxes in a year, which was huge at that time. We were doing a couple in a year, and to do 25 in a year was huge. But, you know, we knew how these guys worked.... but I think you have a bunch of folks at Rocky Flats for whom

it's more important that they have a good professional reputation, more important to win a six-pack of beer, than to get $20 million worth of incentive fee. They were personally motivated to do something where everybody told them they couldn't do it.

We're sitting at a table, and [the DOE site director] and I were across the table from [the CEO and his assistant]. [The CEO] says, "We're going to do 25 glove boxes this year. That's the measure." And I said, "That's great, but I want you to do 50." He says, "No, we're going to do 25." And I said, "No, we want you to do 50." And [the CEO's assistant] gets up and says, "Aw, let's do 50. Piece of cake. Don't worry about it." [The CEO] got a little bit angry, and they called a little time-out. Afterward, [the CEO] brought folks back together and said, "OK, he says he can do 50, and we're going to make him do 50." So 50 was the number. That was one of the examples of a challenge where we tried to outinnovate each other. When all was said and done, I think he got 75 glove boxes done that year, and he got paid for every one of them.

Again, that was one of those turning points where we went from what's the least I could do to what's the most I can do. The next year, 75 wasn't the number anymore, it was over a hundred. So, if you institutionalize the challenge, and if you make it worthwhile for the contractors to go after that, then that's when you start getting the innovation, and that's when you start driving the projects to success and completion.

Contributor 14—Manager, DOE

Usually the pressure for performance at Rocky Flats was not as dramatic as multiplying the output goals by 50. Rather, it involved simply providing individuals with the resources needed to succeed in their work and raising expectations that extraordinary performance was feasible. Bold action, in other words, was exemplified by an abundance posture toward producing output, as is illustrated by this story told by a senior executive at Rocky Flats.

> The workers caught on sooner than middle management. I would walk around the buildings and stop and talk to a shift supervisor and say, "Okay, what's the problem?" One supervisor said, "Well, the problem here is we don't have a PC. Our PC broke." And I said, "Well, are you talking about $1,200 or $1,500? Go down to Radio Shack or CompUSA and buy one." That's what I told him to do. He only needed a $1,200 PC, and we could get back to work. They had been shut down in this building for two or three weeks. Then I called in the general manager or the president of the contractor, and I said, "What's going on with this building? I was just down there, and the shift supervisor said all you needed was $1,200 to go

get a new PC." And the manager said, "No, that's not true. I've had a team looking at that problem for two months now, and it's going to take $100,000 to fix that problem." I said, "Wait a minute. Where is the truth here? Should I believe the guy who is doing the job, or a bunch of people sitting up here in a headquarters building who haven't even been at the work site? They're sitting up here deciding by doing studies. If the guy who has to do the job on a daily basis says he needs $1,200, I say go to Radio Shack, fix it up, and be in operation tomorrow." So the workers got it sooner than the managers. They're excited about it. Someone's listening to them. Someone's going to do something. And the managers ... well, gee, if we listen to the workers, why are they needed? That's a good question.

Contributor 21—Manager, DOE

Incentives to Perform

A very important key to the remarkable level of success achieved at Rocky Flats was the innovative incentive system created both for individual employees and for the company as a whole. Because the closure of the facility in 1989 had taken away the sense of mission from employees, and they had lost pride and purpose in what they were doing, a key challenge was to reignite the positive energy that had previously existed. One mechanism for doing this was the financial incentive system. It was an abundance-centered approach to rewards. The philosophy lying behind this system was described by one of the senior executives at Kaiser-Hill.

> As part of our performance measure structure, we had actually included an incentive program for our employees to share in the profits of the company. Our profits were based on us completing performance measures. So there was a natural fit between motivating the workforce to do the mission work and accomplishing the mission. We also knew that the workforce needed to be motivated. They hadn't been motivated in a positive way for some time. We wanted to reinstill the pride in the workforce that they had during the production days. The performance measures really worked in our favor. They got the workforce motivated and reinstilled the pride that they had had when they were in production. They felt that they had accomplished something. It is not all about coming to work and taking your paycheck home. It is coming to work, feeling like you accomplished something, and going home feeling good about what you did that day.... Our goal is to get it done safely, ahead of schedule, and under budget. That translates into an increased incentive to the company and an increased incentive to the employees. In our new closure contract, our employees are incentivized, just like the company is, to

> help us figure out how to do this safely, faster, and for less money.
>
> Contributor 6—Senior Executive, Kaiser-Hill

Not only was an innovative incentive system established for individual employees, but the organization as a unit also operated on the basis of a completely new incentive system on Department of Energy projects.

> We were the first field office to fully embrace that concept of paying for performance—if you had a stretch goal and if it was a difficult goal, you got paid more. If you did even better, you could make even more money. We also had in there penalties if you didn't do it. So 85 percent of the money was based on objective milestones and measurements. There is no other site in DOE today—even today, ten years later—that is anywhere near 85 percent. In fact, most of them are regressing and going back to an award fee. However, the new contract—since the year 2000—is based 100 percent on incentive. To me, that is the way it should be done.
>
> Contributor 21—Manager, DOE

In traditional contracts with the Department of Energy, the cost of performing the job was assumed to be the same across all vendors. Therefore, DOE negotiated contracts based on the "fee percentage," or the amount of profit to be added to the basic project costs. Because most contracts assumed that costs were not variable, when unanticipated problems arose, the normal strategy was simply to hire more people to address the problem. As a result, the actual cost of projects tended to escalate due to larger numbers of personnel. Cost overruns were typical. At Rocky Flats, for example, the employee base rose from approximately 3,500 employees during production days (pre-1989) to a high of almost 8,000 during the 1989-1995 period. During those years little or no cleanup work was performed, but mandates from CDPHE, DOE, and the EPA led to large numbers of paper studies and record-keeping requirements for which new people were hired. The new Rocky Flats contract, however, was structured differently. CH2MHill's CEO explained that prior to 1995, incentives were in place to *spend more* (i.e., cost-plus contracts). The 1995 contract between Kaiser-Hill and DOE provided incentives to *do more* (i.e., accomplish more work objectives), and the new 2000 contract was focused on *spending less by going faster* (i.e., completion ahead of schedule).

> Our new contract focused on getting things done sooner and attaching more fee to those new activities. For example, the new contract can be illustrated like this:

Old Contract	New Contract
Base profit=$40 million	Base profit=$20 million

Old Contract	New Contract
	Incentive=$20 million (if on time)
	New incentive=$20 million (if ahead of schedule)

Contributor 1—Senior Executive, CH2MHill

In fact, the entire approach to negotiating with the federal government was changed by adopting this new incentive system. CH2MHill's CEO described the process as identifying the expected level of costs incurred, then attaching incentives and penalties to over- and underperformance, respectively. He used the graph shown below to illustrate the way in which the incentive fee was determined.

> In the contracting process, we would negotiate the point on the graph at which a basic fee would be paid. What would be the level of performance—and cost—that would be acceptable? Then a graph was drawn so that if we exceeded that performance—our costs were lower—we would earn more fee. We also drew a graph that showed the penalty we would incur if our costs went higher. A maximum and a minimum point were identified, resulting in the following graph.

Contributor 1—Senior Executive, CH2MHill

Ironically, Kaiser-Hill originally proposed to DOE that no minimum or maximum limit be specified. That is, the company would get nothing if it missed the cleanup and closure goals, but the incentive fee would continue to escalate if the company realized even better than expected cost savings and speed. That proposal was ultimately rejected by both DOE and the board of Kaiser-Hill as being too risky.

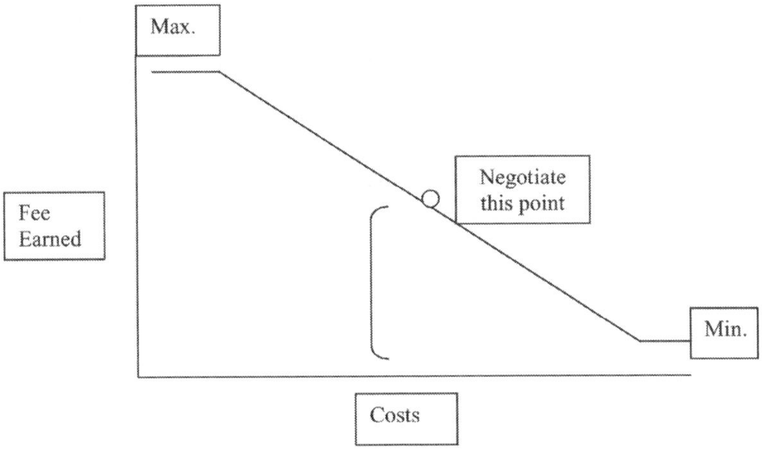

Figure 8.1 AN ILLUSTRATION OF THE INCENTIVE FEE STRUCTURE

The original contract provided for a minimum fee of $150 million and a maximum fee of $460 million, although that changed under a 2004 contract modification that dropped the minimum fee to $75 million and increased the maximum fee to $560 million in order to make sure the contractor [Kaiser-Hill] kept its top personnel around until the end of the project.

Contributor 38—Media Representative

The underlying philosophy of the new incentive system embedded in the contract was focused on providing incentives for spectacular performance. It precisely illustrates the abundance philosophy rather than the deficit gap or problem-solving philosophy. The contract was not open-ended—the company could earn a maximum amount—and a minimum amount was specified even if all performance targets were missed. The two key principles upon which this type of incentive arrangement was based were summarized by the CEO.

> First, force yourself to visualize a spectacular outcome and create an incentive system to reach it. Incentivize people to be outstanding. Second, be more generous with workers than you would normally consider. Provide workers with a lot of payback—lifestyle-changing payback.
>
> Contributor 1—Senior Executive, CH2MHill

To be effective, the incentive system associated with these faster and higher levels of performance could not simply be reserved for the company or for senior executives. Rather, extra incentives had to be made available to employees.

> At least $90 million of the $460 million in profit [by 2003] was distributed in incentives. If we had not done this, we think we would have earned only about $200 million as a company. Sharing the profits with employees created far more revenues than would otherwise have oc-

curred. Plus, it gives employees a sense of pride, success, and career opportunities.

Contributor 10—Senior Executive, Kaiser-Hill

Individual employees were recognized and rewarded with financial incentives when they performed in extraordinary ways. For example:

> One of the issues we were having on the south side was that although we didn't have highly contaminated stuff, we had lots of little stuff that had to go in cargo containers. But the cargo containers wouldn't balance right. So we were doing blocking and bracing and trying to find ways that the cargo would stay balanced so that we didn't have any issues while it was in transit. Well, one of the workers for a subcontractor went home and, in his basement, constructed these boxes for the cargo container that solved the problem. For three months he tried to get his manager to pay attention to him, and the guy just kept blowing him off. Finally, he brought his boxes in, and everybody looked at them and went "Wow, those are perfect." Well, we wrote him a check for $2,500 the next week.

Contributor 9—Senior Executive, Kaiser-Hill

The distribution of financial incentives to all employees was a hallmark of the system. Specifically, whereas salaries were set at market rates at Rocky Flats, benefits were established at levels significantly above market rates. The comments of two former Rocky Flats CEOs are illustrative.

> We have a strong view that incentives drive behavior. Therefore, at least 20 percent of profits were bonused.
>
> Contributor 9—Senior Executive, Kaiser-Hill

> Everyone gets incentive pay. My secretary received $15,000 per year. Most secretaries get $6,000 to $7,000 per year. Average steelworkers earn around $46,000. But with overtime and bonuses they can earn an extra $67,000. So a lot of steelworkers here are earning more than $100,000.
>
> Contributor 10—Senior Executive, Kaiser-Hill

This former CEO personally received approximately 300 percent of an annual salary at the completion of the project. In other words, lifestyle-changing incentives amounted to the opportunity to earn significantly more money than most employees ever thought possible. But, of course, they had to accept the associated risk. The possibility also existed that employees would earn next to nothing since, after 2000, corporate revenues were based almost entirely on incentives. Though it was a completely new way to think about compensation, even officials in the steelworkers union were supportive of the incentive system.

As an example, in one year, $18 million was distributed in incentives, with $8 million going to the executive pool, $8 million going to the general employee pool, an incentive of $4,200 for each union employee, and a completion bonus of $3,000 for each employee. Of course, the incentive system was tied to the completion date, so employees were motivated to complete the project faster rather than prolonging the work just to stay on the payroll. For example, if the project closed in 2005 (60 years early), 100 percent of the available bonus was received. Closure in 2006 would merit a 50 percent bonus, and a 2007 closure date would merit a zero percent bonus. Said one Rocky Flats CEO:

> This is to ensure that people don't slow down just to earn more money. But people are not slowing down to drag this out. They're too excited about what they're doing.

Contributor 10—Senior Executive, Kaiser-Hill

An important feature of the incentive system was the use of "safe units" or "scrip." This innovative system of pay distribution was described this way by one Rocky Flats CEO.

> Incentives were distributed as if we were achieving the actual 1999 cost structure (that is, a total project cost of $3.56 billion). So some

> bonus was given in cash (30 percent), and some was given in safe units. Safe units stay with workers until they leave—sort of like stock options. The safe units increase in value the closer we get to hitting the target. The point is to give everyone a stake in the outcome from the beginning.
>
> Contributor 9—Senior Executive, Kaiser-Hill

Scrip, or safe units, served a function similar to stock options, with the value of the safe units increasing as the organization came closer to accomplishing its objectives. The objectives at Rocky Flats were enormously aggressive in both speed and outcomes, of course, so scrip served as a means to encourage extraordinary performance. For example, the corporate CEO reiterated the philosophy that lay behind the use of scrip.

> This is how we began. Imagine an ideal outcome—an amazingly aggressive schedule or a spectacular result. Now, let's attach the scrip to that outcome. The closer we get to the ideal outcome, the more your scrip is worth. We will give some incentive in cash, but most will be in scrip at first. The workforce, therefore, has an incentive to get the job done faster.... The system makes these assumptions: If we hit the maximum point, here is the amount we're willing to share with workers. The trouble is, we

don't know if we will actually hit the ideal target until the end. So we will issue scrip in place of some of the cash compensation. In 1995 it was 20 percent cash, 80 percent scrip. In 2000 it was 35 percent cash and 65 percent scrip. In 2003 it was 40 percent cash and 60 percent scrip. If we hit the ideal target, the scrip will be worth $1.00 per share. This serves as a retention tool, because if people are laid off or transferred, they keep their scrip. If they quit, they lose it. So competitors cannot afford to hire away our people, since their scrip makes them too expensive for a competing firm to hire.

Contributor 1—Senior Executive, CH2MHill

Employees were incentivized as if they had already achieved the spectacular target—in other words, so that the amount of compensation that could be earned was far higher than that associated with normal or usual performance. However, to create motivation to actually achieve this extraordinary level of performance, part of the compensation was given in scrip. The scrip escalated in value as the spectacular target was approached. Employees were motivated to stay at Rocky Flats to work, therefore, because their normal salary, plus the value of their scrip, priced them out of the competitive market. If they remained until they were laid off as part of closure, their compensation was high enough to be lifestyle changing.

Scrip was also used to create individual incentives for teamwork and performance. The amount of scrip available to a specific employee, for example, was partially determined by his or her individual performance in addition to that of the unit.

> There was peer pressure on the various projects at the site. Plus, there was financial incentive. If my project was doing well, I would get, say, 5,000 units of scrip to distribute. If my project was not doing so well, I might only get 2,000 to distribute. Therefore, the value of the scrip depended on the success of the entire project, so there was enormous pressure for everyone to do well.
>
> Contributor 37—Former Managers, Kaiser-Hill

As might be expected, the level of skepticism was high when the idea of scrip was first introduced. The unions, for example, rejected the idea of scrip and opted for incentive bonuses instead. As it turned out, union employees could have earned much more under the scrip system than under the incentive bonus system, but that outcome was not obvious at the outset. In fact, most employees were leery.

> The union would not accept the idea of scrip. Instead, they selected a bonus system based on our exceeding the schedule. Everyone gets the

> same bonus per hour—which is $2.00 per hour—so, if we complete by December 15, 2005, everyone gets $5,000. If we complete by March 2006, everyone gets $3,000. If we don't finish until December 2006, everyone gets $1,000. The union will actually earn less than if they had opted for scrip instead of a bonus system. But, at first, a lot of people thought scrip was silly. People felt that they wanted to sell scrip for 10 cents. Now people believe that we will hit or exceed the maximum value, so scrip is not sold at all ... even for $1.00 per unit.
>
> Contributor 1—Senior Executive, CH2MHill

As the completion date approached, a slight variation in the scrip incentive system was introduced. To provide an incentive for employees to continue to work at top speed and to exceed the scheduled closure date, half of the scrip to be issued in the last two years of the project was provided in one lump sum, with the other half scheduled to be distributed upon completion.

> For the last 24 months, we took the last years' scrip and gave half up front. The other half will be given in 2005 or 2006, when the project is complete. We are trying to provide an accelerated distribution so that people don't hang around for another year just to accumulate scrip.

The keys to the abundance-oriented incentive system, in other words, were to share a substantial portion of earnings with employees, based on the assumption that the most ideal target had been successfully achieved. The financial incentives were substantial enough that they could potentially provide lifestyle change, but the "safe unit" concept that postponed immediate cash payouts prevented cheating and subversion.

Summary

As a whole, these Market or Compete quadrant factors highlight the roles played by aggressive goals and incentives and the excitement that is associated with visible and substantial progress. In the case of Rocky Flats, success bred success, and the pressure to perform was clearly enhanced by visible progress. One Rocky Flats executive described the positive energy and exhilaration associated with performance that was succeeding even the most optimistic estimates in 2003.

> Well, it's August 2002, and right now we are over $80 million positive cost variance. Right now, we are about $50 million positive schedule variance, I believe. It's so exciting to report that if we keep performing the way we are performing, we have a chance to finish by early or mid-2006. Recall that our contract has a date of December

> 14 or 15, 2006, to be complete. We're ahead of that schedule, and it's so exhilarating.
>
> Contributor 7—Manager, Kaiser-Hill

Even this comment was below ultimate performance achievements, because the project was actually completed in October 2005. Ironically, these achievements could have been even greater, according to a senior executive, if more resources had been provided by DOE. That is, he estimated that the project would have been even further ahead of schedule, and the success even more dramatic, if the project had been provided with more money to spend in the short run. The constraint on spectacular performance was the inability to invest in areas that would produce even greater efficiency and faster progress. In early 2004 he stated:

> If we had another $50 million to spend, we could go even faster, but we are cash-constrained. We even tried to borrow from DOE based on our future allocations, but they would not allow it. We are slower than we could be if we had more resources.
>
> Contributor 1—Senior Executive, CH2MHill

In sum, the Market quadrant identifies enablers that motivate aggressive performance and that manage entities residing in the external environment. In particular, managing external stakeholders and implementing an abundance-based external political strategy, coupled with providing incentives to take bold actions and perform at spectacular levels, were the key enablers that fostered positively deviant behavior at Rocky Flats. Paying attention to external factors as well as the internal factors helped account for success. Figure 8.2 summarizes the theme and key enablers associated with this quadrant.

Among the conclusions to be drawn from these enablers are the following:

- Positive and proactive political strategies must replace more traditional political strategies.
- Competing entities must be coordinated with positive power brokers.
- Adversaries should become stakeholders.
- Multiple external stakeholders should be consolidated and aligned.

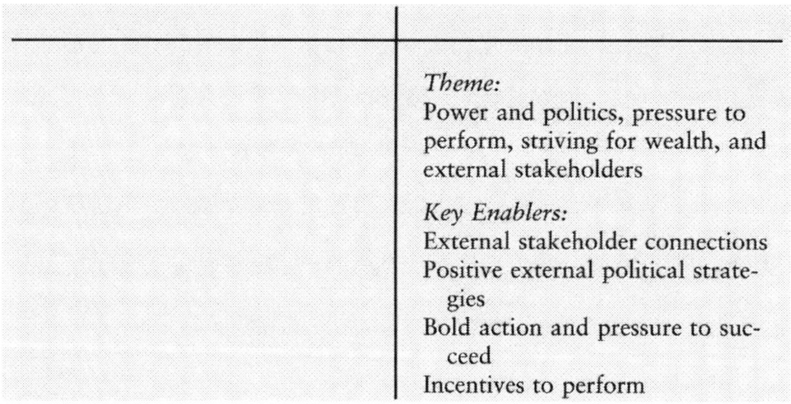

Figure 8.2 KEY ENABLERS IN THE MARKET OR COMPETE QUADRANT

- ***Demanding extraordinary, timely, measurable results over the long term mitigates burnout when linked to an abundance approach.***
- ***Managers should evaluate the performance of workers, and workers should evaluate the performance of managers, with both entailing employment consequences.***
- ***The possibility of lifestyle change should be made available with financial incentives.***
- ***Incentives should be offered in order to visibly change behavior, not merely to signal appreciation.***
- ***Employees should be rewarded as if they have already achieved spectacular performance targets.***
- ***Proactivity, not reactivity or recalcitrance, in sharing performance news builds trust.***
- ***Small wins as well as small problems should be surfaced quickly and early.***

9

Leadership Principles for Spectacular Performance

We have addressed three of the four major questions asked in the book: *How did extraordinary performance occur at Rocky Flats? Why does the abundance approach work, and what explains success? What levers can leaders use to achieve similar results?* This last chapter addresses the final question: *What are the prescriptions for extraordinary success? What is different from conventional leadership?*

The transformational success at Rocky Flats was not supposed to be achievable. No previous organization had successfully accomplished this set of outcomes. No plutonium building had previously been taken down. A thousand glove boxes had never been decontaminated. Radioactive contamination in the ground on such a large site had never before been cleaned up to a standard that exceeded original federal guidelines. No unionized facility had ever worked itself out of a job at this rate of efficiency and enthusiasm. No organization had ever completed this kind of work $30 billion under budget. Even the Government Accountability Office (GAO) had little confidence that closure of a successful Rocky Flats could be achieved in a time frame even close to that targeted.

A high-ranking DOE executive stated that no other current DOE project was being pursued in the same manner as at Rocky Flats, and there was little confidence that this project could meet its own optimistic aspirations.

> Current DOE projects are not being pursued in the same way as Rocky Flats. In fact, there may be a regression toward the old way of doing things instead of toward the Rocky Flats approach.... Organizational culture is the key resistance factor—legacy issues such as the same systems, processes, and aspirations. People think that they can get new results using the same processes, the same teams, and the same culture. That's the definition of insanity.
>
> Contributor 23—Senior Executive, DOE

Changing organizations is a difficult and complicated task, and large-scale transformational changes are especially intractable. Between half and 80 percent of organizational change efforts fail—ranging from relatively simple adjustments, such as a new performance appraisal system or relocating personnel, to more complicated changes, such as downsizing, mergers or acquisitions, or adopting a new competitive strategy (Cameron & Quinn, 2006; Cameron, 1997).

The record is equally poor at the individual level. A well-documented finding in medicine relates to individuals who had recently undergone heart bypass surgery (Deutschman, 2005). They were given a choice by their physicians of changing their lifestyles or of dying. A consistent result over several decades, including thousands of patients, is that only about 10 percent actually make the change. More than 90 percent of people choose death rather than implement major changes in their lives. Opposition to change is universal and persistent.

On the other hand, some especially effective change programs have been devised for heart patients with a success rate approaching 80 percent (Ornish, 1996). These programs emphasize the pursuit of positive factors rather than the avoidance of negative factors. An emphasis on abundance gaps replaces a focus on deficit gaps, so that patients are given something to which they can look forward rather than merely being reminded that they will die without change. An abundance approach dramatically increases the probability of success. This does not mean that physicians or patients ignore negative factors, of course; it means that they target abundance gaps, not deficit gaps, to guide future activities.

This focus on abundance gaps as a predictor of successful change is what explains extraordinary success at Rocky Flats. The adoption of an abundance approach to transformational change—rather than a focus on the obstacles, problems, and failures that had characterized the facility in the past—is the primary key to illuminating how Rocky Flats achieved the impossible. Rather than motivation based on fear—which is often present in a crisis in the short term—long-term change and extraordinary success must rely on positive approaches to change.

Our account of the Rocky Flats story, in other words, centers on what worked, what enabled success, what accounted for spectacular performance. These factors were primarily abundance factors—keys to achieving extraordinary success—and are enablers that literally made the impossible possible. We do not systematically ignore or omit negative or problematic factors, but we report what the individuals and groups associated with Rocky Flats actually stated was the focus of their activities. These were overwhelmingly positive factors—optimistic, forward-looking, meaningful outcomes—for which they were striving.

Trials and errors, blips and bloopers, false starts and missteps occurred along the way, of course, and the changes were not immediate, as pointed out by participants in the process (cited in earlier chapters).

> One cannot underestimate the amount of time and the cultural changes that have to be implemented in order to get large groups of people in various organizations to think about their work in a project fashion.
>
> It took years to change the attitude of the workforce. They hated us at first.
>
> We were slow in engaging the workforce until we got management on the floor with the workers.

In fact, right up until the final days, changes were being made to ensure a successful and safe completion of the project.

> One of the things that we discovered is that hazards become routine. The crews got so confident about their ability to take glove boxes apart and about their ability to solve problems on the spot that they started going beyond the boundaries of the scope, and they stopped stopping work.... That was about the time we said, "You know what? Emphasis on schedule isn't getting us anything." And we literally took down every sign in every building that talked about schedule.... We made the schedule shift because what we wanted to emphasize at that point was do it right the first time. Take whatever time it takes to do it right the first time. In the end, the schedule will take care of itself.
>
> Contributor 9—Senior Executive, Kaiser-Hill

On the other hand, spectacular performance depended on capitalizing on what worked rather than being effective in addressing what didn't. This outcome is consistent with recent scholarly research emphasizing the power of a positive orientation in helping organizations improve (Cameron, Dutton, & Quinn, 2003). Examples of some of these findings will illustrate what we mean.

Research by the Gallup Organization (Clifton & Harter, 2003) found that when workers have a chance to do what they do well at work, productivity is double that of standard organizations. Giving people feedback on their strengths leads to almost one and a half times greater productivity than providing feedback on weaknesses or what went wrong. In other words, an emphasis on positive factors, strengths, and abundance gaps has been shown to produce a great deal more success than a focus on negative factors.

Cameron and colleagues studied the development and manifestation of virtuousness in organizations—institutionalized compassion, forgiveness, integrity, trust, optimism, and so on—and found a link between these factors in organizations and significantly higher performance (Cameron, Bright, & Caza, 2004). That is, profitability, productivity, quality, customer satisfaction, employee retention, and innovation all were higher in organizations demonstrating virtuous behaviors—attributes that represent the highest aspirations of the human condition—compared to normal organizations.

Goddard, Hoy, and Hoy's (2003) research on the performance of schools found that collective efficacy—a sense of collective capability, strength, and positivity—was the major predictor of school success, when school success was measured by test scores, learning, and academic achievement of students. In fact, a positive sense of collective efficacy was more important in accounting for school performance than the racial makeup, socioeconomic status, or previous academic records of the students.

Consistent with these findings, the success at Rocky Flats can be accounted for by an abundance approach to change. Different constituencies attributed the success of the project to different factors, of course, and the number and variety of factors identified were substantial. One of the key lessons learned from this study, in fact, is that spectacular success is not achievable with just a few simple strategies or leadership techniques. For example, when asked to provide a summary of the fundamental enablers of success at Rocky Flats, or to recommend the keys of success to other organizational change efforts, unionized employees attributed success to

> treating employees right, not requiring people to work if they have a safety concern, not wavering on policies, senior executives on the floor with workers, respect and dignity for everyone, well-paid positions, not disadvantaging retirees when Kaiser-Hill goes away, spot bonuses, performance bonuses, and Cold War veteran benefits.
>
> Contributor 12—Union Officers, Kaiser-Hill

First-line supervisors identified a slightly different set of summary factors:

Kaiser-Hill involved the workforce and listened to them. They upgraded the equipment. You had to spend money to earn money. They brought in managers from outside. [Alan] Parker brought the unions and management together. They were team oriented. They said: "This is your mission; no one has done it before, so we can't tell you how. But you're accountable." They are still bringing in the people we need with special expertise. They reward people who have good ideas. There is team thinking in solving problems—everyone has come up with ideas to make this faster. We have constantly changing challenges, quick procedure changes, streamlined organization, and consistent direction and consistent management principles.

Contributor 11—Supervisors, Kaiser-Hill

One former CEO at Rocky Flats summarized the key enablers as

360 strategy and planning, vision and boldness, lifestyle-changing incentives, relentless pressure and tenacity, a singular focus, lots of tactics, changing people so the right people were in the right positions, communication with employees, refusal to behave as the old culture wanted us to behave, and a refusal to go back.

Contributor 9—Senior Executive, Kaiser-Hill

A senior DOE official's summary list of enablers included

> being clear about the task; doing only that which added value, and not doing things that don't; the lifestyle-changing incentive system; efficient downsizing; clear expectations of people, and lots of changes in personnel; accountability for results from everyone, from the contractor to DOE administration; projectizing and measuring; a whole-brain leadership team, including visionaries, implementers, and tacticians; clear meaning and purpose; relationships, trust, and credibility with everyone; great attitudes of employees; the new DOE contract; external constituency support; a culture of innovativeness; and multiple sources of leadership.
>
> Contributor 23—Senior Executive, DOE

Because of their number and variety, we used the Competing Values Framework to organize the various enablers of extraordinary success, highlighting the fact that enablers that were seemingly in conflict with one another are especially needed to ensure high performance. The necessity of this tension is, in fact, an important lesson related to positive deviance. As discussed in chapter 4, the Competing Values Framework separates internal maintenance activities from external positioning activities, and it separates flexibility and change-oriented activities from stability-

and control-oriented activities. Pursuing both orientations at once is an underlying explanation for making the impossible possible. Paradoxical tensions and excellence are connected.

Some of the key enablers at Rocky Flats were categorized as being typical of the Adhocracy or Create quadrant—*a shared vision, symbolic leadership, innovation and creativity, and meaningful work.* Others were typical of the opposite quadrant in the framework, the Hierarchy or Control quadrant—*goal clarity; new government contracts; detailed planning, projectizing, measurement, and accountability; and stable funding.* Some enablers focused on the human side of change, typical of the Clan or Collaborate quadrant—*organizational culture change, collaboration, trust and credibility, and human capital and social relationships.* Other enablers represented the opposite emphasis, a focus on the external environment and on results that are typical of the Market or Compete quadrant—*external stakeholder engagement, external political strategies, bold action and pressure to succeed, and incentives to perform.*

On the surface, these summary enablers may not seem to be unusual or surprising. For the most part, however, they are not commonly practiced in most organizations. In fact, the explanation of the dramatic success achieved at Rocky Flats can be recapitulated by contrasting conventional leadership principles prior to 1995 with the abundance approach that characterized Rocky Flats after 1995. These conventional principles were almost universal prior to 1995, but they began to be supplemented by abundance principles upon the arrival of Kaiser-Hill. By the time the closure contract was signed in 2000, abundance principles permeated the Rocky Flats facility. We summarize below the transitions made at Rocky Flats from conventional leadership principles used before 1995—which are typical of most organizations—to abundance principles, which led to extraordinary performance.

Conventional Leadership Principles Versus Abundance Leadership Principles

The following leadership principles summarize what was learned from the spectacular success at Rocky Flats. They incorporate the enablers that were illustrated in the previous chapters. That is, this discussion highlights the differences between abundance-oriented practices and conventional practices, and it demonstrates the fact that abundance-oriented leadership is usually positively deviant in most organizations.

Admittedly, we have highlighted an unusually large number of leadership principles, but we adopted this strategy on purpose. We want to draw attention to the fact that multiple levers are needed, multiple leadership practices are necessary, and multiple initiatives are required to enable spectacular success. Making the impossible possible is not a single-digit endeavor. We propose that each of these principles was essential to Rocky Flats' success. These leadership principles were illustrated in the quotations reported in earlier chapters, so we provide only a brief summary here.

It is also important to note that the headline descriptors that characterize *conventional leadership principles* and *abundance leadership principles* are not meant as binary opposites. They are better thought of as points on a continuum where the left-hand point is focused on reaching satisfactory or effective performance. The right-hand point is focused on reaching positive deviance and extraordinarily successful performance. In most cases they are not mutually exclusive. Elements of both types of leadership principles are often typical of extraordinary success.

CONVENTIONAL PRINCIPLES	ABUNDANCE PRINCIPLES
General Leadership Principles	
1. Problem-solving and deficit gaps	1. Virtuousness and abundance gaps

Managers in organizations usually focus on diagnosing and addressing problems, challenges, and obstacles. In fact, successful managers are typically defined as successful problem-solvers. Moreover, a great deal of emphasis in business education and management training is placed on the case method—the analysis of problems and issues in organizations which lead to recommendations regarding how to resolve them. This orientation occurs for good reason, of course, since organizations are often fraught with problems, organizations may fail if they don't pay attention to weaknesses and liabilities, and some problems can be lethal. Adopting a Pollyanna perspective, wearing rose-colored glasses, or just thinking positively is not sufficient to produce extraordinary performance.

At Rocky Flats, problems were not ignored or overlooked, but leaders also focused on abundance gaps—the differences between effective performance and extraordinary performance. Leaders worked to close those gaps. That is, they focused less on obstacles than on opportunities, less on impediments than on virtuousness. They worked toward the highest achievement possible. From our discussion in chapters 1 and 2, we concluded that

- The impossible is made possible by the abundance approach to change.
- An abundance approach to change helps produce a heliotropic effect.
- Unlocking heliotropic effects in organizations, and among employees, leads to extraordinary performance.
- Adopting an abundance approach also produces amplifying and buffering benefits, so an up-

ward spiral of improvement can be created as a result of abundance leadership.

- Regardless of external circumstances—whether difficult and resistive or comfortable and conducive—adopting an abundance approach to change is always possible.

CONVENTIONAL PRINCIPLES	ABUNDANCE PRINCIPLES
2. A single heroic leader	2. Multiple leaders playing multiple roles

Accounts of the heroic leader are ubiquitous in the popular business press and in scholarly accounts of successful organizational change. It is comforting to believe that a single individual can turn an organization around, lead the team to victory, or create success. Conversely, when organizations do not do well, the leader usually takes the blame, gets fired, or is vilified. When the team loses, the coach gets the boot. The story of Rocky Flats makes clear, however, that multiple leaders in multiple locations representing multiple groups are essential for success to be achieved. No single leader could have produced these results. In most organizations, in fact, a single leader cannot produce extraordinary success. Change, especially transformational change, is always a product of multiple leaders. Dramatically successful leadership is always plural. From our analysis in chapters 1 and 3, we concluded that

- Leadership is embodied in multiple individuals and has multiple sources.
- Three different leadership roles are necessary for spectacular change to occur—idea champion, sponsor, and orchestrator.

CONVENTIONAL PRINCIPLES	ABUNDANCE PRINCIPLES
3. One leader from beginning to end	3. A continuity of leaders

Successful leaders are usually assumed to enact the change process from beginning to end. Models of transformational leadership include steps such as creating readiness for change, overcoming resistance, articulating a vision, generating commitment, and institutionalizing the change (Cameron, 2005a). It is almost always assumed that a single leader initiates these steps and leads the organization to a successful conclusion. Heroes finish the job. At Rocky Flats, however, multiple successors at the facility itself, in DOE, in the Colorado governor's office, in the steelworkers union, and in community groups each experienced leadership transitions, but each maintained a consistency of direction. Continuity of vision, goals, and aspirations was maintained. At the same time, of course, each leader brought his or her own special strengths and emphases to the project, but the consistency of the abundance orientation was never lost. Multiple leaders acting in conjunction and coordination with one another were necessary. From our analysis in chapter 3, we concluded that

- Continuity and consistency in leadership are required over time.

CONVENTIONAL PRINCIPLES	ABUNDANCE PRINCIPLES
4. Congruence and consistency	4. Paradox and contradiction

Most models of organizational success are based on the idea that strategies, structures, culture, routines, incentives, and managers' styles must be consistent and aligned. Effectiveness is assumed to be based on congruence. Leaders typically are charged with coordinating the various aspects of their organizations. Popular approaches to corporate strategy emphasize alignment. Of course, alignment is crucial in organizations, as evidenced in research by Cameron and Mora (2003), in which the success or failure of mergers and acquisitions could be predicted with 95 percent accuracy, depending on the congruence and alignment of the two organizations' cultures.

At Rocky Flats, however, simultaneous opposites were also present, and conflicting strategies were part of the reason for dramatic success—such as a focus on taking care of people along with tough and demanding expectations for performance; risk-taking and innovation along with careful planning and tight controls; a focus on external stakeholder involvement along with building internal trust and collaboration; and a focus on measurement, milestones, and predictability along with symbolic messages attached to a long-term vision. An important insight from the

Competing Values Framework is that simultaneous opposites, tensions, and paradox are indicative of and necessary for extraordinary performance. From our analysis in chapter 4, we concluded that

- The successful leadership of extraordinary change requires the pursuit of simultaneously conflicting strategies.

Principles Related to the Adhocracy or Create Quadrant

This quadrant emphasizes activities that facilitate innovation and risk, and foster visionary thinking, through symbolic leadership.

CONVENTIONAL PRINCIPLES	ABUNDANCE PRINCIPLES
5. Left-brain visions—logical, rational, and sensible—with SMART goals	5. Right-brain visions—symbolic, emotional, and meaningful—with profound purpose

Virtually all organizations have vision statements. They are printed on laminated cards, explained in the front of annual reports, and articulated in various ways to employees and shareholders. They are usually statements of values, goals, and aspirations for success. By and large, employee behavior is not affected much by vision statements. It is driven more by SMART goals. SMART goals are Specific, Measurable, Aligned, Reachable, and Time-bound. Much evidence exists suggesting that setting SMART goals is more likely to lead to achievement than is merely articulating an organizational vision statement. In the presence of strong pressure to achieve an aggressive goal in a short amount of time, it is understandable that the energy and effort of employees would be focused on achieving short-term goals and immediate tasks.

At Rocky Flats, specific goals were also attached to a special kind of vision. The vision was embedded in stories, symbols, profound purpose, and symbolic activities such as the removal of razor wire fences, guard towers, and headquarters buildings. Symbolic, emotional, and right-brain elements received a substantial amount of emphasis. The source of positive energy and of steady progress became attached to the inspiring vision more than to immediate goals. Short-term achievements became part of a broader goal. The presence of a vision with profound purpose ensured that a focused goal orientation was embedded in an orientation toward abundance. From our analysis in chapter 5, we concluded that

- A positive vision of abundance must take priority over a problem-centered or deficit-based vision.
- The vision must not emerge from the senior leader alone; it must be created by and shared among all relevant constituencies.
- Effective visions must have more emphasis on right-brain elements than on left-brain elements, so that imagery provides inspiration.
- Positively deviant goals guiding organizational performance must come from multiple sources, not just from the top of the organization.

CONVENTIONAL PRINCIPLES	ABUNDANCE PRINCIPLES
6. Consistency, stability, and predictability	6. Revolution and positive deviance

Especially when an organization is engaged in work where safety is at a premium and mistakes cannot be tolerated (for instance, a severe accident or fire would have destroyed all the success accomplished at Rocky Flats up to that point, not to mention endangering the entire eastern slope of the Rocky Mountains), a safe, predictable, and stable orientation is typical and understandable. Maintaining consistency and continuity is typically assumed to be the chief prerequisite of success. At Rocky Flats, however, revolutionary thinking and innovativeness were also encouraged and supported. Solving problems as they arose, experimenting with new procedures, and challenging rules in the service of achieving more efficiency and effectiveness were typical of almost all workers—top to bottom. As a result, more than 200 innovations were created by employees who aimed at finding ways to accomplish work better, faster, and safer. Some efforts failed, but many led to extraordinary success. From our analysis in chapter 5, we concluded that

- Leaders must strive for positive deviance, so that aspirations represent revolutionary, not merely successful, performance.
- Leaders must institute symbolic events that signal the ideal future.

CONVENTIONAL PRINCIPLES	ABUNDANCE PRINCIPLES
7. Personal benefits and advantages	7. Meaningfulness beyond personal benefits

Most motivational systems in organizations focus on providing benefits to employees in order to generate commitment and engagement. Financial incentives, opportunities for promotion, and flexible working hours are examples of ways in which employee commitment is encouraged. Employees stay engaged because they obtain the benefits that they want. Obtaining an advantage over others and building personal stature are fundamental assumptions in an achievement-oriented society. At Rocky Flats, however, personal benefits were supplemented by a profound purpose associated with the work. People stayed engaged because they were devoted to the meaningfulness of the vision and the benefits that would accrue to others beyond their lifetimes. Instead of "I got what I want, so I'll stay engaged," at Rocky Flats the motive was "I believe in, and care deeply about, what we are doing, so I'll go the extra mile." Meaningfulness trumped greed. A sense of calling in the work dominated a mere careerist orientation. This sense of calling could not be superimposed by top management but had to be individually accepted. From our analysis in chapter 5, we concluded that

- The objective must include a profound purpose, or meaningfulness, beyond personal benefit and immediate outcomes.

CONVENTIONAL PRINCIPLES	ABUNDANCE PRINCIPLES
8. Organizations absorb the risks of failure and benefits of success	8. Employees share the risks of failure and rewards from success

In conventional government contracts, and in almost all organizational contracts with employees, the organization accepts the majority of the risk of failure. If revenues sink, or if unexpected negative events occur, employees still receive financial remuneration and the organization absorbs the loss (assuming that ethical lapses have not occurred). With the exception of decisions to downsize, requests for concessions in wages and benefits, or, alternatively, offering unexpected bonuses, organizations absorb financial losses or reap the benefits of extraordinary success while employees retain the same level of compensation. At Rocky Flats, however, employees accepted a major portion of the risk of failure because a substantial part of their compensation was in the form of scrip. If the organization did not achieve goals, or it earned less than expected, remuneration to employees would have been severely affected. Employees would have earned much less had success not been achieved. On the other hand, they also were in a position to earn a great deal more if they were successful. From our analysis in chapter 5, we concluded that

- Employees must share in the risk of failure, so that the financial burden of missteps and mistakes is not borne entirely by the organization.

- The source of the contract—or the governing entity—and the recipient of the contract must share risk equally.

Principles Related to the Hierarchy or Control Quadrant

This quadrant emphasizes activities that carefully control processes and maintain stability in goals and funding.

CONVENTIONAL PRINCIPLES	ABUNDANCE PRINCIPLES
9. Downsizing at the expense of people	9. Downsizing for the benefit of people

A great deal of evidence suggests that downsizing produces a variety of negative consequences in organizations. Organizational performance almost always deteriorates but, most important, workers are harmed, lose trust, and bear the personal cost of job elimination (Cameron, 1998). Rigidity and resistance tend to escalate, anger and depression permeate the climate, and leaders tend to be scapegoated and criticized. At Rocky Flats, however, the focus was on using downsizing to produce advantages for employees. These advantages included long-term health insurance coverage, Cold War veterans benefits, high levels of incentive pay upon project completion, and, where possible, continued employment within the larger CH2MHill parent corporation or DOE when Rocky Flats was closed. Importantly, employees benefited financially to an unusually high degree from the rapid closure of the facility. In place of harm, employees realized important benefits. From our analysis in chapter 6, we concluded that

- Downsizing in the workforce must provide advantages and benefits rather than displacement and harm.

CONVENTIONAL PRINCIPLES	ABUNDANCE PRINCIPLES
10. Commitments and priorities based on environmental demands	10. Unalterable commitments and integrity at all costs

It is common for organizations to publicly proclaim that "people are our most important resource," then eliminate their jobs when difficult financial conditions arise. People change, in other words, from being defined as human resources to being defined as human liabilities when environmental conditions deteriorate. Investments in the development of employees—in the form of educational benefits, leadership training, or family leave—are almost always the first to be reduced in tight financial times. Saying one thing and doing another regarding human resources is common practice in organizations. Moreover, changes in environmental demands, alterations in contract provisions, and shifting amounts of risk are likely to cause priorities to change in organizations. Maintaining adaptability by shifting organizational priorities and commitments is an oft-cited strategy for success.

At Rocky Flats, however, a consistent theme among leaders—from senior executives to union stewards and supervisors, and from congressmen to the governor's office—was that all commitments would be kept. Period. Trust and credibility were crucial to the success of the project, and trust was almost entirely dependent on the demonstration of absolute integrity, consistency in keeping promises, and follow-through on commitments. In addition, key priorities remained consistent and firm regardless of environmental conditions and external pressures—clean it up, make it safe, close it down, and engage only in activities that add value. Thus, the overarching priorities were unwavering even if the tactics to achieve those goals were adapted continuously. From our analysis in chapter 6, we concluded that

- Leaders must never compromise the integrity and trustworthiness of the organization, or themselves, for any reason.

CONVENTIONAL PRINCIPLES	ABUNDANCE PRINCIPLES
11. Managing the contractor, attaching resources to performance	11. Managing the contract and ensuring stable funding

It is typical for fastidious monitoring and regular reporting to be required of contractors with whom the federal government—particularly DOE—does business. This is also typical of most contracts in which one organization holds another accountable for results, as in subcontracting or partnership arrangements, as well as in circumstances where managers hold subordinates accountable for expectations associated with contracted obligations. Accountability is required of the recipient of the contract to prove that commitments have been met and outcomes have been achieved. Obtaining resources is dependent on demonstrating progress or accomplishment.

In the case of Rocky Flats, the new contract shifted the focus from managing the contractor (Kaiser-Hill) to ensuring that the contract provisions were clear and consensual, and included incentives for success and penalties for failure. Emphasis was placed on ensuring that the contract was appropriate for giving responsibility to the contractor, and then Kaiser-Hill was allowed to manage the work. Specifications regarding how the work was to be accomplished, and even when specific activities were to be completed, were not included. Importantly, stable resources were guaranteed for the duration of the project. Managing the contract, not the contractor, and ensuring secure resources, while contrary to most conventional arrangements, enabled organizational empowerment, which led, in turn, to remarkable success. From our analysis in chapter 6, we concluded that

- Contracts—or governing entities—should focus on outcomes, not effort, and must offer broad discretion regarding means and methods.
- The contract—or the expectations, vision, goals, and standards—not the contractor—the workers and managers—should be carefully managed.
- Stable resources must be ensured for those engaged in the pursuit of positive deviance.

CONVENTIONAL PRINCIPLES	ABUNDANCE PRINCIPLES
12. Ultimate responsibility and accountability for measurable success at the top	12. Responsibility and accountability for measurable success apply to everyone, including workers, managers, regulators, community organizations, and funders

Responsibility and accountability for attaining results ultimately rest at the top of most organizations. Reports of measurable outcomes usually end up in the hands of senior executives who are assumed to be the strategic decision makers. In that way, senior managers maintain ultimate responsibility for success or failure. In federal contracts, in particular, the senior executives of the contracting firm are held exclusively responsible for obtaining expected results. At Rocky Flats, however, the responsibility for measuring and ensuring results rested with multiple constituencies. Communicating the results of these measures was pointed not just upward but to multiple stakeholders—from community groups to state officials and DOE staff members on site—and measurement became a distributed responsibility rather than a centralized one. Data were shared widely and openly, and measurements occurred not merely because an inspector or regulator required it. Moreover, several stakeholders were made accountable for specific aspects of the process—workers for dismantling contaminated buildings, managers for hitting contract targets, community organizations for advocacy activities, DOE for establishing receiver sites, and Congress for stable funding.

No single entity had complete responsibility for ensuring success, yet these multiple entities were aligned, and accountable, in their activities in order to achieve the desired result. From our analysis in chapter 6, we concluded that

- Multiple stakeholders must share equal responsibility and accountability for extraordinary performance.

CONVENTIONAL PRINCIPLES	ABUNDANCE PRINCIPLES
13. Adaptability and addressing work challenges as they arise	13. Engaging only in value-added activities

When faced with literally hundreds of tasks, unknown risks, challenges never before encountered, and aggressive time deadlines, it is common for organizations to address the critical issues as they arise. Since, by definition, first-time and highly uncertain work is unpredictable, organizations must respond to immediate demands. Remaining flexible is lauded as an organizational strength under most circumstances. At Rocky Flats, however, a cardinal rule was to avoid activities that did not add direct value to the ultimate objective, and to ensure that each activity had a defined scope, budget, time line, and priority. With some notable exceptions where activities were undertaken for symbolic purposes—such as knocking down guard towers or refurbishing a peace garden—the focus was on engaging only in activities that helped achieve the ultimate objective. Though the agility and flexibility to respond to shifting work demands and challenges was maintained, a rigorous control system guided Rocky Flats work activities so that wasted effort, side trips, and non-value-added work were avoided. From our analysis in chapter 6, we concluded that

- Every value-adding activity must be planned, budgeted, and measured, and non-value-adding activities must be avoided.
- The myriad activities and targets must be consolidated into a few key success factors.

Principles Related to the Clan or Collaborate Quadrant

This quadrant emphasizes activities that develop human capital and interpersonal relationships, and nurture a collaborative culture within the organization.

CONVENTIONAL PRINCIPLES	ABUNDANCE PRINCIPLES
14. Building on and reinforcing the current culture	14. Introducing challenges that the culture cannot address

One major reason for failure in organizational change efforts is that the attempted changes contradict the organization's current culture. Challenging or contradicting core values and assumptions is always strongly resisted. Hence, efforts at cultural change are seldom successful, and the modal tendency in organizations is to reinforce and build on the current culture rather than attempt to change it. The primary purpose of culture, in fact, is to maintain stability in an organization's current functioning.

The strategy at Rocky Flats, however, was to introduce challenges that the current culture was not capable of handling, thus forcing an overhaul of the existing values, processes, and basic assumptions. Cultural change was at least partly motivated by making it clear that the traditional values, traditional assumptions, traditional attitudes, and traditional paradigms were not sufficient to achieve the vision of the future. A new abundance-oriented culture was developed in order to replace the traditional one that would not work. From our analysis in chapter 7, we concluded that

- Challenges and opportunities must be created that make the current culture appear inadequate and incapable.

CONVENTIONAL PRINCIPLES	ABUNDANCE PRINCIPLES
15. Decision-making and leadership at the top	15. Employee and union partnership in planning, decision-making, training, evaluation, and discipline

Traditionally, the job of leaders at the top of the organization is to establish plans, goals, and direction. Responsibility for elements such as the incentive system, discipline, training, and important decisions rests with the top management team. Moreover, disagreements between union members' perspectives and management's perspectives are common, and top management usually ends up as the entity in charge of an organization's new direction. A typical reaction by unions to proposed major changes is simply to wait until a replacement team comes in to launch still another new set of initiatives. Passive resistance and, sometimes, outright conflict are typical. Such was the case at Rocky Flats prior to 1995.

Achieving spectacular success at Rocky Flats, however, was dependent on a great deal of listening to and involvement of multiple stakeholders. For example, union officials took on the responsibility of safety training—on their own time—as well as disciplining coworkers. One Rocky Flats CEO, in particular, made it his primary objective to ensure a full and productive partnership with the union. Whereas unions, by definition, are in the business of preserving jobs, the three unions at Rocky Flats actively assisted in the elimination of jobs as part of their major responsibility. Changes in supervisors and managers occurred if subordinates rated these people as acting inconsistently with organizational values and demonstrating poor treatment of workers. Community groups were involved in establishing cleanup standards. Key decisions were often made in collaboration with union members, managers, regulators, and community representatives. From our analysis in chapter 7, we concluded that

- Collaboration among adversaries must be created.
- The abundance approach must be fostered among antagonists.
- Managers and employees should evaluate one another's performance, and both sets of evaluations must have employment consequences.

CONVENTIONAL PRINCIPLES	ABUNDANCE PRINCIPLES
16. Need-to-know information-sharing and physical separation	16. Early, frequent, and abundant information-sharing and colocation

Common practice in organizations engaged in downsizing, not to mention those engaged in highly secretive activities and potentially harmful work, is to share information only on a need-to-know basis. Keeping information close to the vest and avoiding the hassles of explaining details is the typical pattern. Hence, workers are frequently frustrated by not knowing what they want to know on a timely basis. Especially when downsizing is undertaken, communication is almost always restricted (see Cameron, 1998). Similarly, it is almost always the case that evaluations of performance and, therefore, decisions about employment are unidirectional from the top down. Many leaders in organizations experiencing job elimination have reported feeling a siege mentality and, therefore, trying to avoid direct contact with the workforce whose jobs are being eliminated (Cameron, 1994).

At Rocky Flats, however, the rule of thumb was to share information early and often, provide feedback to both internal and external constituencies on a frequent basis, and err on the side of overcommunication. Workers and managers evaluated each other, and those evaluations carried employment consequences. The headquarters building at Rocky Flats was purposely destroyed early in the project in order to co-locate managers and workers in the same facilities and have them share information. They also built in redundancy of safety monitors onsite and tried to preemptively communicate information to community groups and the media offsite—even when the news was unpleasant. An attitude of transparency and an inclination toward dialogue with external constituencies was typical. From our analysis in chapter 7, we concluded that

- Managers and workers should be co-located to enhance collaboration.
- Overcommunication and preemptive information-sharing should be the norm.

CONVENTIONAL PRINCIPLES	ABUNDANCE PRINCIPLES
17. Long-term employment, personal relations, and the use of specialists	17. Long-term employability, professional relations, and retraining

It was not unusual to find employees at Rocky Flats who were the second or third generation employees in their families. A pervading assumption was that nuclear weapons would be needed into the foreseeable future, and the facility would be a source of employment for generations to come. Worker security was an important benefit provided by Rocky Flats. Similarly, job security continues to be a driving force in most unionized environments. However, a common rule of thumb is not to use the workforce who built the facility, or who operated it during production, to tear it apart. Those employees not only have a vested interest in preserving the status quo and protecting their previous worksite, but they don't have the necessary expertise to dismantle the facility and clean it up. Builders and demolition experts are not trained in the same way.

At Rocky Flats, however, the same individuals who operated the facility were hired to dismantle it. They had to prove their capability, of course, and new roles and new skills had to be developed. But investing in and preserving the jobs of the current unionized employees was a key factor in the success achieved. The assumption was made that those who constructed and ran the site best knew the nuances of the system, so their general expertise was supplemented with the specific expertise needed to dismantle the facility. Of course, downsizing the workforce was part of the mission of the facility, so all employees knew that they would eventually lose their jobs. The focus shifted, therefore, from worker employment to worker employability. CH2MHill, the parent company of Kaiser-Hill, took on the responsibility of assisting laid-off employees find employment either within the company in other locations, or through partnerships with the state of Colorado to assist with employment in the greater Denver area. In addition to providing supplementary training and education opportunities, the company advertised the skills and capabilities of soon-to-be-available Rocky Flats employees in newspapers, and it organized job fairs to bring potential employers to the site. Importantly, it allowed nonmanagement workers who would be laid off to choose, within constraints, the timing of their departure rather than controlling when these employees left, thus helping them retain key benefits and accommodate the transition to new employment. Such measures helped make a difficult transition for workers occur more successfully and led to high commitment among employees who remained at the site. From our analysis in chapter 7, we concluded that

- Ensuring trust trumps measurement, control, plans, or communication strategies, so integrity must be maintained at all costs.
- Positive safety nets must be provided for at-risk employees.

Principles Related to the Market or Compete Quadrant

This quadrant emphasizes activities that engage external stakeholders and attach incentives to rigorous, uncompromising performance standards.

CONVENTIONAL PRINCIPLES	ABUNDANCE PRINCIPLES
18. Managing the media	18. Openness with the media early and often

It is generally acknowledged that the media can be a powerful force, positively or destructively, for individuals or organizations. Traditionally, the media had not been a friend or an advocate of Rocky Flats. Having uncovered evidence of accidents or possible escape of radioactive pollution decades before, the media maintained the viewpoint that Rocky Flats was covering up, being deceptive, and stonewalling information flows. Most media coverage of Rocky Flats was skeptical and critical. Under such conditions, it is easy to understand why reluctance to cooperate fully with the media would be predictable. When engaged in pursuing secret goals, risky endeavors, and unpopular work activities, the tendency of most organizations would be to attempt to manage the media by sharing only the news that puts the organization in a positive light. Mistakes would be likely to be hidden, and spinning what news had to be shared in a favorable light would be predictable and understandable.

At Rocky Flats, however, information was shared before it had to be, including information about errors or aberrations. It was not unusual to make announcements of potential problems before anyone outside the facility was aware of them, and to report what was being done to address the issue. Trust and credibility were built by consistent openness with the external news outlets. From our analysis in chapter 8, we concluded that

- Proactivity, not reactivity or recalcitrance, in sharing performance news builds trust.

- Small wins as well as small problems should be surfaced quickly and early.

CONVENTIONAL PRINCIPLES	ABUNDANCE PRINCIPLES
19. Keeping adversaries at a distance and using protective political strategies	19. Making adversaries stakeholders, building relationships, and using positive political strategies

Most organizations become adept at maintaining barriers between themselves and antagonistic external constituencies. Traditionally, renegade stockholders, environmental groups, or protesters were systematically kept at bay by organizations so that these adversaries did not disrupt successful goal accomplishment. As a protective mechanism, certain federal regulatory agencies, the state health department, and community groups had only restricted entry to the Rocky Flats facility for several decades prior to 1989. Physical barriers, armed guards, and information management fostered a culture of secrecy. Employees at Rocky Flats did not share information about their work even with neighbors and friends. Complete isolationism is impossible, of course, so most organizations interact with outside groups, regulators, and legislators through a political process. Politicking by organizations is commonly associated with manipulating important resource providers, ingratiating powerful constituencies, or pressuring power brokers. Protecting Rocky Flats from undue encroachment by federal regulators, government overseers, and activist groups was traditionally an important part of its political strategy.

After 1995, however, leaders at Rocky Flats initiated visits to churches, chambers of commerce, public schools, government agencies, and other interested constituencies to invite participation, express views, and build relationships. Efforts were made to obtain onsite access for these groups in order to diminish the sense of adversarial, secrecy-cloaked relationships. Steps were taken to actively engage such groups—for example, listening to their concerns, involving them in establishing soil pollution standards, and seeking input from them in creating an overall vision for the site. Meetings and focus groups were held at these constituencies' home facilities. Analogous actions were taken at the federal level, where efforts increased to proactively communicate with Congress and regulatory agencies.

In addition, after 1995 the political strategy at Rocky Flats changed focus. It mainly emphasized positive factors such as articulating an inspiring vision to external constituencies and then delivering measurable, verifiable results that led to the accomplishment of that vision. The key emphasis of this positive political strategy was not sugarcoating information or delivering only good news. Rather, it was designed to build trust with important constituencies by producing exceptional results, providing information before it was required, and creating partnerships based on respect and confidence. Logrolling, lobbying, and defensive manipulations were replaced by nontraditional positive influence techniques. From our analysis in chapter 8, we concluded that

- Positive and proactive political strategies must be created.
- Competing entities must be coordinated with positive power brokers.
- Adversaries should become stakeholders.

CONVENTIONAL PRINCIPLES	ABUNDANCE PRINCIPLES
20. Clear, stable performance targets that meet standards coming from the top	20. Escalating performance, virtuousness, and positive deviance taggets from multiple sources

A common rule of thumb in organizations is to establish a clear performance target and then align incentives that achieve the goal. In an environment that is heavily monitored, policies and procedures are rigid, reporting requirements are burdensome, and safety is of utmost concern, it is common for organizations to concentrate on basic requirements and hitting standards exactly. The presence of tight controls almost always fosters responses that focus on meeting minimum requirements. Moreover, these standards, targets, and goals are almost universally handed down from the top of the organization or by the outside regulator.

At Rocky Flats, positive deviance, innovation, and virtuousness also characterized the organization's approach to regulations. Exceeding federal standards for soil cleanup, achieving targets faster and cheaper than required, and fostering employee development even in the midst of downsizing were typical outcomes and quite contrary to mere compliance. Achieving positive deviance rather than acquiescence to stated standards was the goal. Furthermore, targets were constantly refined and altered. Specific objectives in 1995 were not the same as they were in 1998 or 2001. Expectations for performance became even more aggressive as progress was made.

Less than 24 months before the project was completed, for example, the completion goal was 12 months longer than the actual closure date (i.e., it was set at December 2006). What is also unusual is that the escalating goals, targets, and standards came from a coordinated effort among multiple constituencies. Community groups helped establish a standard for soil pollution that exceeded the federal standard by a factor of 13. Union supervisors helped establish a goal for glove box removal that was 25 times more aggressive than the previous performance standard. In other words, the source of performance standards at Rocky Flats did not reside solely in the office of the CEO, the regulators, or past achievement. From our analysis in chapter 8, we concluded that

- Demanding extraordinary, timely, measurable results over the long term mitigates burnout when linked to an abundance approach.

- Multiple external constituencies should be consolidated and aligned.

CONVENTIONAL PRINCIPLES	ABUNDANCE PRINCIPLES
21. Organizational financial benefit from outstanding success	21. Financial generosity and benevolence with employees

Typical financial arrangements in contract work center on the profit margin to be allocated to the contractor upon task completion. Organizations are remunerated on the basis of their costs to complete the work plus a percentage "award fee." Because the award fee is fixed, the organization must keep employee compensation within a narrow range. Employee compensation is defined as a cost that must be kept under control. Furthermore, it is typical to retain as much of the earnings as possible to reinvest in the organization, distribute to stockholders, retain in reserves to maintain flexibility, or stockpile in preparation for new opportunities. The organization, in other words, typically benefits most from financial success. Few organizations distribute an unusually large portion of their revenues to employees.

At Rocky Flats, however, Kaiser-Hill adopted a stance in which employees were the primary beneficiaries of task completion. Based on a negotiated "incentive fee," employee compensation was not fixed. The "scrip" system—employees were paid a portion of their compensation in scrip, assuming that they had already achieved spectacular success—allowed employees to benefit from outstanding performance.

A larger percentage of the incentive fee was allocated to employees than had ever been done previously. The goal was to give people enough financial remuneration that it would change their lifestyles. That is, lifestyle-altering compensation was an explicit objective associated with the project. Generosity rather than stinginess was the value. By the time the project was completed, for example, union workers had the possibility of significantly increasing their annual compensation to well beyond what any other company could afford to pay them. From our analysis in chapter 8, we concluded that

- The possibility of lifestyle change should be made available through financial incentives.
- Incentives should be offered in order to visibly change behavior, not merely to show appreciation.
- Employees should be rewarded as if they have already achieved spectacular performance targets.

Summary

We have recounted the story of an organization making the impossible possible—achieving such extraordinary success that, if it had not actually been accomplished, would have been unbelievable. We have documented—using the accounts of those involved in the change—the key enablers and the crucial practices that accounted for this success. These enablers have been categorized as representing four themes. One theme focuses on innovation, risk-taking, visionary thinking, and symbolic leadership (Adhocracy or Create quadrant). Another theme focuses on the opposite—maintaining stability, carefully controlling processes, having precise objectives, and practicing financial discipline (Hierarchy or Control quadrant). Pursuing these two themes simultaneously—that is, fostering chaos and control at the same time—helped foster positive deviance. We identified a third theme focusing on supportive interpersonal relationships, developing human capital, practicing openness, and nurturing a collaborative culture (Clan or Collaborate quadrant). A fourth theme focuses on the opposite—power and politics, pressure to perform, striving for wealth, and importance of external stakeholders (Market or Compete quadrant). Pursuing these two themes simultaneously—that is, fostering both collaboration and competition—helped explain positive deviance at Rocky Flats.

From an analysis of these various enablers, a number of conclusions were drawn about what leads to positively deviant success. For example, we identified adopting an abundance framework, simultaneously implementing conflicting strategies, relying on multiple sources of leadership, creating an inspiring vision, using symbolic leadership, highlighting the meaningfulness of the work, articulating clear goals, creating innovative government contracts, fostering detailed planning, projectizing the work, measuring precisely, maintaining accountability, assuring stable funding, initiating culture change, collaborating with multiple constituencies, building trust and credibility, developing human capital and social relationships, engaging external stakeholders, using positive external political strategies, fostering bold action, initiating pressure to succeed, and using innovative incentives to perform as among the factors that played an important role in this unusual organizational triumph. These many factors have been summarized into 21 leadership principles meant to guide leadership behavior in creating positively deviant performance.

It is worth repeating that documenting the spectacular success at Rocky Flats is important mainly because these enablers and principles may be applicable to other organizations and to other circumstances. The inherent interest in Rocky Flats resides in the extent to which these factors can be translated into prescriptions for leaders in other types of organizations. This book makes the case that Rocky Flats serves as an important source of inspiration and guidance for leaders in almost any situation in which major change and positively deviant performance are desired. Our belief is summarized by a quotation of Mohandas Gandhi when he was in the midst of leading his own positively deviant success and trying to make the impossible possible:

> Keep your thoughts positive, because your thoughts become your words. Keep your words positive, because your words become your behavior. Keep your behavior positive, because your behavior becomes your habits. Keep your habits positive, because your habits become your values.

Keep your values positive, because your values become your destiny.

APPENDIX I

Caveats and Alternative Views of Rocky Flats' Success

Our emphasis on the achievements at Rocky Flats and the key enablers of successful outcomes may give rise to legitimate concerns that we have ignored contrary data or unfairly biased this account toward the positive. Any story that sounds too good to be true raises questions about whether alternative explanations can account for, or temper, the purported success, or call into question whether success has really been achieved at all. At least two questions should be considered: First, what level of consensus exists that success has been achieved? In other words, the question might be asked: "Success according to whom?" Second, given that what constitutes success in any circumstance is context-dependent, what were the standards upon which success was judged? In other words, the relevant question is: "Success compared to what?"

We want to be clear that, as would be expected, there are stakeholders who consider the cleanup and closure process of Rocky Flats less than spectacular. Disagreement about the implications of nuclear proliferation, national security, public health, community safety, and federal policy related to Rocky

Flats are all likely to color definitions of success and result in a range of views about outcomes.

While we attempt to summarize some of the key concerns about the Rocky Flats cleanup and closure our intent is not to advocate for the desirability or validity of any particular perspective. We are not, for example, taking up the question of whether the 50-year mission of Rocky Flats was desirable. Our consideration is limited to the performance of Kaiser-Hill once the firm received the charge to clean up and close the facility. We must also remind readers that our goal is to consider organizational performance *within* the cleanup and closure standards that were established through complex public policy machinations, not to address the adequacy of such standards.

By way of analogy, much energy has been devoted to understanding Wal-Mart's distribution strategy. It is widely recognized as world-class. To recognize and learn from such success does not mean that one must endorse the firm's overall approach nor fail to consider social consequences of a firm's strategy. Evaluating the success of an organizational actor, or an aspect of that actor's performance, also does not mean that one embraces the "rules of the game" within which such performance occurred.

Thus, analyzing organizational achievements within the context of a nuclear weapons facility is not akin to advocating nuclear proliferation or militarism. Examining the organizational performance that was required to achieve cleanup and closure is not based on the claim that we have the authority or expertise to evaluate the government's cleanup and closure standards. Our claim is simply that achieving those goals represents a remarkable accomplishment and that there is much to be learned from such performance.

Whereas the results achieved at Rocky Flats are measurable and therefore not in question, the extent to which they represent laudable, or even sufficient, performance is a matter of opinion. In this appendix, we highlight some of the concerns about Rocky Flats' performance during cleanup and upon closure. Our hope in doing so is to better define the boundaries of successful performance in this context.

Success According to Whom and Compared to What?

The first reservation relates to the extent to which an unqualified success was really achieved, and whether or not multiple constituencies would all agree that adequate standards of cleanup have been met. There is widespread recognition that Rocky Flats was the site of some of the country's most severe environmental nuclear contamination during its years of active operation, thereby threatening worker health, surrounding communities, and the natural environment. Subsequent analyses suggested that the high level of secrecy maintained at the site, along with the assertion that the Atomic Energy Act shielded it from state and federal environmental regulation, may have amplified the dangers of its operation. Three reservations were expressed by specific constituencies regarding the final state of closure at Rocky Flats.

One concern raised by some stakeholders was that the final levels of soil and water cleanup were not as stringent as they should have been. A second concern was that the process of involving community stakeholders in cleanup decisions was not sufficiently consultative. Third, some suggested that Rocky Flats' performance was not as successful as touted because of problems involving safety incidents and financial penalty. We briefly describe the basis for each of these concerns.

Transforming what was once among the most dangerous nuclear sites in the world to an end state as a wildlife refuge certainly represents an incredible change. Yet, an essential question relates to how clean the end state will be, or how much plutonium will remain in the soil once the facility is cleaned up. Some level of background radiation occurs naturally in all environments. The measure used to calculate remaining plutonium is picocuries per gram of soil. The final cleanup level at Rocky Flats is 50 picocuries per gram (50 pCi/g); some community stakeholders pushed for a standard of 35 pCi/g, based on the recommendations of an independent review conducted by Radiological Assessments Corporation.

Level of Cleanup. One of the reasons for the site being designated as a wildlife refuge, rather than land that could be open to development, is that a wildlife refuge poses less risk to human safety. It does not result in full-time occupancy of the site. It therefore can allow for a less stringent background cleanup level. In the case of a wildlife refuge, calculations about possible risk to human health are based on those of a park ranger working on the site. This risk calculation indicated that such a worker would have slightly higher than a 1 in 500,000 chance of developing cancer by spending a career working on the site, compared to working at any other wildlife refuge.

Another important consideration in determining the ultimate use of the Rocky Flats site was a response to the public's demand for more open space. Proposals had been made, and investigations conducted, to determine if the site could be turned into an industrial park. However, because of the distance from major transportation arteries and the Denver metropolitan area, no firms were willing to relocate to this location, and plans for industrial development or human habitation were abandoned. The open space option was by far the most favored land use.

Concerned stakeholders counter, however, that given the more than 24,000-year half-life of plutonium, it is not reasonable to assume that the site will remain uninhabited for thousands of years. Organizations such as the National Academy of Science have pointed to the risks of assuming that a current land use designation—such as that of wildlife refuge—will endure over hundreds of years. Therefore, they contend, a more reasonable end state cleanup standard is to calculate the risk of residual contamination to someone who is both residing on and cultivating food for personal consumption on the site.

This debate about the different levels of residual contamination centers primarily on cost. The Department of Energy, the Colorado Department of Public Health and Environment, and the Environmental Protection Agency, mindful of the expense of cleaning up and closing a number of sites around the country, have advocated a "risk-based" approach, meaning that these agencies favor allowing for a somewhat greater calculated risk in certain locations in return for more funds to reduce risk in other locations. This approach is currently representative of the federal law. In other words, in areas that are not likely to be inhabited by human beings, higher levels of contamination can be tolerated, whereas more stringent cleanup standards are required when risk to human health is higher. In the case of Rocky Flats, saving large sums of money through rapid closure provided a financial incentive to accept a less stringent cleanup standard when risk to long-term human exposure was deemed less substantial.

Control of Industrial Zone. The Department of Energy is maintaining control of an approximately 1,000 acre parcel area encompassing the industrial zone within Rocky Flats, rather than ceding the entire site to the Department of Fish and Wildlife for conversion to parkland. Because the industrial zone is the area where active nuclear production occurred, this area had the greatest contamination risk. The Department of Energy will continue to monitor this zone. While such monitoring may be precautionary it has raised concerns among some stakeholders who question why the DOE should need to maintain control over this part of the site if the cleanup is complete.

Soil Depth. Another criticism regarding the cleanup levels at Rocky Flats relates to the depth at which the measurement is taken. More specifically, the revised contract in 2000 allowed for a concentration of 50 picocuries of plutonium per gram of soil to remain in the top three feet of soil, but at a depth of three to six feet, the level is allowed to rise to 1,000 picocuries per gram. Below six feet, risk-based standards are applied before additional soil remediation actions are taken. That is, if the risk is deemed sufficient, additional soil cleanup would need to occur. Critics contend that geologic changes over time could result in significant safety issues or the need for more cleanup. Therefore, they consider this standard of cleanup to be short-term and representative of irresponsible stewardship.

Proponents, on the other hand, contend that the contamination below three feet is comparatively minimal to begin with—far short of the specified standard—and this approach concentrates funds on significantly lowering the surface risk, hence providing maximum benefit from the allocated monies. They also contend that the geology of the site makes major subsurface movement unlikely, and removing any deep contaminant would result not only in greater cost but also in major environmental harm. That is, the possibility of spreading any remaining contamination to other areas is even greater if large amounts of soil are significantly disturbed.

Still another area of concern relates to the claim that the standards and methods of measuring contamination levels and determining health risks are themselves faulty or inadequate. Cleanup also means that contaminated materials must be transported elsewhere in the United States. Thus there are risks posed by the transportation of such materials from Rocky Flats to receiver sites. Whereas the risk posed by the existence of these materials might be removed from the Rocky Flats site, it is still present at the facilities to which the waste is transported. These receiver sites, of course, are far from populated areas, and the materials are stored more securely and permanently than they were at the Rocky Flats site. Nevertheless, the contaminated material does not go away. Long-term future risk may still be present.

Stakeholder Influence. The major criticism of the stakeholder dialogue process for negotiating cleanup standards at Rocky Flats was based on the initial 1996 cleanup agreement signed by the Department of Energy (DOE), the Colorado Department of Public Health and Environment (CDPHE), and the Environmental Protection Agency (EPA). This agreement allowed for 651 picocuries per gram of radiation to remain in the soil (compared with the final standard of 50 Picocuries per gram for soil down to a depth of three feet that was achieved at the site). The 651 pCi/g standard would have left Rocky Flats substantially more contaminated than many Pacific island test sites that the government had cleaned up after its atomic bomb detonations. Moreover, this initial agreement contradicted the recommendations of groups that had been convened to represent community interests in the cleanup process. In 1995 the Rocky Flats Future Site Working Group recommended that the site be cleaned up to original background levels, although they acknowledged that the technology did not exist to attain this standard, and no requirement existed at any nuclear site to achieve this level of decontamination. They stated a preference to extend the time line of cleanup over generations, if necessary, in order to reach a pristine level of soil contamination.

This recommendation for complete cleanup was endorsed by the two DOE-funded citizen advisory bodies—the Rocky Flats Local Impacts Initiative and the Rocky Flats Citizens Advisory Board. Thus, the first cleanup agreement (the 1996 RFCA), allowing for a 651 pCi/g level of radiation on the site, was met with strong criticism. Complaints centered on both the cleanup standard itself and the seeming disregard of the input of these two stakeholder groups. Public outcry led the DOE to commission another independent review of the cleanup plan. That recommendation called for a 35 pCi/g cleanup level at Rocky Flats.

Dangerous Precedent. Finally, there is the concern that the accelerated cleanup approach pioneered by Rocky Flats represents a dangerous precedent. Critics of accelerated cleanup contend that it represents the acceptance of comparatively lower cleanup levels and aggressive cost and time schedules which may establish a detrimental precedent for other DOE cleanup sites. In an effort to constrain the overall cost of cleanup of nuclear facilities and to reduce major risk more quickly, shortcuts may be taken in other cleanup efforts. Rocky Flats' aggressive standards could constrain the possibility of addressing risks that emerge in the process of cleanup. In addition, it could make more stringent cleanup levels difficult to achieve because cost and time constraints would not allow for it.

As a case in point, the Rocky Flats site closed months ahead of even the most optimistic 2003 estimates (October 2005 rather than December 2006). Such acceleration saved even more money for the DOE and financially benefited Kaiser-Hill for realizing those savings. Concerned stakeholders assert that in the face of such savings, more resources could be directed to higher cleanup levels while still realizing closure far ahead of the 70-year cleanup schedule and below the initial $36 billion budget.

Clearly, there are understandable reasons for a spirited and critically important debate about the cleanup levels selected at Rocky Flats. Again, our focus is not to defend one standard over another but to describe extraordinary organizational performance within the scope of the standard that was established. This may seem convenient, as it would be hard to applaud an organization for quickly and skillfully achieving an outcome that was widely considered problematic and dangerous. On the other hand, viewpoints contrary to those described in this appendix are presented in the book's chapters, and being cognizant of the complexities associated with defining success and declaring victory are important to acknowledge. Our primary goal in explaining the controversies surrounding Rocky Flats is to provide enough background for readers to make their own determinations about the extent to which this is truly an exemplary story of positive deviance, as we contend.

Safety Concerns

The site improved its safety and operating performance dramatically over a period of years from 1995 onward. It began with safety records far worse than other sites within the DOE complex and achieved far better performance by the time of closure. On the other hand, the site did not avoid controversy regarding safety. In fact, the DOE penalized Kaiser-Hill for a range of infractions by reducing the fees paid for performance. Given the potential seriousness of risks in a nuclear setting, even minor safety errors that do not compromise health and safety can carry hundreds of thousands of dollars in penalties. Kaiser-Hill noted that emphasizing safety was essential to achieving accelerated closure, inasmuch as any compromise of health or safety could result in major stoppages and slowdowns. Nevertheless, the following by academic and journalist Len Ackland, former editor of the *Bulletin of Atomic Scientists* and author of *Making a Real Killing: Rocky Flats and the Nuclear West,* appeared in the *Bulletin of Atomic Scientists* (2001 vol.57, p.6).

> Whether Kaiser-Hill has been doing so with proper attention to safety has been a point of contention with Energy's Barbara Mazurowski. Last January 5 [2001] she sent a blistering memo to Bob Card, then Kaiser-Hill's president. She ticked off several concerns including "inadequate management—at every level and in each project—to ensure safe, productive operations." She listed the $410,000 in fines (fee reduction penalties) that the Energy Department levied against the company during the previous 11 months. She demanded that the company develop a "comprehensive corrective action plan."
>
> "Back in January and previously, everybody was pretty much doing their own thing here," Mazurowski explained in her direct, soft-spoken manner during a recent interview. "We as a site were not focused on safety measures that would improve our performance." And that troubled

Mazurowski, who ran an Energy Department high-level nuclear waste vitrification project in West Valley, New York, before becoming Rocky Flats manager in June 2000. "At West Valley I learned that without a good safety program you can't achieve peak performance." While the Energy Department fines didn't get Kaiser-Hill's attention, the January 5 memo did, she said. And today, "Kaiser-Hill and [DOE] are perfectly aligned in what we have to do to be successful here."

Alan Parker (then President of Kaiser-Hill at Rocky Flats) echoed that sentiment, attributing some of the problems between Energy and Kaiser-Hill to miscommunication. "There were a series of very small events going on that were really irritating and troubling to [DOE]. We were watching those and letting them know we had it under control but they wanted more significant action," he said. "After the January 5th letter we gave them exactly what they wanted."

If everything was cleared up early this year, why then did the Energy Department hit Kaiser-Hill in July with a $385,000 fine, the biggest to date? Mazurowski explained that the fine resulted from violations of the Price-Anderson Act, which regulates nuclear issues such as procurement, procedural compliance, and process control. She noted that all the events cited occurred before her January 5 memo to Kaiser-Hill, that the timing of the fine resulted from a typical lag in paperwork

> processing, and that the findings did not indicate worker injury. Indeed, Energy's announcement of the fine stated, "While none of the violations presented a serious threat to worker health and safety, the events could serve as precursors to more serious incidents."

Ackland's article described incidents that occurred in 2000 and early 2001, and it was clear in more recent interviews with personnel at Rocky Flats and at DOE that the current Rocky Flats leadership had greatly increased safety protocol and performance. Their greatest fear was a significant safety violation or accident that would jeopardize the entire project. Many of the stories we heard from DOE and Kaiser-Hill employees described a climate of mistrust between the contractor and the regulator dating back to the years before Kaiser-Hill took over the project, when a plethora of unattainable "paper milestones" were required by DOE, new nuclear facility standards were superimposed, and preparations were being made for resumption of production. The climate was consistent with Ackland and Mazurowski's depictions of the site. The new DOE standards and requirements imposed in the mid-1990s were the factors that produced the fines and fee reductions described in Ackland's article. However, a significant transformation had occurred by the time the site closed in 2005; mutual distrust had been replaced with an effective level of shared priorities and trust, as reflected in Parker's statement above.

Beyond violations of protocol and procedure that carried stiff penalties but did not result in injury or harm to individuals, Rocky Flats was never free of safety concerns. For example, in October 2000, 11 workers were found to have "elevated levels of internal plutonium." Kaiser-Hill immediately launched an investigation, the results of which were inconclusive but indicated that the exposure was most likely from airborne radioactivity during cleanup. The dose of radiation to which the workers were exposed did not come close to exceeding regulatory limits for worker exposure on such a site. Nevertheless, very serious responses were made to the incident. Measures were instituted to ensure that workers emphasized safety over work deadlines. All workers, in fact, had the authority to stop work if they suspected safety concerns, and the number of safety monitors on the site increased steadily. As of July 2004, the total recordable case rate—the number of occupation related incidents requiring more than basic first aid multiplied by 200,000 labor-hours—was 1.0 at Rocky Flats, half the average for DOE facilities. The lost workday case rate (restricted days away from work) was 0.2, one quarter of the average for DOE facilities. In other words, a number of years were required for the dramatic improvement to occur in safety performance, and at no time was safety not a significant concern at the site.

Post-Cleanup Issues

Though it is outside the scope of cleanup and closure, it should be noted that since the time of the Rocky Flats completion of cleanup in October 2005, issues have arisen regarding the payment of benefits to former Rocky Flats employees. Specifically, disagreements have occurred regarding qualification of workers whose employment ended just shy of junctures that would have entitled them to greater health and retirement benefits. Some workers have felt disadvantaged because they worked just short of the required time, or were just beneath the required age, to receive specific benefits. To be fair, benefit payments are being handled by the Department of Labor, not Kaiser-Hill or the Department of Energy. Moreover, some state and federal officials are working to see if benefit qualifications can be amended to extend more broadly the benefits desired by these former Rocky Flats employees. These issues clearly have serious consequences for former workers over time, and perhaps could affect the ability of other facilities to replicate similar levels of performance. If workers have concerns about postemployment coverage, they may be reticent to perform to the same level as workers at Rocky Flats. On the other hand, these issues did not affect the organizational dynamics or leadership principles associated with the cleanup and closure at Rocky Flats.

Additional Resources

Sources that can provide more information and a critical perspective about Rocky Flats are listed below. Inasmuch as the objectives of these publications are different from ours, they need not be defined as contradictory or inconsistent with our presentation. By and large, their intent, as illustrated above, is to surface ongoing disagreements with the standards and performance criteria that governed Rocky Flats operations.

Ackland, Len. (1999). *Making a Real Killing: Rocky Flats and the Nuclear West.* Albuquerque: University of New Mexico Press.

Bulletin of Concerned Scientists. http://www.thebulletin.org.

Rocky Mountain Peace & Justice Center. http://www.rmpjc.org/.

Readers who want to investigate more detailed aspects of the Rocky Flats project may find these references of interest.

Colorado Department of Public Health and Environment's Hazardous Materials and Waste Management Division, http://www.cdphe.state.co.us/hm/rf/rfhom.asp.

EPA's Superfund sites in the region, http://www.epa.gov/region8/superfund/sites/co/rocky.html.

Rocky Flats Citizen Advisory Board, http://www.rfcab.org.

Rocky Flats Closure Project, http://www.rfets.gov.

Rocky Flats National Wildlife Refuge, http://rockyflats.fws.gov/.

Summary

This appendix explores critical viewpoints of and possible alternative explanations for the extraordinary success at Rocky Flats. We delineated the major concerns of some stakeholder groups—that cleanup of residual contamination at the Rocky Flats site is not sufficient, that corners may have been cut or safety concerns ignored in order to achieve the results, or that various constituencies' viewpoints were not taken sufficiently into account. Such concerns are legitimate and understandable, and divergent opinions on such matters are to be expected. Our contention is that, within the scope of the cleanup agreement that was negotiated, the performance of Kaiser-Hill remains extraordinary in its timing, cost, quality, and outcomes. The firm's success is not incompatible with the critical perspectives discussed in this chapter, which focus mostly on the adequacy of the standards to which Kaiser-Hill was held.

APPENDIX II

Research Methods

We made visits in the fall of 2003 and the summer of 2004 to the Rocky Flats site, where we conducted interviews with senior managers (e.g., CEO and former CEOs; COO, CFO, strategic planning director), steelworkers union members, the president of the steelworkers union, and supervisors and middle managers. We also interviewed corporate officers at CH2MHill, the parent company of the firm responsible for the cleanup (e.g., chairman, vice chairman, CFO, business group presidents) in 2003, 2004, and 2005, as well as several former Rocky Flats employees. We interviewed senior staff members in the Department of Energy (DOE) at their offices in Washington, D.C. We obtained organizational records from Rocky Flats personnel (to whom we owe a huge debt of gratitude) as well as from external news organizations (e.g., ABC's *Nightline,* the *Denver Post*), the Colorado Department of Public Health and Environment, the Department of Energy, and public records. Performance measurements were obtained from official records, and explanations of enablers and organizational processes relied on verbatim quotations from employees, regulators (e.g., EPA), citizen action groups (environmental advocacy organizations), and oversight agencies (e.g., DOE). In total, we conducted individual and small group interviews with more than 35 people at Rocky Flats.

In addition to the face-to-face interviews, we analyzed approximately 24 hours of videotaped interviews and their written transcriptions. These interviews were conducted in the fall of 2002 by a subcontracted firm, and funded by DOE and Kaiser-Hill. The interviews were carried out as part of their efforts to understand and learn from the legacy of Rocky Flats. None of those interviews had been analyzed prior to our receiving them. Interview subjects on those tapes included a broad cross section of stakeholders, among them elected officials in Colorado, other representatives from the state of Colorado, staff members of the Environmental Protection Agency, local community groups from the Rocky Flats area, U.S. congressmen who were involved in the project, and Rocky Flats site managers from both the DOE and Kaiser-Hill. We obtained videotaped interviews for 27 individuals. Combining these with our in-person interviews, we obtained data from more than 60 individuals. In a few instances we conducted in-person interviews with people who had also provided a videotaped interview. This gave us the chance to ask follow-up questions and chart progress. We also interviewed half a dozen former employees at Rocky Flats who had left the facility before our study began.

Data were gathered primarily during the process of closure and cleanup, largely between the fall of

2002 and the summer of 2003, rather than after the project had been completed in the fall of 2005. In other words, respondents were describing processes as they were unfolding, not retrospectively after the project had ended. It is important to note, however, that our interviews and those on the videotapes were conducted after the site had enjoyed several years of success, and contributors did reflect on and describe events regarding the history of the site.

The primary analysis of key enablers occurred during the last two years of the project's existence. In fact, one respondent indicated that his greatest fear was that Rocky Flats leadership "would spike the ball on the five-yard line"—that is, they would celebrate completion before completion had actually been accomplished—or that a major accident would occur that would negate all of the success achieved up to that point. On the one hand, writing this story before the project was completed and judged to be an unequivocal success represented something of a risk. Things could have fallen apart, the closure could have been postponed, a major failure could have occurred, or some divergence from the idea could have emerged. On the other hand, the dramatic successes along the way to final completion were so notable that many leadership principles could have been learned even if deadlines were missed or completion got sidetracked. Fortunately, the project was completed successfully and ahead of even the most optimistic time lines and budget projections.

One caveat is in order. Despite this being a remarkable story of success, we promised to maintain confidentiality and anonymity for the individuals who provided us with insights and quotations. Therefore, only in rare cases have we identified a statement with a particular person, and then only after having obtained permission from the individual being cited. Not all data we collected were glowingly positive, of course, and we obtained candid information by ensuring that names would not be associated with individual comments. Hence, we have referenced all quotations, but not with contributors' names.

References

Adler, P.S., and Kwon, S. (2002). "Social capital: Prospects for a new concept." *Academy of Management Review* 27: 17–40.

Asch, S.E. (1952). *Social Psychology.* New York: Prentice-Hall.

Baker, W., Cross, R., and Wooten, M. (2003). "Positive organizational network analysis and energizing relationships." In K.S. Cameron, J.E. Dutton, and R.E. Quinn (eds.), *Positive Organizational Scholarship: Foundations of a New Discipline.* San Francisco: Berrett-Koehler.

Barney, J. (2001). *Gaining and Sustaining Competitive Advantage.* Upper Saddle River, NJ: Prentice-Hall.

Batson, C.D. (1994). "Why act for the public good? Four answers." *Personality and Social Psychology Bulletin* 20: 603–610.

Bolino, M.C., Turnley, W.H., and Bloodgood, J.M. (2002). "Citizenship behavior and the creation of social capital in organizations." *Academy of Management Review* 27(4): 505–522.

Bright, D., Cameron, K.S., and Caza, A. (2006). "The amplifying and buffering effects of virtuousness in downsized organizations." *Journal of Business Ethics* (in press).

Buckingham, M., and Clifton, D.O. (2001). *Now, Discover Your Strengths.* New York: Free Press.

Burke, W.W. (2002). *Organization Change: Theory and Practice.* Thousand Oaks, CA: Sage.

Cameron, K.S. (1986). "Effectiveness as paradox: Conflict and consensus in conceptions of organizational effectiveness." *Management Science* 32: 539–553.

______. (1994). "Strategies for successful organizational downsizing." *Human Resource Management Journal* 33: 89–112.

______. (1997). "Techniques for making organizations effective." In D. Druckman, J. Singer, and H. Van Cott (eds.), *Enhancing Organizational Performance,* pp.39–64. Washington, DC: National Academy Press.

______. (1998). "Strategic organizational downsizing: An extreme case." *Research in Organizational Behavior* 20: 185–229.

______. (2003). "Organizational virtuousness and performance." In K.S., Cameron, J.E. Dutton, and

R.E. Quinn (eds.), *Positive Organizational Scholarship,* pp.48-65. San Francisco: Berrett-Koehler.

_____. (2005a). "Leading positive change." In D.A. Whetten, and K.S. Cameron, *Developing Management Skills.* Upper Saddle River, NJ: Prentice-Hall.

_____. (2005b). "Organizational effectiveness: Its demise and reemergence through Positive Organizational Scholarship." In K.G. Smith and M.A. Hitt (eds.), *Great Minds in Management: The Process of Theory Development.* New York: Oxford University Press.

Cameron, K.S., Bright, D., and Caza, A. (2004). "Exploring the relationships between organizational virtuousness and performance." *American Behavioral Scientist* 47(6): 766–790.

Cameron, K.S., Dutton, J.E., and Quinn, R.E. (eds.). (2003). *Positive Organizational Scholarship.* San Francisco: Barrett-Koehler.

Cameron, K.S., Kim, M.U., and Whetten, D.A. (1987). "Organizational effects of decline and turbulence." *Administrative Science Quarterly* 32: 222–40.

Cameron, K.S. and Mora, C. (2003). "Corporate culture and financial success of mergers and acquisitions."

Working paper, Ross School of Business, University of Michigan.

Cameron, K.S., and Quinn, R.E. (2006). *Diagnosing and Changing Organizational Culture.* San Francisco: Jossey-Bass.

Cameron, K.S., Quinn, R.E., DeGraff, J., and Thakor, A.V. (2006). *Competing Values Leadership.* Cheltenham, UK: Edward Elgar.

Caza, A., Barker, B., and Cameron, K. (2004). "Ethics and ethos: The amplifying and buffering effects of ethical behavior and virtuousness." *Journal of Business Ethics* 52: 169–78.

Cialdini, R.B. (2000). *Influence: The Science of Persuasion.* New York: Allyn Bacon.

Clifton, D.O., and Harter, J.K. (2003). "Investing in strengths." In K.S. Cameron, J.E. Dutton, and R.E. Quinn (eds.), *Positive Organizational Scholarship: Foundations of a New Discipline,* pp.111–121. San Francisco: Berrett-Koehler.

Cole, R.E. (1993). "Learning from learning theory: Implications for quality improvement in turnover, use of contingent workers, and job rotation policies." *Quality Management Journal* 1: 9–25.

Colorado Department of Public Health and Environment (CDPHE). (2004). *Rocky Flats Historical Public Exposure Studies.* Denver: CDPHE.

Collins, J. (2001). *Good to Great: Why Some Companies Make the Leap and Others Don't.* New York: Harper Business.

Cooney, R. (1987). *The Power of the People: Active Nonviolence in the United States.* Philadelphia: New Society Publishers.

Cooperrider, D.L. (1990). "Positive image, positive action: The affirmative basis of organizing." In S. Srivastva, and D.L. Cooperrider, *Appreciative Management and Leadership.* San Francisco: Jossey-Bass.

Cooperrider, D.L., and Whitney, D. (1999). *Appreciative Inquiry.* Williston, VT: Berrett-Koehler Communications.

Csikszentmihalyi, M. (1990). *Flow: The Psychology of Optimal Experience.* New York: Harper Perennial.

Danner, D.D., Snowden, D.A., and Friesen, W.V. (2001). "Positive emotions in early life longevity: Findings from the nun study." *Journal of Personality and Social Psychology* 80: 804–813.

Darwin, C. (1989). *The Power of Movement in Plants.* Reprinted, New York: New York University Press.

Department of Energy Office (DOE) of Environment Management. (1995). *Estimating the Cold War Mortgage: Baseline Environmental Management Report.* Washington, DC: U.S. Government Printing Office.

Deutschman, A. (2005). "Change or die." *Fast Company* (May), pp.52–62.

Dienstbier, R.A., and Zillig, L.M. (2002). "Toughness." In C.R. Snyder and S.J. Lopez (eds.), *Handbook of Positive Psychology,* pp.515–527. New York: Oxford University.

Dutton, J.E., Frost, P.J., Worline, M.C., Lilius, J.M., and Kanov, J.M. (2002). "Leading in times of trauma." *Harvard Business Review,* pp.54–61.

Dutton, J.E., and Heaphy, E.D. (2003). "The power of high quality connections." In K.S. Cameron, J.E. Dutton, and R.E. Quinn (eds.), *Positive Organizational Scholarship: Foundations of a New Discipline.* San Francisco: Berrett-Koehler.

Emmons, R.A. (2003). "Acts of gratitude in organizations." In K.S. Cameron, J.E. Dutton, and R.E. Quinn (eds.), *Positive Organizational Scholarship:*

Foundations of a New Discipline. San Francisco: Berrett-Koehler.

Fineman, S. (1996). "Emotion and organizing." In S.R. Clegg, C. Hardy, and W.R. Nord (eds.), *The Handbook of Organizational Studies,* pp.543–564. Thousand Oaks, CA: Sage.

Fredrickson, B.L. (1998). "What good are positive emotions?" *Review of General Psychology* 2: 300–319.

______. (2003). "Positive emotions and upward spirals in organizations." In K.S. Cameron, J.E. Dutton, and R.E. Quinn (eds.), *Positive Organizational Scholarship: Foundations of a New Discipline.* San Francisco: Berrett-Koehler.

George, J.M. (1995). "Leader positive mood and group performance: The case of customer service." *Journal of Applied Social Psychology* 25: 778–794.

Gittell, J.H., Cameron, K.S., and Lim, S. (2006). "Relationships, layoffs, and organizational resilience: Airline industry responses to September 11th." *Journal of Applied Behavioral Sciences* (in press).

Goddard, R.D., Hoy, W.K., and Hoy, A.W. (2003). "Collective efficacy beliefs: Theoretical developments, empirical evidence, and future directions." *Educational Researcher* 33: 3–13.

Gottman, J.M. (1994). *Why Marriages Succeed or Fail.* New York: Simon and Schuster.

Hamel, G., and Prahalad, C.K. (1994). *Competing for the Future.* Boston: Harvard Business School Press.

Kaiser-Hill. Company promotional materials and Web site.

Kirschenbaum, D. (1984). "Self-regulation and sport psychology: Nurturing an emergent symbiosis." *Journal of Sport Psychology* 8: 26–34.

Kotter, J. (1996). *Leading Change.* Boston: Harvard Business School Press.

Krebs, D. (1987). "The challenge of altruism in biology and psychology." In C. Crawford, M. Smith, and D. Krebs (eds.), *Sociobiology and Psychology.* Hillsdale, NJ: Lawrence Erlbaum.

Lawler, E.E. (2000). *Rewarding Excellence: Pay Strategies for the New Economy.* San Francisco: Jossey-Bass.

Losada, M., and Heaphy, E. (2004). "The role of positivity and connectivity in the performance of business teams." *Journal of Applied Behavioral Science* 47: 740–765.

March, J.G. (1994). *A Primer on Decision Making: How Decisions Happen.* New York: Free Press.

Mitroff, I.I. (1998). *Smart Thinking for Crazy Times: The Art of Solving the Right Problems.* San Francisco: Berrett-Koehler.

Moore, L. (2004). *Rocky Flats: A Local Hazard Forever.* Denver, CO: Rocky Mountain Peace and Justice Center.

New York Times. (2005). "Rocky Flats nuclear cleanup declared complete." October 14, p.A21.

Obmascik, M. (2000). "Price of Peace." *Denver Post,* June 25.

Ornish, D. (1996). *Reversing Heart Disease: The Only System Scientifically Proven to Reverse Heart Disease Without Drugs or Surgery.* New York: Ivy Books.

Ornstein, R., and Sobel, D. (1987). *The Healing Brain.* New York: Simon and Schuster.

Quinn, R.E. (1988). *Beyond Rational Management.* San Francisco: Jossey-Bass.

_____. (2004). *Building the Bridge as You Walk on It.* San Francisco: Jossey-Bass.

Quinn, R.E., and Cameron, K.S. (1983). "Organizational life cycles and shifting criteria of effectiveness: Some preliminary evidence." *Management Science* 29: 33–51.

_____. (1988). *Paradox and Transformation: Toward a Theory of Change in Organization and Management.* Cambridge, MA: Ballinger.

Quinn, R.E., and Rohrbaugh, J. (1983). "A spatial model of effectiveness criteria: Towards a competing values approach to organizational analysis." *Management Science* 29: 363–377.

Rosenthal, R., and Jacobson, L. (1968). *Pygmalion in the Classroom: Teacher Expectations and Pupils' Intellectual Development.* New York: Holt, Rinehart and Winston.

Ryff, C.D., and Singer, E. (1998). "The contours of human health." *Psychological Inquiry* 8: 1–28.

Seligman, M.E.P. (1991). *Learned Optimism.* New York: Knopf.

_____. (2002a). *Authentic Happiness.* New York: Free Press.

_____. (2002b). "Positive psychology, positive prevention, and positive therapy." In C.R. Snyder and S. Lopez (eds.), *Handbook of Positive Psychology,* pp.3-9. New York: Oxford University Press.

Seligman, M.E.P., and Csikszentmihalyi, M. (2000). "Positive psychology: An introduction." *American Psychologist* 55: 5–14.

Sethi, R., and Nicholson, C.Y. (2001). "Structural and contextual correlates of changed behavior in product development teams." *Journal of Product Innovation Management* 18: 154–168.

Snowden, D. (2002). *Aging with Grace: What the Nun Study Teaches Us About Leading Longer, Healthier, and More Meaningful Lives.* New York: Bantam.

U.S Department of Energy. *Rocky Flats Closure Project.*http://192.149.55.183/.

Watson, T. (2005). Quoted in *Poor Man's College.* Aapex Software, #9757.

Weick, K.E. (2006). "The role of values in high risk organizations." In E. Hess and K.S. Cameron, *Values Based Leadership.* New York: Cambridge University Press.

Wilde, O. (1892). *Lady Windermere's Fan.* Act 3.

Photo Credits

Figure 1: Courtesy of the Rocky Flats Cold War Museum
Figure 2: Courtesy of Kaiser-Hill/U.S. Department of Energy
Figure 3: Courtesy of Kaiser-Hill/U.S. Department of Energy
Figure 4: Courtesy of Kaiser-Hill/U.S. Department of Energy
Figure 5: Courtesy of Kaiser-Hill/U.S. Department of Energy
Figure 7: Courtesy of Kaiser-Hill/U.S. Department of Energy
Figure 8: Courtesy of Kaiser-Hill/U.S. Department of Energy
Figure 9: Courtesy of Kaiser-Hill and Pixel Kitchen Inc.
Figure 10: Courtesy of Kaiser-Hill/U.S. Department of Energy
Figure 11: Courtesy of Kaiser-Hill/U.S. Department of Energy
Figure 12: Courtesy of Kaiser-Hill/U.S. Department of Energy
Figure 13: Courtesy of Kaiser-Hill/U.S. Department of Energy
Figure 14: Courtesy of Kaiser-Hill/U.S. Department of Energy
Figure 15: Courtesy of Kaiser-Hill/U.S. Department of Energy

Figure 16: Courtesy of Kaiser-Hill/U.S. Department of Energy
Figure 17: Courtesy of Kaiser-Hill/U.S. Department of Energy

About the Authors

KIM CAMERON University of Michigan

Kim Cameron is professor of management and organization at the University of Michigan Business School and professor of higher education in the School of Education at the University of Michigan. Professor Cameron has served as dean and Albert J. Weatherhead professor of management in the Weatherhead School of Management at Case Western Reserve University, as associate dean and Ford Motor Co./Richard E. Cook professor in the Marriott School of Management at Brigham Young University, and as a department chair and director of several executive education programs at the University of Michigan. He also has been on the faculties of the University of Wisconsin-Madison and Ricks College. He organized and directed the Organizational Studies Division of the National Center for Higher Education Management Systems in Boulder, Colorado.

Dr. Cameron's research on organizational downsizing, effectiveness, quality culture, virtuousness, and the development of management skills has been published in more than 80 articles and 10 books: *Coffin Nails and Corporate Strategies* (Prentice-Hall), *Developing Management Skills* (HarperCollins), *Diagnosing and Changing Organizational Culture* (Jossey-Bass), *Organizational Decline* (Ballinger), *Organizational Effectiveness* (Academic Press), *Paradox and Transformation* (Ballinger), *Positive Organizational Scholarship* (Berrett-Koehler), *Competing Values Leadership* (Edward Elgar), and *Leading with Values* (Cambridge University Press). His current research focuses on the virtuousness of and in organizations and its relationship to organizational success. He is one of the founders of the Center for Positive Organizational Scholarship at the University of Michigan, and this work was recognized as one of the 20 highest impact ideas of 2004 by the *Harvard Business Review.*

Dr. Cameron received B.S. and M.S. degrees from Brigham Young University, and M.A. and Ph.D. degrees from Yale University. He served on the National Research Council, was president of Bay Asset Funding Corporation, and was a Fulbright distinguished scholar. He is a graduate of Leadership Cleveland, class of 2000, and a recipient of the Organizational Behavior Teaching Society's Outstanding Educator Award. He currently consults for a variety of business, government, and educational organizations in North America, South America, Asia, Africa, and Europe.

He is married to the former Melinda Cummings and has seven children.

MARC LAVINE Boston College

Marc H. Lavine is a doctoral student and instructor in the Department of Organization Studies at the Wallace E. Carroll School of Management at Boston College. His interests are in the domains of corporate social responsibility, ethics, leadership, and nonprofit and public management. His current research focuses on the role that an organization's social purpose plays in individual well-being and organizational peak performance. For more than a decade Lavine led and founded nonprofit, educational, and leadership development initiatives in the United States and abroad. He has consulted for multinational firms, nonprofit organizations, and public schools on issues of social responsibility, organizational learning, and strategic growth. Lavine received his B.A. from Earlham College and his M.B.A. and M.A. in education from the University of Michigan.

About the Center for Positive Organizational Scholarship

This study was conducted by the Center for Positive Organizational Scholarship (POS) in the Ross School of Business at the University of Michigan. The Center consists of a group of faculty members who examine the enablers, motivations, and effects associated with remarkably positive phenomena—how they can be identified, why they work, how they are facilitated, and how researchers and managers can capitalize on them. POS does not adopt one particular theory or framework, but draws from the full spectrum of organizational and psychological theories to understand, explain, and predict the occurrence, causes, and consequences of positive phenomena.

Research at the Center focuses on three types of phenomena. One is performance that represents positive deviance—that is, extraordinarily positive performance or achievement that is well beyond expectations. A second relates to an affirmative bias—that is, phenomena that are oriented toward positive strengths rather than weaknesses, positive communication rather than negative communication, or positive possibilities rather than problems. A third relates to goodness or virtuousness—that is, the highest potential of human beings or the best of the human condition. Research investigations to date have included projects on change, communication patterns, compassion, emotions, energy, forgiveness, efficacy, high reliability systems, leadership, meaningfulness, positive deviance, resilience, sustainability, thriving at work, and virtuousness.

In addition to conducting research, faculty members at the Center for Positive Organizational Scholarship teach a weeklong executive education program at Michigan—"Leading the Positive Organization"—and consult with a variety of profit and not-for-profit organizations. The goal is to assist organizations in implementing tools and procedures that will markedly enhance performance of individual employees and the organization as a whole. A variety of practical techniques have been developed for enabling positively deviant performance.

To learn more about POS at the University of Michigan, visit http://bus.umich.edu/positive.

About Berrett-Koehler Publishers

Berrett-Koehler is an independent publisher dedicated to an ambitious mission: creating a world that works for all.

We believe that to truly create a better world, action is needed at all levels—individual, organizational, and societal. At the individual level, our publications help people align their lives and work with their deepest values. At the organizational level, our publications promote progressive leadership and management practices, socially responsible approaches to business, and humane and effective organizations. At the societal level, our publications advance social and economic justice, shared prosperity, sustainable development, and new solutions to national and global issues.

We publish groundbreaking books focused on each of these levels. To further advance our commitment to positive change at the societal level, we have recently expanded our line of books in this area and are calling this expanded line BK Currents.

A major theme of our publications is "opening up new space." They challenge conventional thinking, introduce new points of view, and offer new alternatives for change. Their common goal is changing the underlying beliefs, mind-sets, institutions, and structures that keep generating the same cycles of problems, no matter who our leaders are or what improvement programs we adopt.

We strive to practice what we preach—to operate our publishing company in line with the ideas in our books. At the core of our approach is *stewardship,* which we define as a deep sense of responsibility to administer the company for the benefit of all of our stakeholder groups: authors, customers, employees, investors, service providers, and the communities and environment around us. We seek to establish a partnering relationship with each stakeholder that is open, equitable, and collaborative.

We are gratified that thousands of readers, authors, and other friends of the company consider themselves part of the BK community. We hope that you, too, will join our community and connect with us through the ways described on our Web site, www.bkconnection.com.

Be Connected

Visit Our Web Site

Go to www.bkconnection.com to read exclusive previews and excerpts of new books, find detailed information on all Berrett-Koehler titles and authors, browse subject area libraries of books, and get special discounts.

Subscribe to Our Free E-Newsletter

Be the first to hear about new publications, special discount offers, exclusive articles, news about best-sellers, and more! Get on the list for our free e-newsletter by going to www.bkconnection.com.

Participate in the Discussion

To see what others are saying about our books and to post your own thoughts, check out our blogs at www.bkblogs.com.

Get Quantity Discounts

Berrett-Koehler books are available at quantity discounts for orders of ten or more copies. Please call us toll-free at (800)929-2929 or e-mail us at bkp.or ders@aidcvt.com.

Host a Reading Group

For tips on how to form and conduct a reading group in your workplace or community, see our Web site, www.bkconnection.com.

Join the BK Community

Thousands of readers of our books have become part of the BK community by participating in events featuring our authors, reviewing draft manuscripts of forthcoming books, spreading the word about their favorite books, and supporting our publishing program in other ways. If you would like to join the BK Community, please contact us at bkcommunity@bkpub.com.

A

B

C

D

E

F

G

I

J

K

L

M

N

O

P

S

T

U

V

Books For ALL Kinds of Readers

At ReadHowYouWant we understand that one size does not fit all types of readers. Our innovative, patent pending technology allows us to design new formats to make reading easier and more enjoyable for you. This helps improve your speed of reading and your comprehension. Our EasyRead printed books have been optimized to improve word recognition, ease eye tracking by adjusting word and line spacing as well as minimizing hyphenation. Our EasyRead SuperLarge editions have been developed to make reading easier and more accessible for vision-impaired readers. We offer Braille and DAISY formats of our books and all popular E-Book formats.

Printed in Dunstable, United Kingdom

91343661R00261